IMAGES
of America

AROUND DALLASTOWN

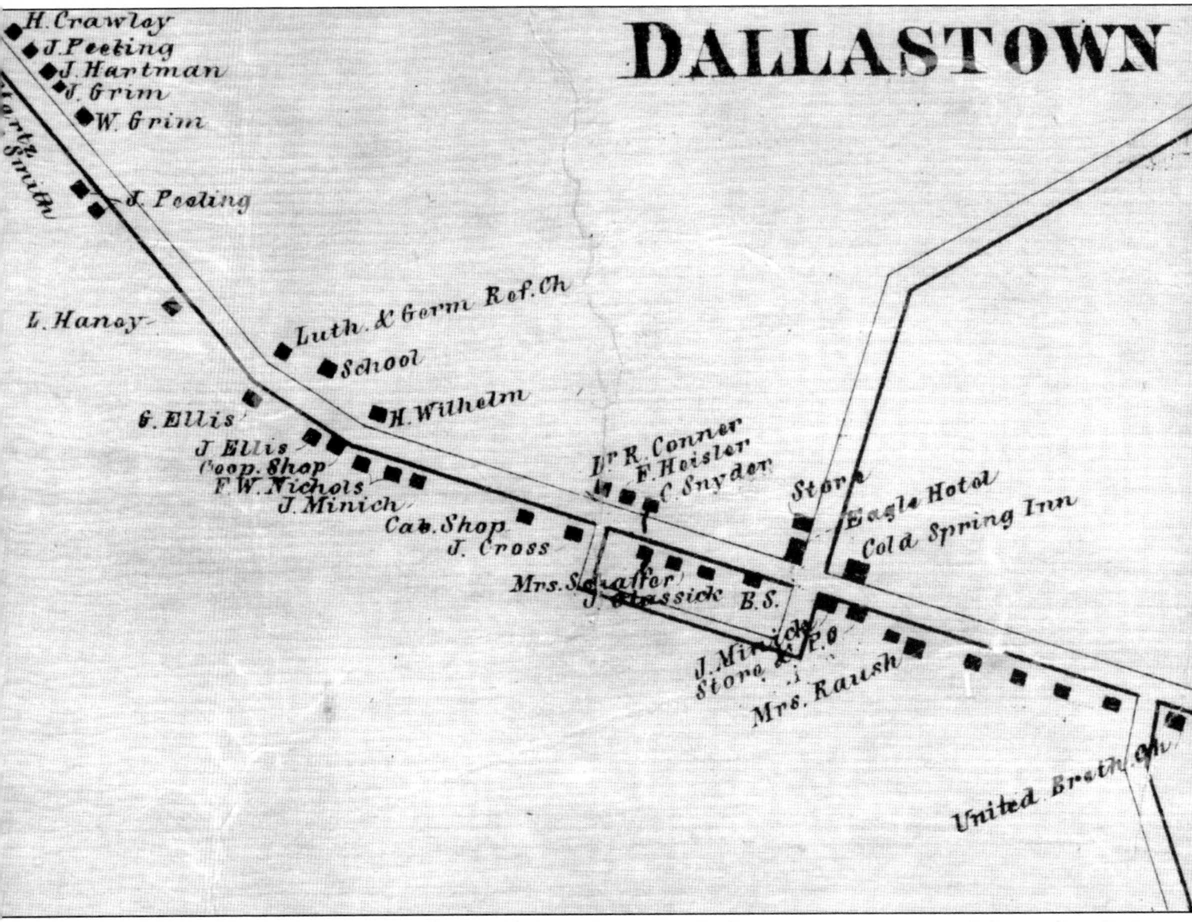

This early map of Dallastown depicts the town six years before it was incorporated. It is a detailed map from *Shearer's Map of York County, Pennsylvania*, by D.J. Lake in 1860. It shows private residences, as well as early churches, businesses, and hotels. Main Street runs from top left to bottom right of the image. (Courtesy of Dallastown Area Historical Society.)

On the Cover: Volunteer members of Dallastown Rescue Fire Company No. 1 are shown posing in front of their hand-drawn hose and ladder wagon. This firefighting apparatus is parked in front of the fire engine house at 118 East Main Street around 1914. The building was dedicated in June 1914 and was used by the fire company until 1981. (Courtesy of Dallastown Area Historical Society.)

IMAGES
of America

AROUND DALLASTOWN

Richard C. Saylor and Michael L. Sentz Jr.

ARCADIA
PUBLISHING

ISBN 978-1-4671-3481-1

Published by Arcadia Publishing
Charleston, South Carolina

Printed in the United States of America

Library of Congress Control Number: 2015955476

For all general information, please contact Arcadia Publishing:
Telephone 843-853-2070
Fax 843-853-0044
E-mail sales@arcadiapublishing.com
For customer service and orders:
Toll-Free 1-888-313-2665

Visit us on the Internet at www.arcadiapublishing.com

To our late friends and Dallastown Area Historical Society board members Beverly Scott, Jean Capatch, Helen Ehrhart, Yvonne Raab, and Louise Strayer. We miss you!

Contents

ACKNOWLEDGMENTS

The Dallastown Area Historical Society was founded in 2000 by Mayor Beverly Scott and Dallastown native Richard C. Saylor. Since then, the historical society has had a number of board members and many other members who have helped to make it thrive and grow. We would like to thank everyone who has contributed time, labor, and donations to make the society what it is today. Borough manager Connie L. Stokes and the borough council have provided invaluable assistance to the historical society throughout its development. Catherine Bankoske, current president of the society, has been consistently supportive of the authors and this book project.

Kathryn M. Patterson, an original board member of the historical society, provided greatly appreciated assistance with the preparation of this book. Her experience in editing and layout of printed materials was instrumental in the preparation of this work. Jeanne M. Saylor assisted the authors with identifying a number of the book's images. Railroad historians Kurt Bell and Rudy Fischer helped the authors achieve a better understanding of trolley and railroad history in and around Dallastown. Cathy Bankoske and Lance Wolf each provided information from their personal recollections of Dallastown history. Thank you, to all of those listed above.

The authors would also like to thank the many individual contributors who provided images for this book from their personal collections. The preponderance of images in this book were culled from the collections of the historical society. Unless otherwise noted, all images are from the Dallastown Area Historical Society.

INTRODUCTION

Dallastown Borough was incorporated in 1866, one year after the American Civil War concluded. However, people of European descent had been living in the Dallastown area since 1736. Part of the Dallastown area was an open common used as a parade ground or muster area for local militia during the Revolutionary War era.

Simon Plymire obtained a hotel license in the Dallastown area in 1840, followed two years later by a store opened by James Edgar. In 1841, James Peeling, former sheriff of the city of York, purchased 95 acres of land, including what would become Dallastown. Peeling, born in 1823 in York County, initially used the land for cultivation but later sold off part of the land as lots. Located seven miles southeast of York, Pennsylvania, the town sits on an inclined plane 656 feet above sea level overlooking the Codorus Valley.

The town was named in 1844 in honor of George Mifflin Dallas, a Philadelphia lawyer and politician who was vice president of the United States during the presidency of James K. Polk. In 1847, the Dallastown Post Office was established by the authorities in Washington, DC.

Two of the early industries in Dallastown were basketmaking and cigar manufacturing. Before the town was named in 1844, the area was noted for its basketmaking. Two types of baskets were the most popular: bushel baskets for farmers and three-peck baskets for shipping oysters. These oak baskets were made by hand in large numbers by the local populace and sold in York and Baltimore. This trade continued in earnest until the late 1860s when basketmaking became a largely mechanized industry. Thereafter, the basketmaking profession in Dallastown suffered a steady decline. In 1881, there were still four full-time basket-makers in the borough: John Daugherty, Jacob M. Grim, Rufus Grim, and Jesse Hildebrand. By 1904, only one person in Dallastown continued to list his profession as basket manufacturer. Rufus Grim, of 49 West Main Street, continued the time-honored local occupation of basketmaking through 1917.

As the basketmaking industry was in decline in Dallastown, the cigar-making industry was beginning to grow. In 1860, William Wireman built a factory to make cigars in Dallastown. This was the first of many such factories to be built in the 19th century in the borough. After the Civil War, the cigar manufacturing industry in the town really took off. A number of large factories were erected, and even more small shops were started around the town. In 1883, the York City directory listed 24 cigar manufacturers in Dallastown. The next year, the United States Revenue report described that the town shipped 25 million cigars to market and had 38 cigar factories. During this period, Dallastown led all towns in York County in the cigar-making industry. Firms who operated large cigar factories included George W. Conaway, Dallastown Cigar Company, A.F. Fix, John C. Heckert, Hose & Brillhart, Hamilton D. Kauffman, Samuel Kauffman, Adam Kohler, Perrie McCoy, John W. Minnich, New York Factory, William H. Raab & Son, Park G. Shaw, and Jacob H. Spotz.

Wooden box factories also were created in late 19th-century Dallastown to support the burgeoning cigar industry. The three largest box factories were Michael Hose, Charles Kohler & Company, and Merchants Cigar Box Factory.

By 1907, there were 1,200 cigar manufacturing factories in York County with an annual production of 300 million cigars. In Dallastown in 1907, there were over 307 people who listed their occupations as being part of the cigar industry. Jobs like tobacco strippers, cigar makers, cigar manufacturers, and cigar packers easily employed more people in the town than any other industry. In fact, the cigar industry employed more people than any other industry in the entire county in that year. And not all of these people worked in a cigar factory; many residents of Dallastown worked in the cigar industry in their homes or outbuildings. Numerous children assisted with stripping tobacco to prepare it for use in cigars. This went on throughout the first half of the 20th century.

It was widely reported in January 1917 that the cigar manufacturers in Dallastown could not keep up with all of the orders they were receiving due to lack of laborers. Manufacturers raised the wages for making cigars from 17¢ per hundred for rolling to 22¢ per hundred. By August 1917, it was reported that Dallastown was experiencing an industrial boom and that all houses and rooms in town were rented. And still, a number of factories could not keep up with their orders due to the scarcity of cigar makers.

The population in Dallastown Borough was 287 in 1870; in 1900, there were 1,181 residents, and by 1907, a total of 1,800 people lived in the town. This population boom was directly related to the increase in industry in the town, the majority of which was related to the cigar manufacturing industry.

Farming continued to be a way of life for many people in the Dallastown area in the late 19th century as well. In 1883, a city directory listed 88 separate individuals as being farmers in and around the town. This area of York County has traditionally had a strong farming community, established on some of the most fertile soil in the region.

One of Dallastown's most important documentarians was photographer William Mitchell Bigler. Bigler married Elizabeth "Lizzie" A. Thompson on November 27, 1890, in York, Pennsylvania. In 1898, he was listed in a city directory as a cigar maker living in Windsor, Pennsylvania. By 1904, the Biglers had moved to Dallastown, and he had changed his profession to that of photographer. They resided at 86 West Main Street. Bigler continued to document the town and the people in it for over 40 years. During this time, he took many important images of street scenes, bird's-eye views, and portraits of Dallastown and its residents. In the 1940 United States census, Bigler, age 73, is still listed as an active photographer who owned his own studio at 266 West Main Street in Dallastown. William M. Bigler died on December 28, 1954, at the age of 88 at the Odd Fellows Home of Pennsylvania.

Fraternal organizations such as the Odd Fellows played a very important role in the community life of Dallastown Borough in its first two centuries of existence. Six different societies are listed in the 1904 city directory as existing in Dallastown. One was the Dallastown Musical Association, which included the Dallastown Boys Band; this junior band fed into the Dallastown Band. The five others were fraternal organizations, including Daughters of Liberty; Daughters of Rebekah; Independent Order of Odd Fellows; Junior Order of United American Mechanics, Golden Star Council; and the Patriotic Order Sons of America. All of these societies met in the Minnich Building located at 11–13 East Main Street, except the Patriotic Order Sons of America, which met in the Sechrist Building at 135 East Main Street. The Patriotic Order Sons of America was founded in 1847 as a patriotic and fraternal organization. It is open to male American citizens who are 16 years or older.

The Independent Order of Odd Fellows was originally a fraternal organization modeled on the British Independent Order of Odd Fellows service organizations of the 18th century. The American version split with the British in 1843 and took the name Independent Order of Odd Fellows. The Daughters of Liberty was a female auxiliary to the Order of United American Mechanics. Its membership was restricted to white women 16 years or older who were born in the United States. The Daughters of Rebekah was initially a female auxiliary of the Independent Order of Odd Fellows. These lodges were first founded in the United States in 1851.

The Junior Order of United American Mechanics, Golden Star Council was originally a Nativist organization that was the youth affiliation of the Order of United American Mechanics. It held anti-Catholic sentiments but eventually abandoned these tenets and became a general fraternal organization. It became independent of the Order of United American Mechanics in 1885.

By 1927, fraternal organizations in Dallastown had grown to also include the Fraternal Temple Association, Knights of the Mystic Chain, Senior Order United American Mechanics, and the Patriotic Order of Americans.

Before train, trolley, or automobile travel became prevalent in Dallastown, stagecoach lines were the most important form of public transportation in the area. Daily stage lines connected Dallastown with the city of York. V. Frank Taylor operated one such line, which left the Farmers' Hotel at 101 South George Street in York at 2:00 p.m. daily (except Sundays) for Dallastown via the village of Spry.

In 1898, the Dallastown Railroad Company was incorporated to build a branch line into the borough of Dallastown. The Dallastown station on the Maryland & Pennsylvania Railroad (also known as the Ma & Pa) was opened on May 20, 1899. The station was located on a level lot near the corner of East Maple and North Walnut Streets. It measured 21 feet high and was 60 feet long by 24 feet wide. The station had a slate roof with wooden walls and wooden platforms on the west and south sides. It had a passenger waiting room, an agent's office, and a large freight room. On March 14, 1902, the Dallastown Railroad Company sold the branch line to the Maryland & Pennsylvania Railroad.

For many years, the Maryland & Pennsylvania Railroad agent in Dallastown was Charles J. Taylor, who assumed this position around 1912. Taylor was born in 1889 and lived until 1970. He was married to Amelia M. Taylor, and together they had four children and, for a time, lived on North Park Street Extended in Dallastown. Taylor served as agent for the Maryland & Pennsylvania Railroad until at least 1940. During this same era, he also served as an agent for the Adams Express Company, the American Railway Express, and the South Eastern Express Company. Taylor was also a successful dairy and hog farmer who owned three York County farms. The Dallastown station was closed on October 6, 1957, and the building was thereafter used for storage by the railroad until it was destroyed by fire in June 1959.

Before the station opened in 1899, railroad service to Dallastown reached only as close as the vicinity of the corner of North Walnut Street and Fruitlyn Drive. This was known as the Dallastown station stop on the narrow-gauge Peach Bottom Railway as early as 1875. From there, horse-drawn buggies or wagons relayed passengers, mail, or freight south on North Walnut Street for about one mile into the borough. It continued to be called the Dallastown stop as various small-gauge railroad companies operated along this line in the 1880s and 1890s. However, shortly after the 1899 opening of the 1.25-mile Dallastown Branch, which terminated at the Dallastown station on East Maple Street, the original Dallastown stop was renamed Relay by the York Southern Railroad. The Ma & Pa was converted to standard gauge in 1901. Interestingly, in March of that same year, the Ma & Pa ran a special train from the Relay station to Washington, DC, for the inauguration of Pres. William McKinley.

The York & Dallastown Electric Railway Company was organized in 1892 to construct a line from York south to Dallastown. In 1901, the York County Traction Company purchased control of the area's electric lines. It reorganized the Dallastown line into the York & Dallastown Railway Company and began construction of the line in March 1901. The distance between York and Dallastown, by trolley, was 7.1 miles and the trip took about 30 minutes.

The York & Dallastown Street Railway opened on July 27, 1901. At 10:00 a.m. on opening day, Dallastown had a celebration, including speeches from prominent citizens and music from the Dallastown Band. The mayor of Dallastown swore in four additional policemen during the first week that trolley service began, according to the borough's newspaper, the *Dallastown Advocate*.

The town council passed a law in 1902 that the trolley only be permitted to travel seven miles per hour throughout the borough. Nevertheless, a number of residents continued to complain about the speed at which the motormen drove the trolley cars through town. In 1907, the York & Dallastown Street Railway Company merged with the York Railways Company. The trolley continued service in the borough until February 1939. It was discontinued, in part, due to the rise of the automobile industry and the ubiquitous nature of cars and trucks owned by the residents of the town, which decreased the trolley line's patronage. York Railways Company was also denied the right to sell its surplus electric power for additional revenue to new city tracks by the Pennsylvania Utility Commission, which also pushed it into receivership in 1937. When trolley service stopped, bus lines were added to most of the towns formerly connected via the trolley system.

The people of Dallastown very devout town from its inception, and one of the earliest ordinances of the borough adopted in October 1866 was that "any person who shall sit or stand at the doors or windows or in or out of any church or other place of worship or nearby and through loud conversation or by laughing, puffing tobacco smoke, or running to or from place of worship in a disorderly manner and hallooing either before or after worship or any lawful assemblage or in this boro or any person who shall encourage or assist them in so doing each of them on conviction and at discretion of the Justice of the Peace or Chief Burgess forfeit and pay a fine of not less than One Dollar and not exceeding $25."

St. John's Blymire Church, or the United Church of Christ, was located south of Dallastown in 1758 by Martin Blymire. St. Paul's Lutheran and Reformed Church was built in the borough of Dallastown in 1856. In 1888, the Lutheran congregation built its own church, Christ Evangelical Lutheran Church, on West Main Street. The first United Brethren in Christ church was built in the town in 1850, on the present site of the old fire hall now occupied by the Dallastown Area Historical Society. St. Joseph's Catholic Church was founded in 1850 by Germanic citizens who emigrated from the various principalities of Baden, Bavaria, Hannover, Hesse, Prussia, and Westphalia. In 1908, Trinity Evangelical United Brethren Church was built on South Charles Street.

The Dallastown area has been inhabited predominantly by Pennsylvania Germans since the early 19th century. Many recognizably Germanic names dominated the town's city directories and telephone books throughout the 19th and 20th centuries.

Over the years, the town has evolved from an employment center into a bedroom community, as numerous businesses have either closed or moved out of the borough in the last several decades, including the town's banks, Wagman Ornamental Iron Works, River's Garage, and C. Joseph Deller and Sons. Dallastown's population in the 2010 census was 4,087 residents.

This book is a celebration of Dallastown's history and its people through the medium of photography. It has been created to coincide with the borough's sesquicentennial in 2016.

One

Street Scenes

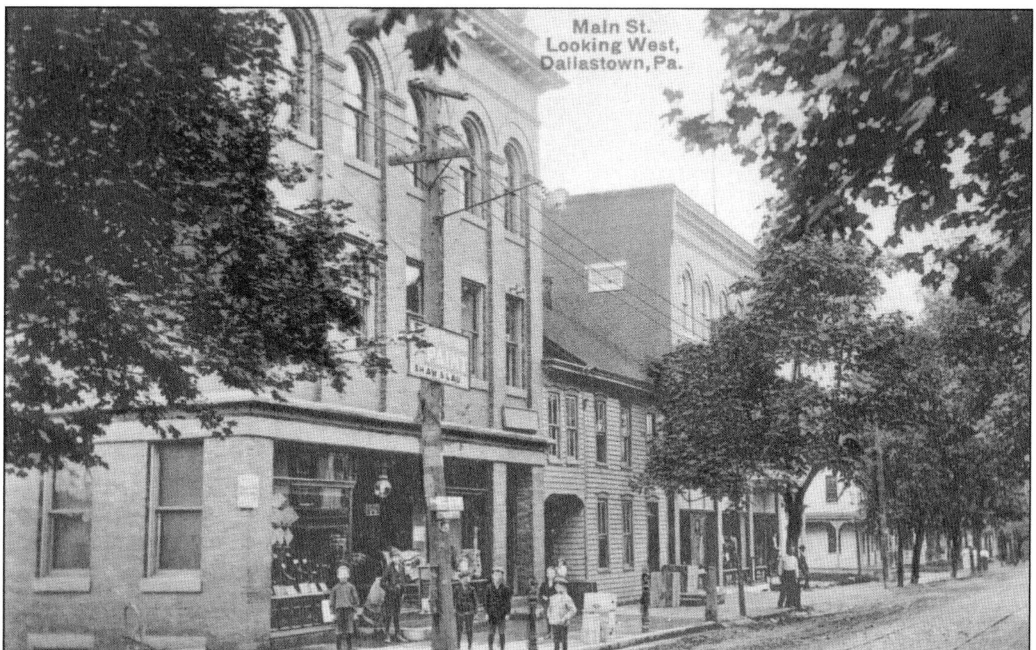

This postcard depicts the Hose Building at the southwest corner of Main and Walnut Streets on the town square in Dallastown. The structure was built by Michael Hose. On the street level of the three-story building is the Shaw & Lau general merchandise store, shown sometime between 1904 and 1909. The building is long gone, but the location currently houses the town's Turkey Hill Minute Market.

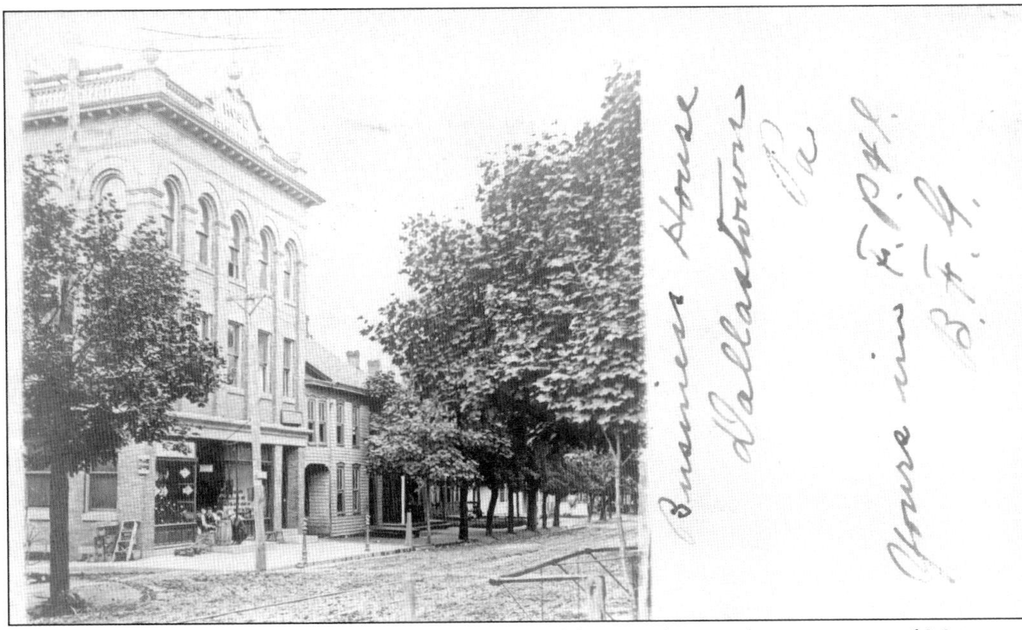

Mailed in 1906, this postcard shows the Hose Building at the southwest corner of Main and Walnut Streets in Dallastown. The owner, Michael Hose, was the proprietor of both a cigar box–manufacturing factory and a cigar manufacturing business by 1900. He was married to Mary Adelaide Keesey in 1883. The view is looking west along West Main Street. Trolley tracks are visible on the unpaved street. (Courtesy of Tom Taylor.)

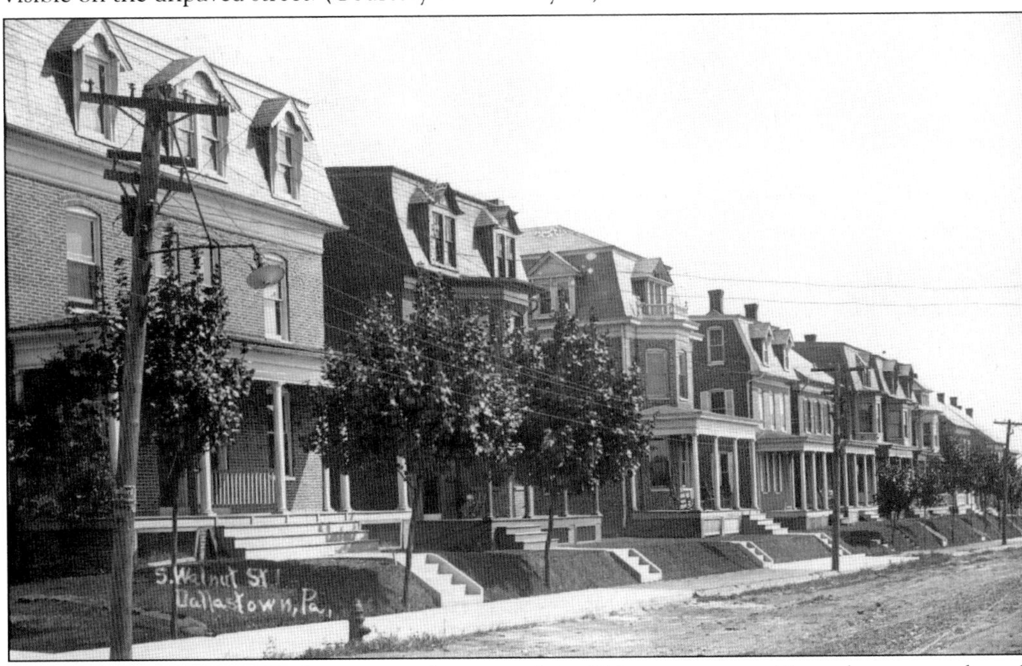

South Walnut Street in Dallastown is shown in this 1913 street scene. Note the unpaved road. The buildings in the image are family residences on the east side of the street, at the corner of East Howard and South Walnut Streets. A number of businesses were on the west side of the street, such as the Lyric Theatre and the New York Cigar factory. (Courtesy of Tom Taylor.)

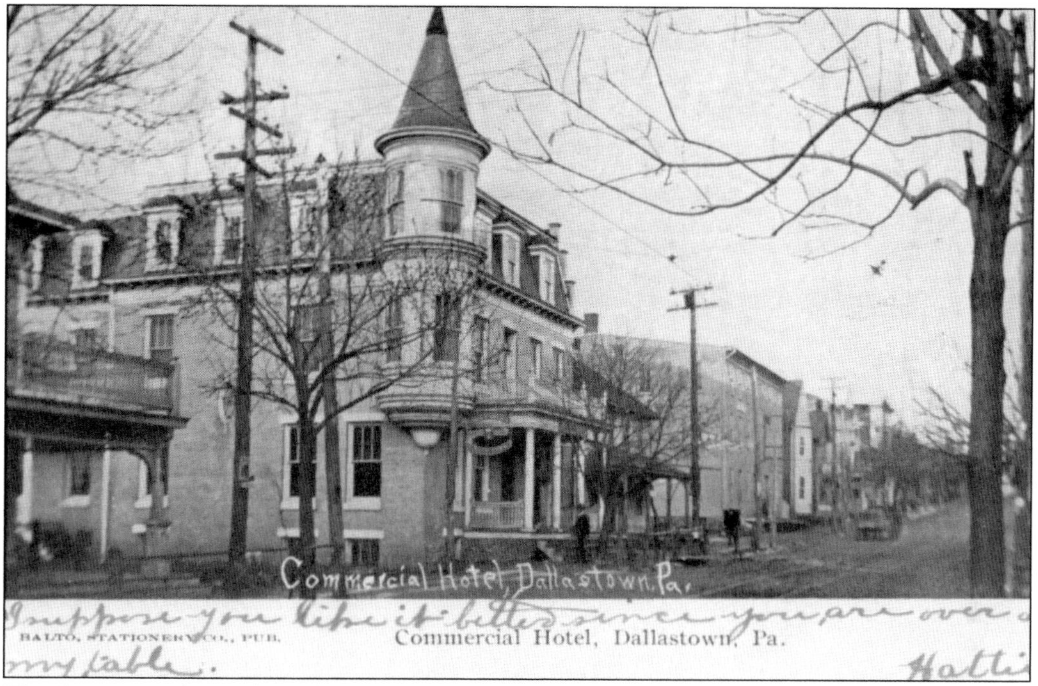

The Commercial Hotel was located at the corners of East Main and North Walnut Streets on the square in Dallastown. This postcard's view is looking east along Main Street. The ground floor of this building housed numerous businesses over the years, including a cigar store, pool hall, greeting card and magazine shop, soda fountain, and an arcade. This structure is currently used as an apartment building. (Courtesy of Cathy Bankoske.)

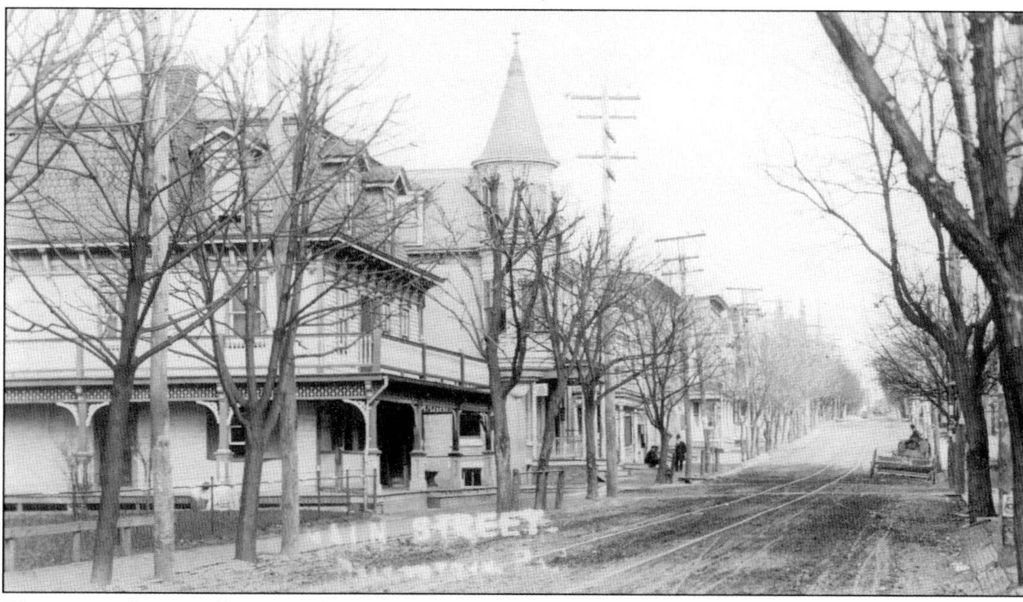

This scene from Dallastown depicts the north side of the town's square. The first two buildings on the left side of the postcard are the Eagle Hotel and the Commercial Hotel. Both of these establishments were constructed in the 19th century. The view looks east along Main Street, sometime between 1904 and 1918. (Courtesy of Tom Taylor.)

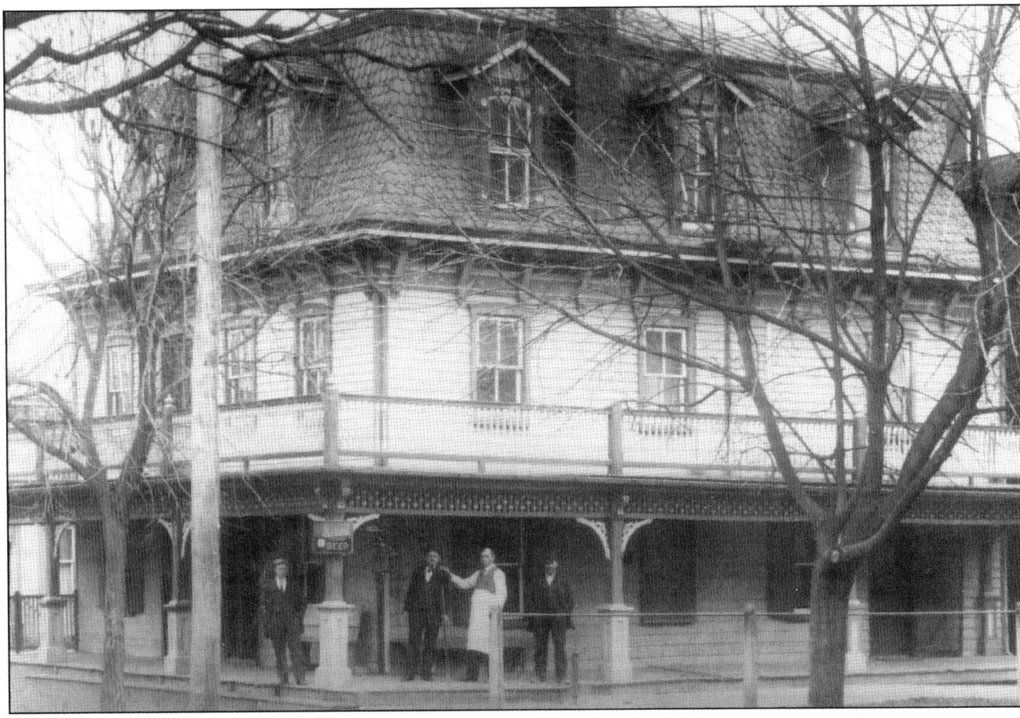

The Eagle Hotel was located on the town square of Dallastown at the corner of West Main and North Walnut Streets. The building was one of the first constructed in the town and appears on an 1860 map of the settlement. The site was later the location of Zarfoss Hardware store. (Courtesy of Roger Fuller.)

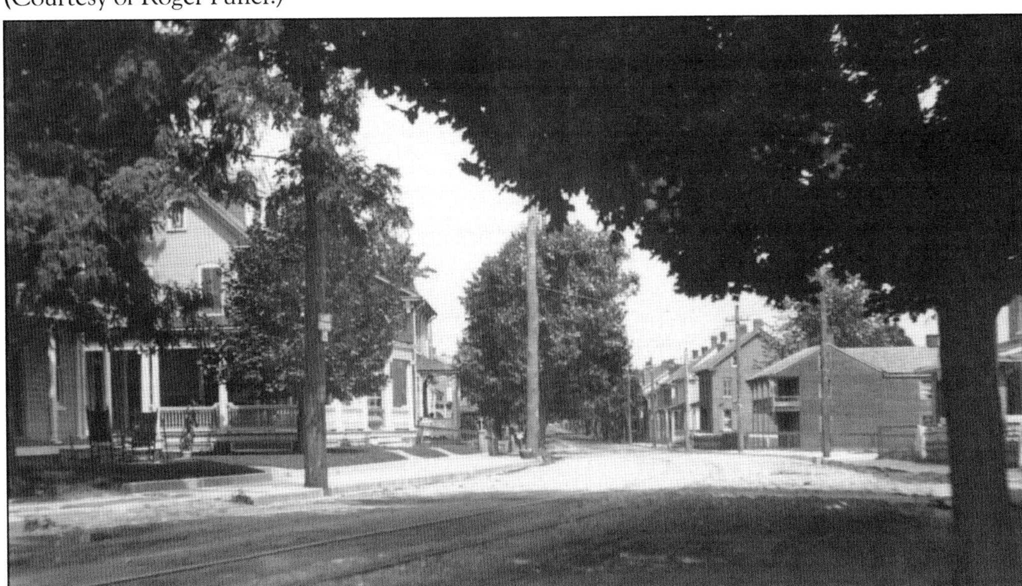

This view of West Main Street in the vicinity of School Street is looking east. Taken around 1902, this photograph depicts the way the west end of town looked from the 1880s forward, with the exception of the trolley tracks that are visible in the center of the unpaved street. The tracks were laid in town in 1901.

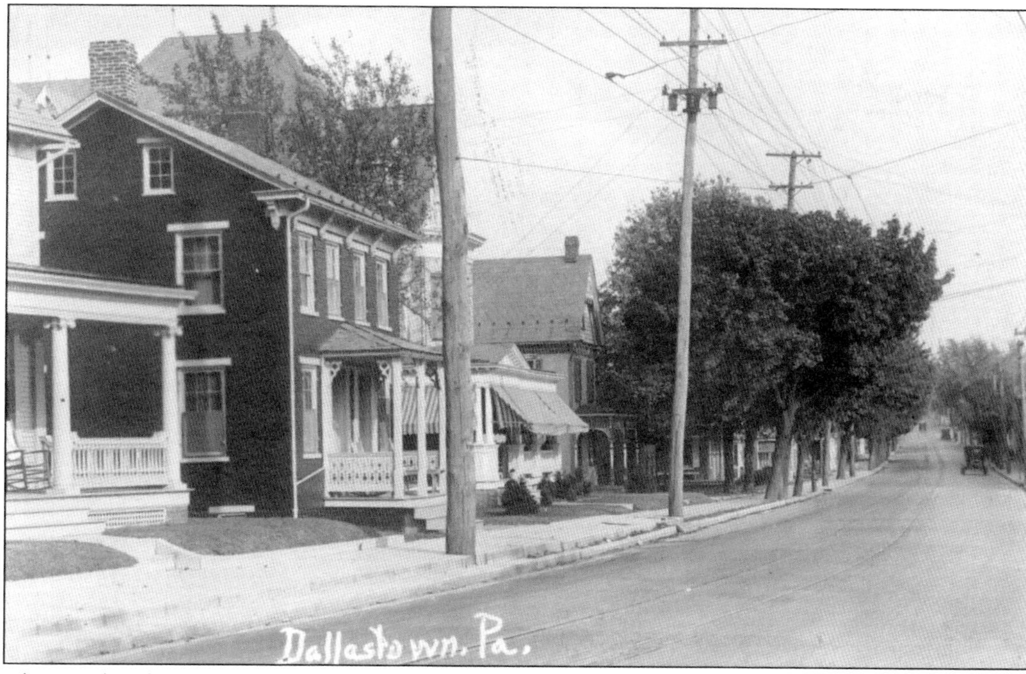

The north side of West Main Street, across the road from Christ Evangelical Lutheran Church, is the focal point of this c. 1920 photograph. The trolley tracks are still visible, but the street is now paved. A number of automobiles are visible driving east along tree-lined Main Street. (Courtesy of Cathy Bankoske.)

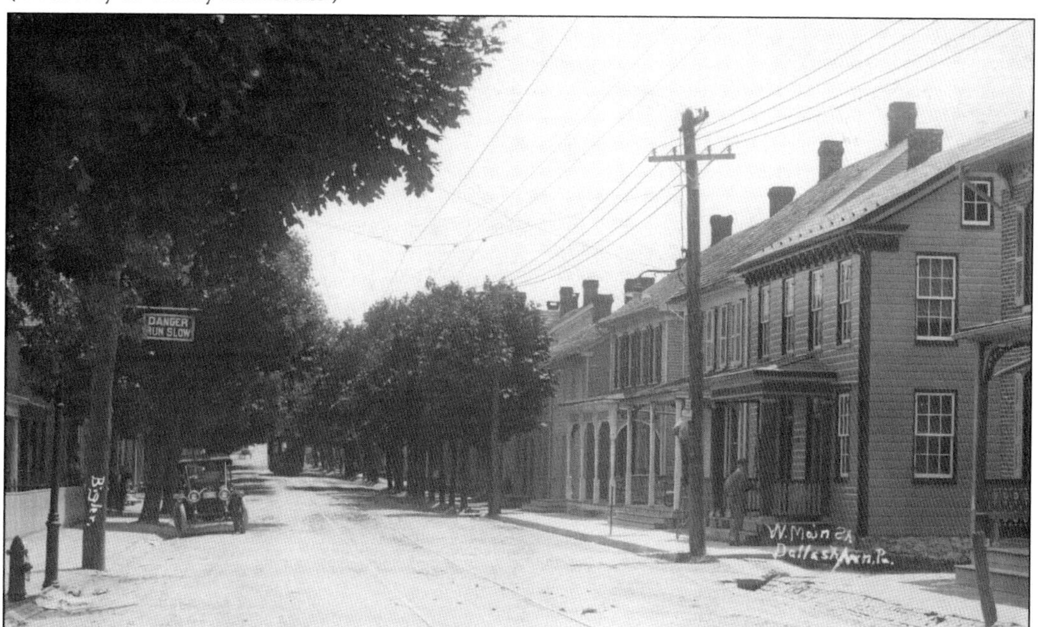

This postcard of West Main Street in Dallastown shows the trolley running along the tracks on the unpaved street between 1907 and 1915. Note the early traffic sign at left warning drivers: "Danger Run Slow." The speeds of both trolleys and automobiles were a great concern of the town's government in the first part of the 20th century. (Courtesy of Roger Fuller.)

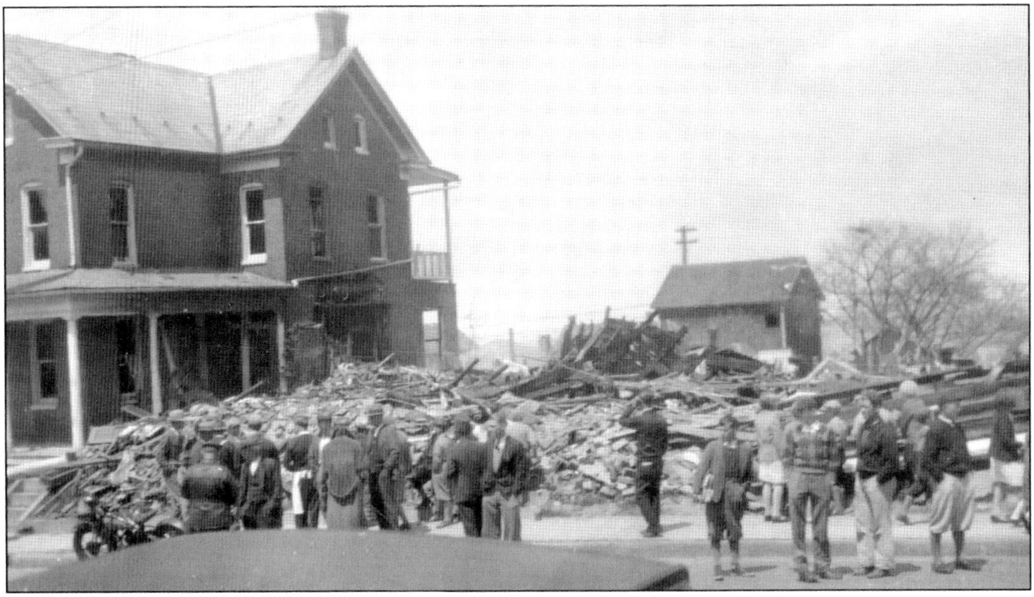

The site of a house explosion and fire at 359 East Main Street in Dallastown is depicted in this photograph. Townspeople are shown gathered around the area of debris. The gas explosion occurred on April 27, 1933, and completely destroyed the home of Archibald Grim and damaged the John Myers house next door as well. Injured were Priscilla Grim, Harry Keller, Charles Keller, and Earl Myers. The explosion was heard for miles around the accident site.

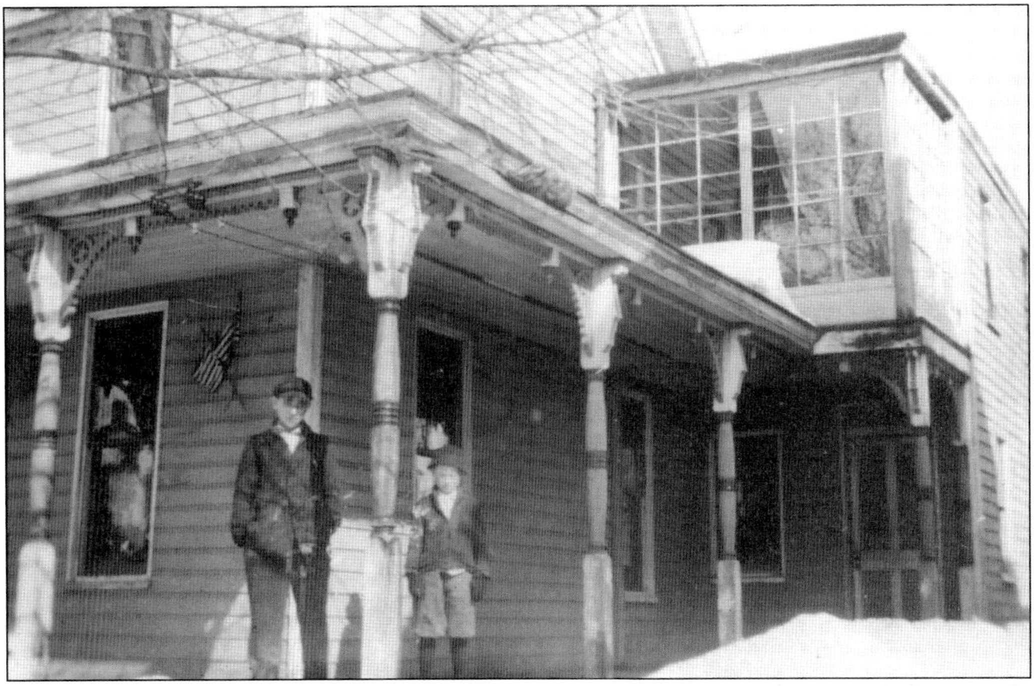

Grim family members pose on their porch at 387 West Main Street in this c. 1930 photograph. The image was taken during the winter season as evidenced by the snow piles. Years later, Joan Shirley (Grim) Hoffman ran a beauty shop in this building from the 1950s to the 1960s. It also continued to be used as a family home. (Courtesy of Priscilla Hoffman.)

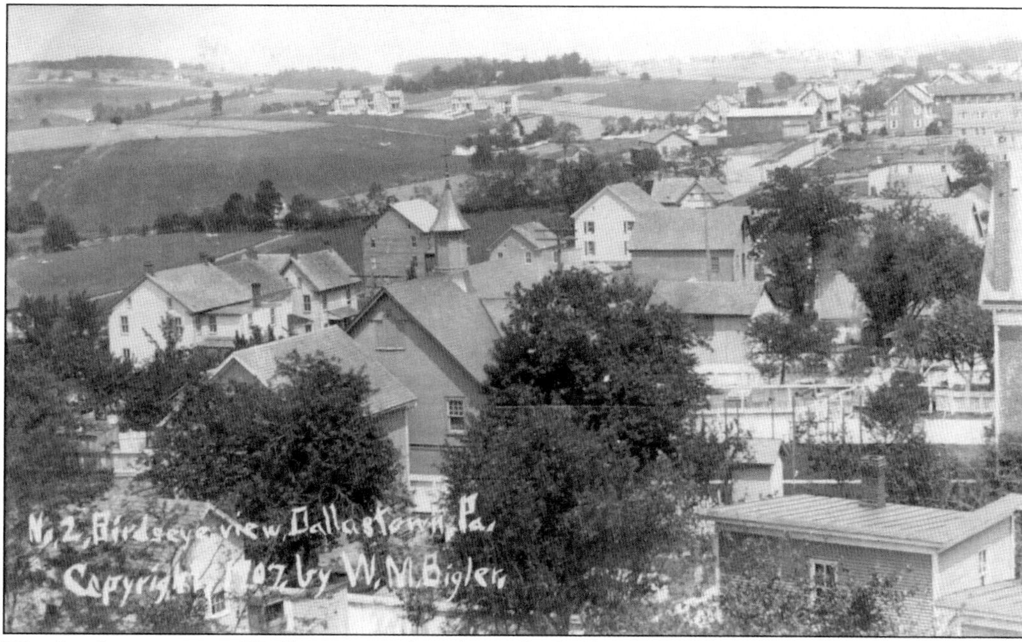

This bird's-eye view of Dallastown, taken from the bell tower of the public school at the corner of School Place and West Main Street, is looking northeast. It was taken in 1907 by Dallastown photographer William M. Bigler. House-lined Maple Street starts at the left edge of the image and runs diagonally to the center. Lombard Street, running to Yoe, is located in the upper left background of this postcard. (Courtesy of Jeffrey L. Deller.)

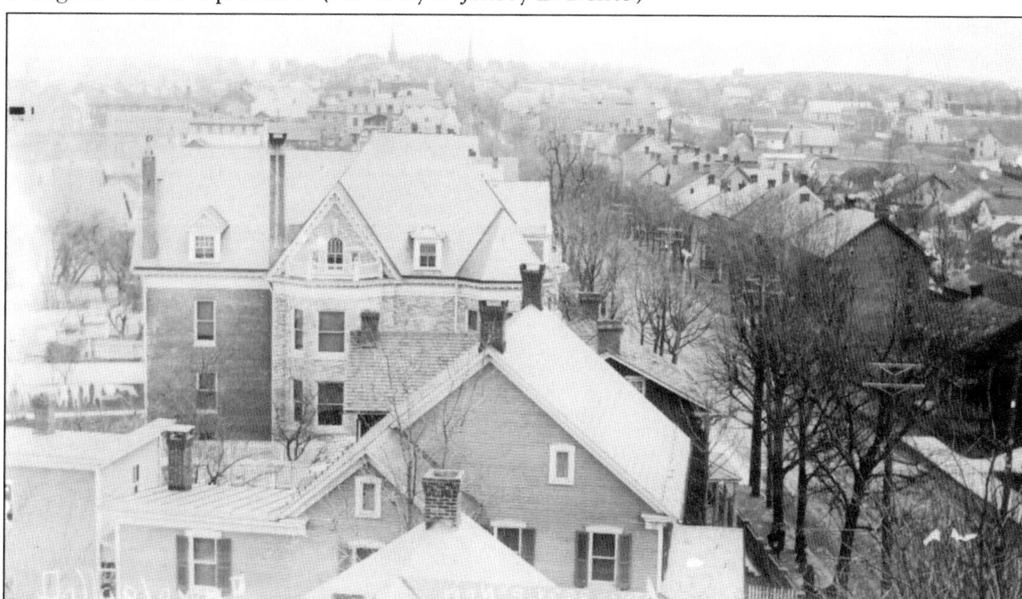

Standing in the old public school's bell tower at the corner of School Place and West Main Street, Dallastown photographer William M. Bigler took this bird's-eye photograph with a view looking southeast along West Main in 1907. The Commercial Hotel's turret is visible in the distance, on the north side of the street, as is St. Joseph Catholic Church's steeple. (Courtesy of Jeffrey L. Deller.)

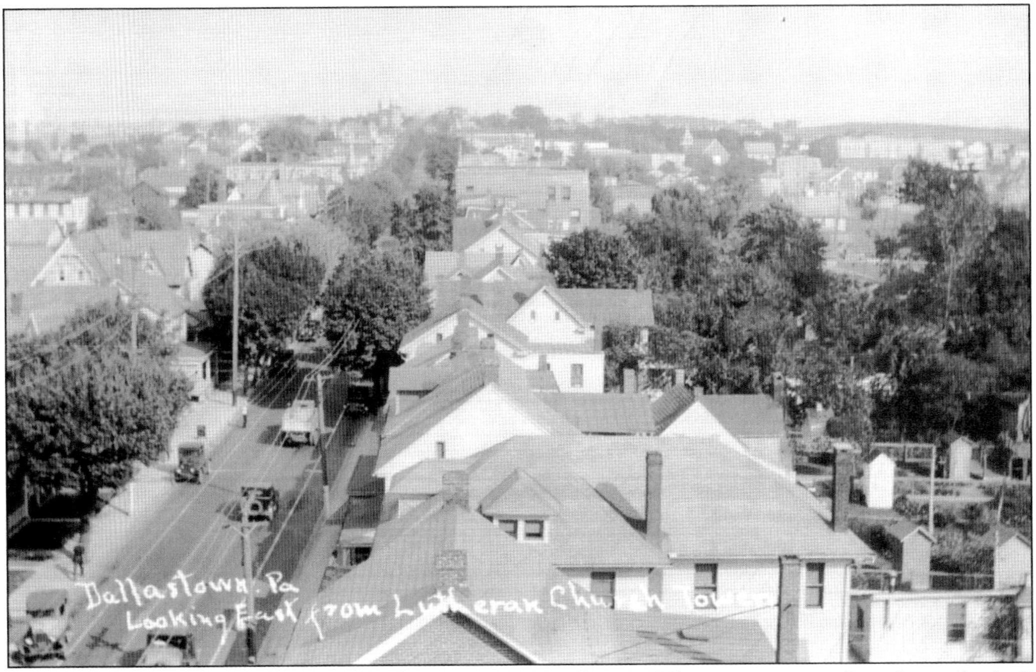

This bird's-eye view is looking east along West Main Street. The image was taken from the bell tower of Christ Evangelical Lutheran Church. Bethlehem United Methodist Church and St. Joseph Catholic Church steeples are visible in the distance. Numerous outhouses and small gardens can be seen in the lower right corner of this photograph.

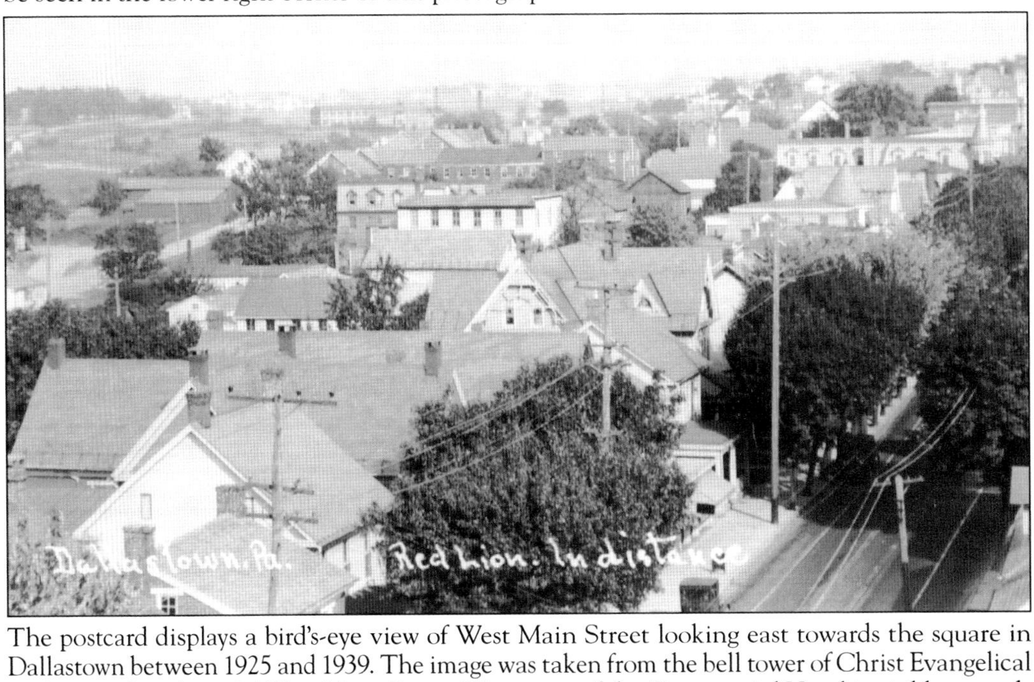

The postcard displays a bird's-eye view of West Main Street looking east towards the square in Dallastown between 1925 and 1939. The image was taken from the bell tower of Christ Evangelical Lutheran Church at 126 West Main Street. The turret of the Commercial Hotel is visible towards the right side of the image above the trees. The neighboring town of Red Lion can be seen in the upper left background. (Courtesy of Tom Taylor.)

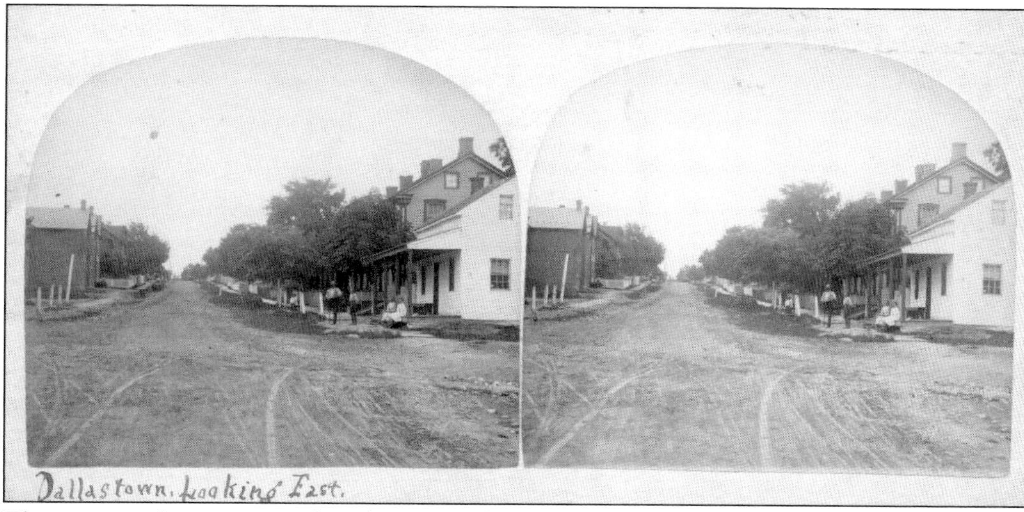

The view in this stereograph, taken around the 1880s, looks east along East Main Street in Dallastown. Note the dirt roads and that there are no telephone lines or trolley tracks. A man near the right street corner is missing his right leg and is using crutches in order to stand. (Courtesy of Tom Taylor.)

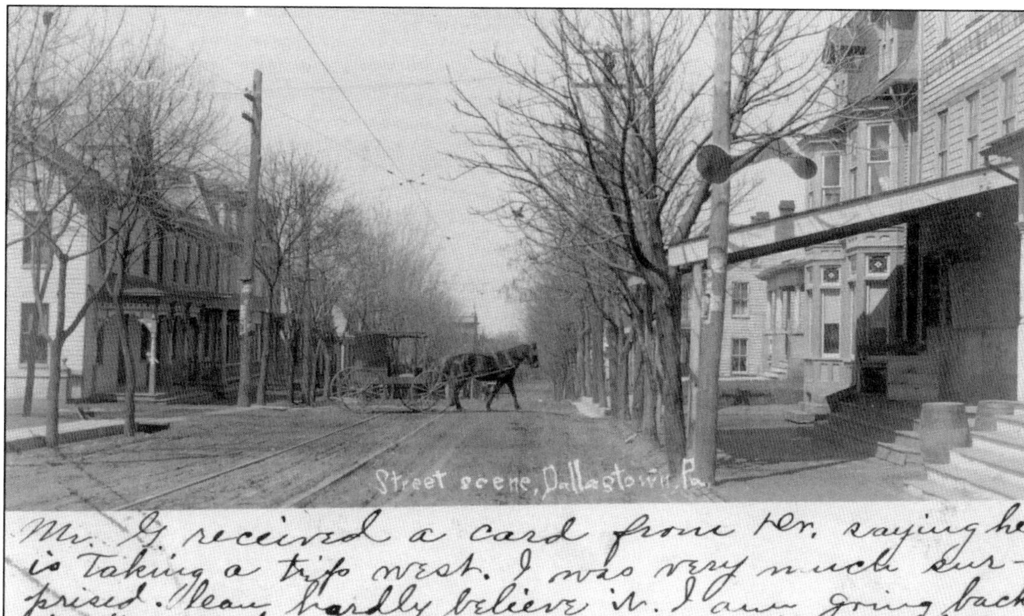

With a view looking west, this postcard image was taken on East Main Street in Dallastown sometime between 1901 and 1907. The top of the Hose Building can be seen in the center background of the image, on the left side of the road. The street is made of dirt, and trolley tracks are visible in the center of the road. A horse and buggy are shown crossing East Main Street. (Courtesy of Tom Taylor.)

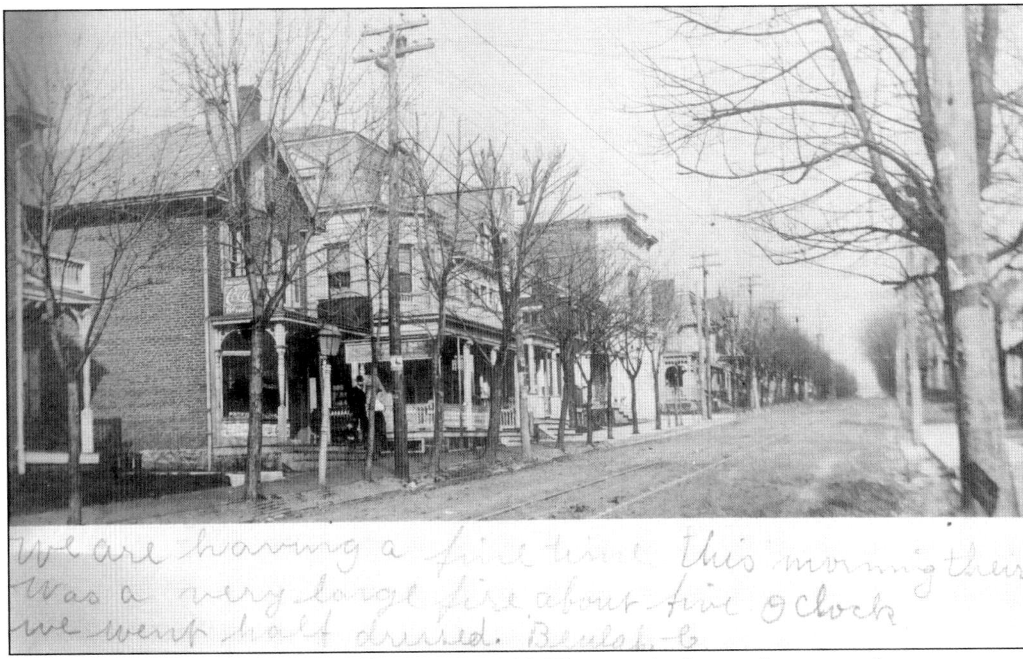

This postcard was mailed from Dallastown in 1908. The view looks east from near the town square along East Main Street. George A. Meyers's pharmacy is visible on the left side of the street, and Meyers and his wife, Amanda, are standing on the front steps of the business. Farther east on the same side of the road is the First National Bank of Dallastown. (Courtesy of Tom Taylor.)

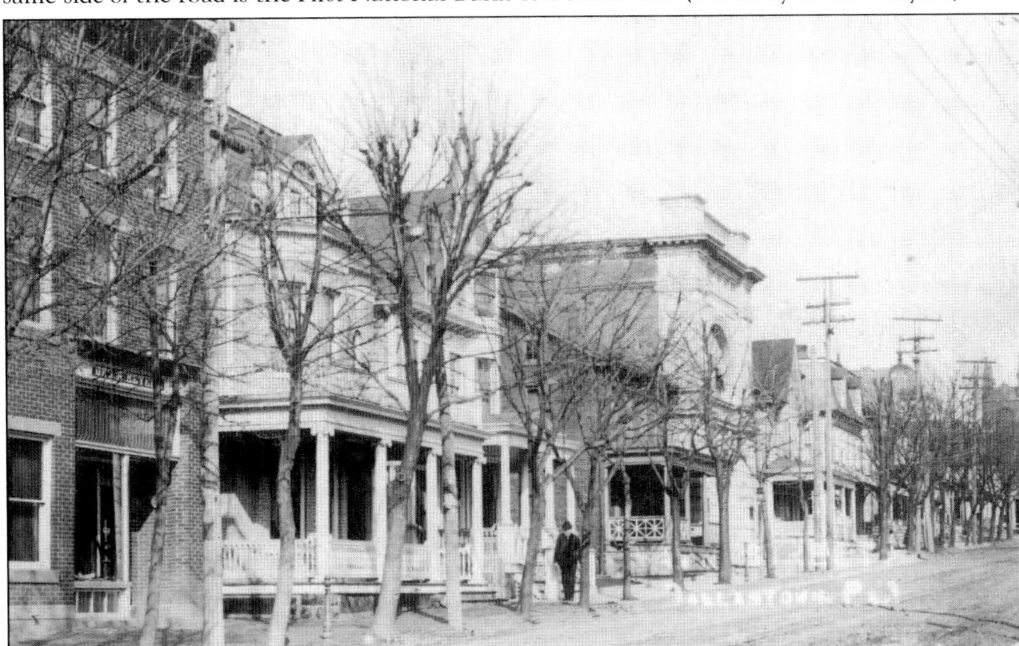

Approximately 11 years after the previous image was made, this postcard photograph was taken from practically the same location. The view looks east along East Main Street in Dallastown. George A. Meyers's pharmacy is visible on the north side of the street, but by 1919, it had a new facade. (Courtesy of Tom Taylor.)

This view of a street scene in Dallastown looks east along East Main Street. The image was taken between 1904 and 1918 from the south side of the street near St. Joseph Catholic Church. Two boys run in the unpaved road near the tracks as a trolley car is visible at the intersection of Park and Main Streets. A sign attached to a tree in the bottom left of the postcard advertises "Crystal Ball Cigars." (Courtesy of Tom Taylor.)

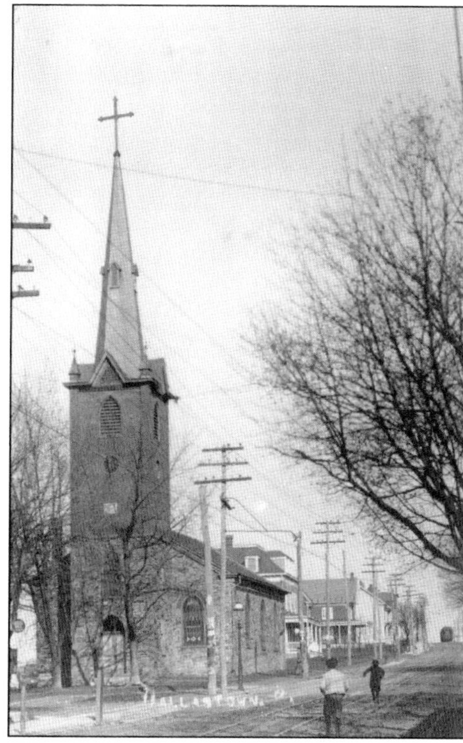

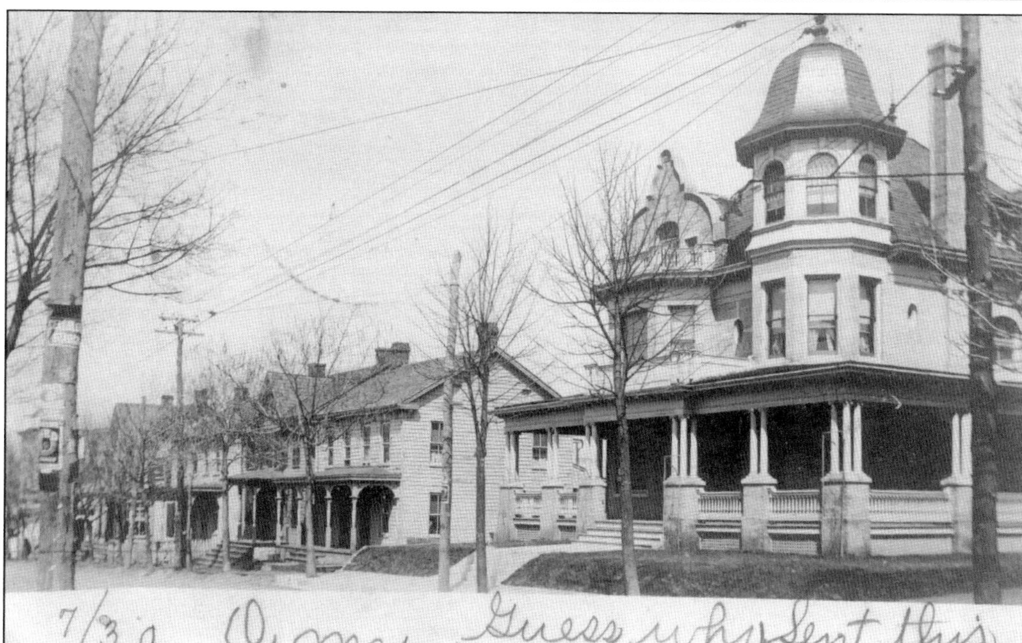

William Henry Raab's house, located at 83 East Main Street, is on the far right side of this postcard image from 1906. This view looks west along the north side of East Main Street. Raab served four terms as postmaster of Dallastown, was an incorporator of the First National Bank of Dallastown, and belonged to the Patriotic Order Sons of America and the Ancient Order Knights of the Mystic Chain. (Courtesy of Tom Taylor.)

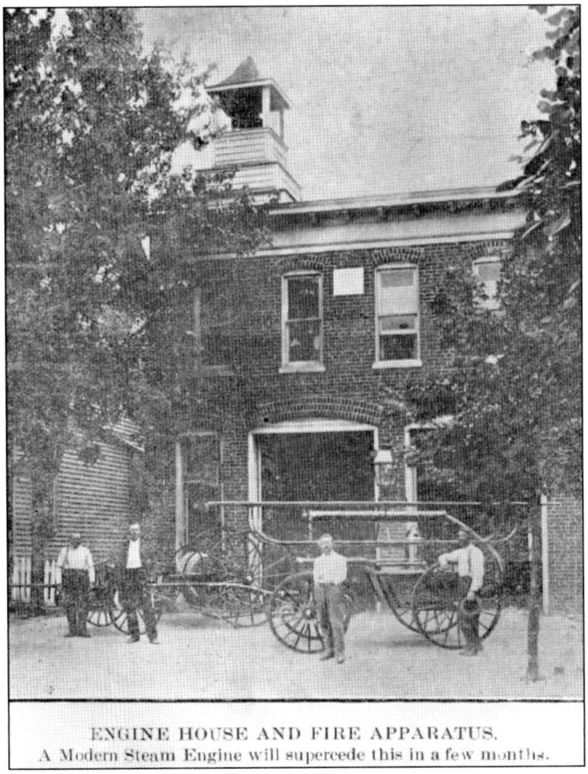

Dallastown's Rescue Fire Company No. 1 was founded in March 1892, with W.L. Glatfelter as the first president. The original Dallastown firehouse is depicted in this c. 1900 image along with the company's first hand-drawn hose and ladder cart and hand pumper. This firehouse was used until a new one was built in 1913. (Courtesy of Roger Fuller.)

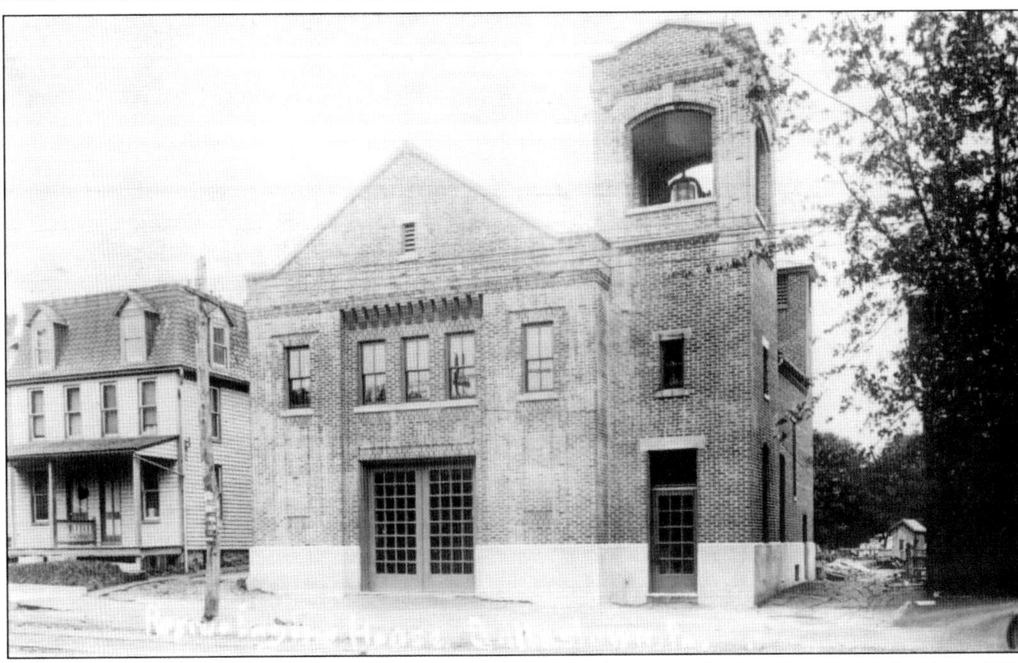

The second Dallastown Rescue Fire Company's engine house is depicted as it was built in 1913 at 118 East Main Street. It is a large two-story brick building that housed trucks and equipment on the first floor and meeting rooms, a small recreation room, and the Chief Burgess office on the second.

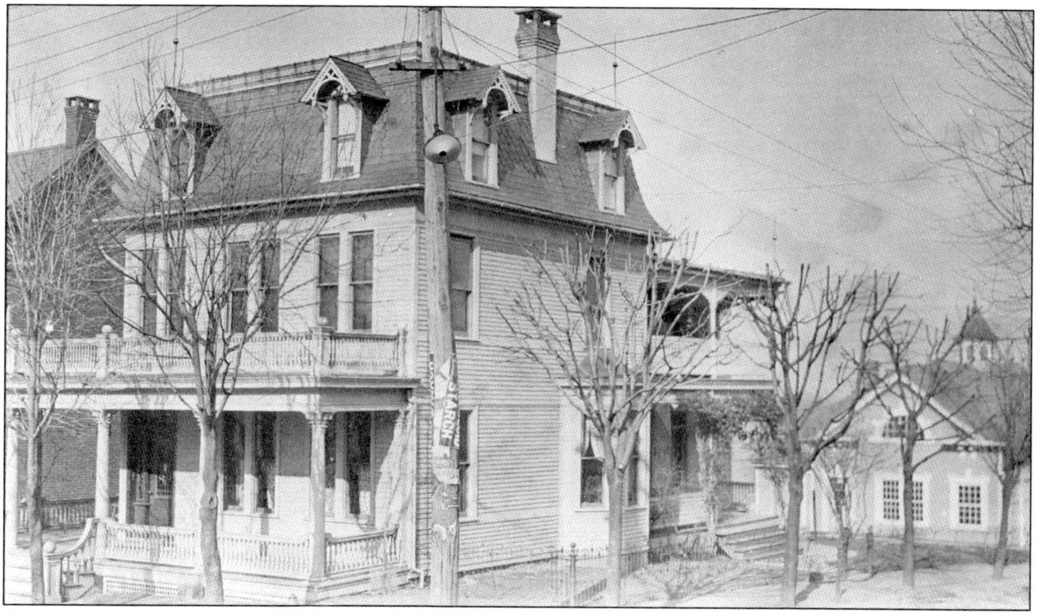

Cigar manufacturer John W. Minnich's house is depicted on this postcard. The house is located at 157 East Main Street, on the northwest corner of East Main Street and North Pleasant Avenue. This image was taken before 1905, as there is not yet a side porch on the west side of the house. Minnich, born on January 21, 1860, owned J.W. Minnich Cigar Factory in Dallastown. (Courtesy of Lance Wolf.)

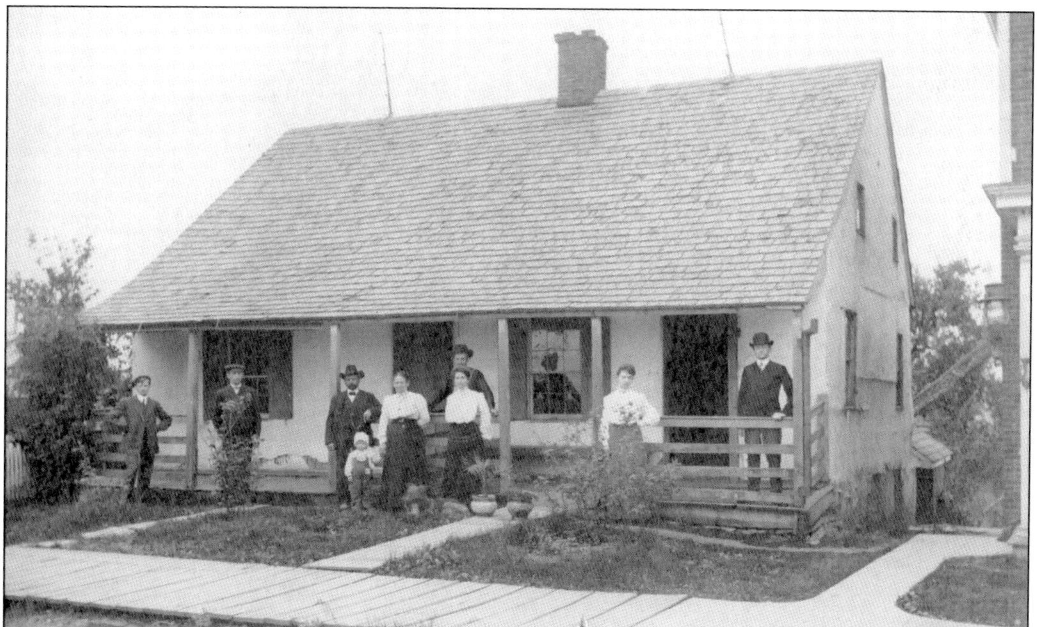

The house in this c. 1906 image was located between 300 and 316 East Main Street in Dallastown. Martin Valentine Simon and his wife, Carolyn Margaret Wagman, built a new home next to this one, which was then torn down. From left to right are John F. (son), Henry C. "Harry" (son), Martin, James Walter Simon (grandson), Carolyn, Valentine Martin "Walter" (son), Euphemia (daughter), Gertrude C. (daughter), and James Lewis (son). (Courtesy of Cathy Bankoske.)

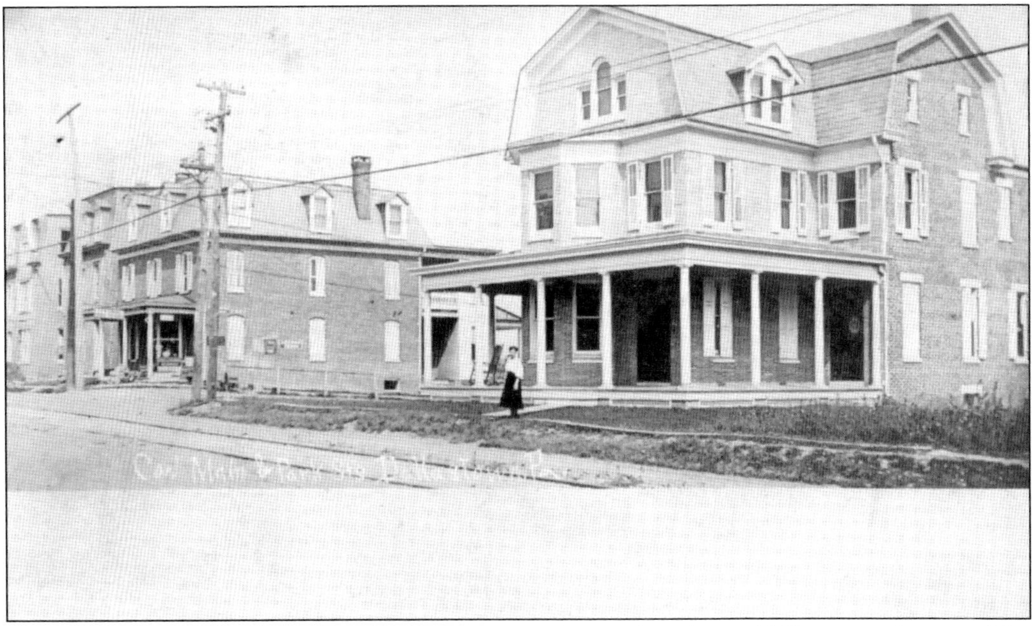

The corner of North Park and East Main Streets is depicted in this c. 1907 postcard image. The building on the left, 377 East Main Street, had a grocery store on the first floor that was run by Henry Joseph Ryer in the 1920s and 1930s. Ryer and his wife, Marie, rented a house at 438 East Main Street for their family residence, according to the 1940 federal census.

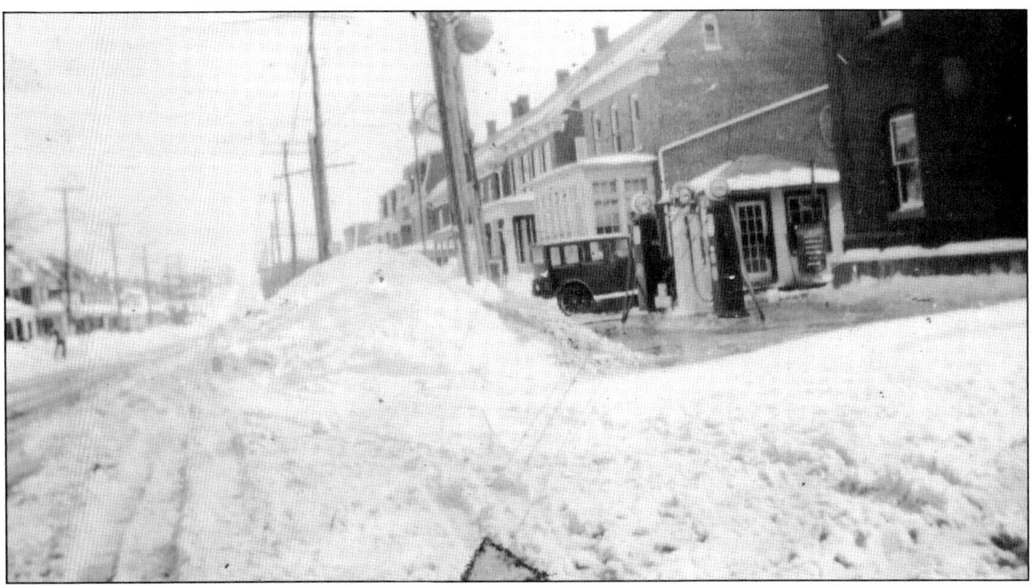

Carson Landis's service station was located at 400 East Main Street, near the corner of the intersection with South Park Street. This image of the gas pumps and the south side of East Main Street was taken during the winter around 1935. Carson Landis was born in 1901 and died in 1985. (Courtesy of Cathy Bankoske.)

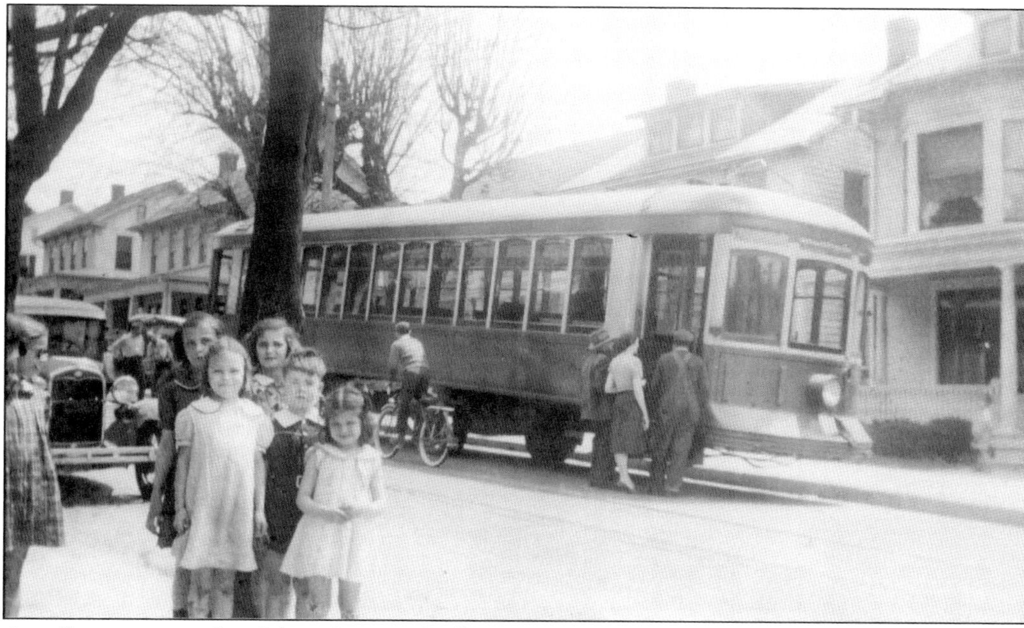

A trolley car stopped on Main Street in Dallastown is depicted in this photograph. Children from town pose in the forefront of the c. 1930s image. Trolley car No. 319 is off its tracks and is hooked up to a truck for towing. Derailments such as this were not terribly unusual for trolleys.

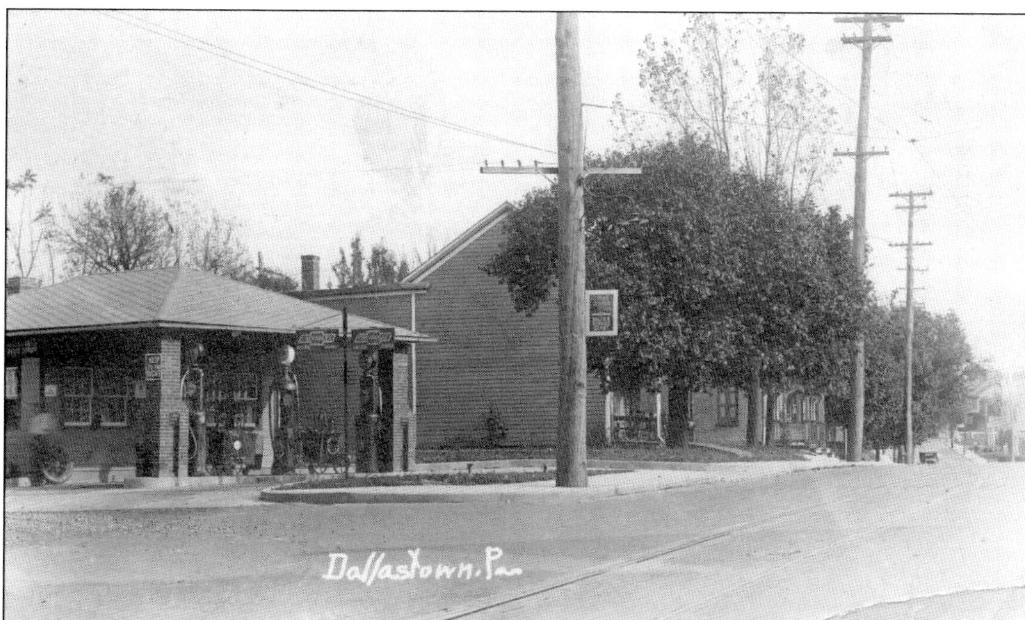

This 1927 postcard of Carr Motor Company Inc. in Dallastown shows its service station and visible gas pumps on the left side of the image. The business was managed by Jere E. Carr. This station and garage was located at 397 West Main Street. Note the trolley tracks on the paved street. This company was listed in city directories from 1923 to 1928. (Courtesy of Barry Arnold.)

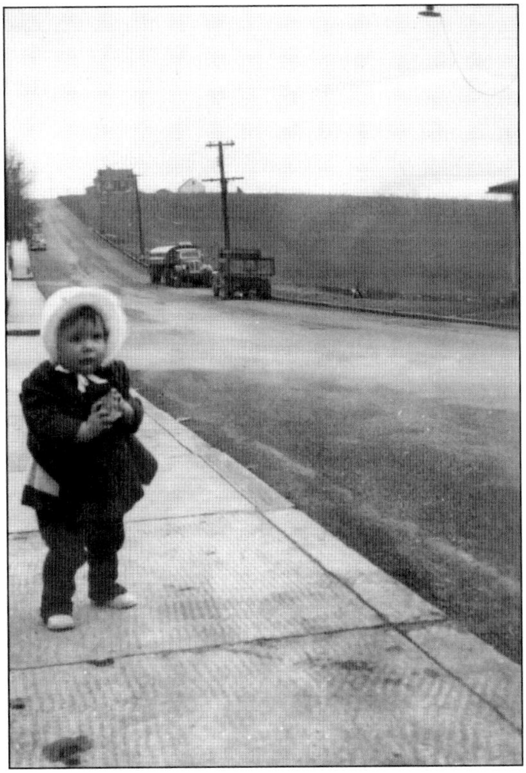

This image depicts South Park Street being paved in 1950. On the right side of the image, there is a great amount of farmland. Near the bottom left of the photograph is Rosena R. Deller, standing on the sidewalk near the intersection of South Park and East Frederick Streets. (Courtesy Michael L. Sentz Jr.)

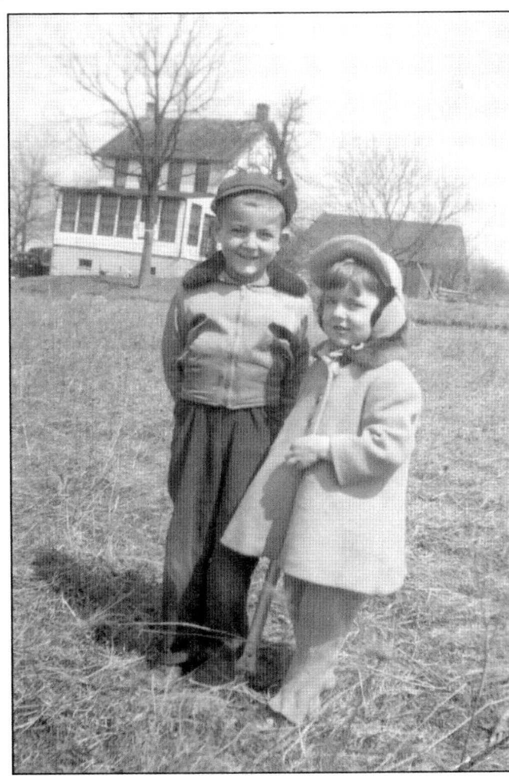

Rick and Jane Steinfelt, children of Joseph and Elizabeth (Eck) Steinfelt, pose in front of the Eck family farmhouse around the 1940s. The Eck family home was located on the east side of South Park Street, opposite Mellinger Drive, in RD No. 1 Dallastown. The farmhouse was burned down in the fall of 1986. The farm property was converted into a housing development in the 1990s. (Courtesy of Jeanne M. Saylor.)

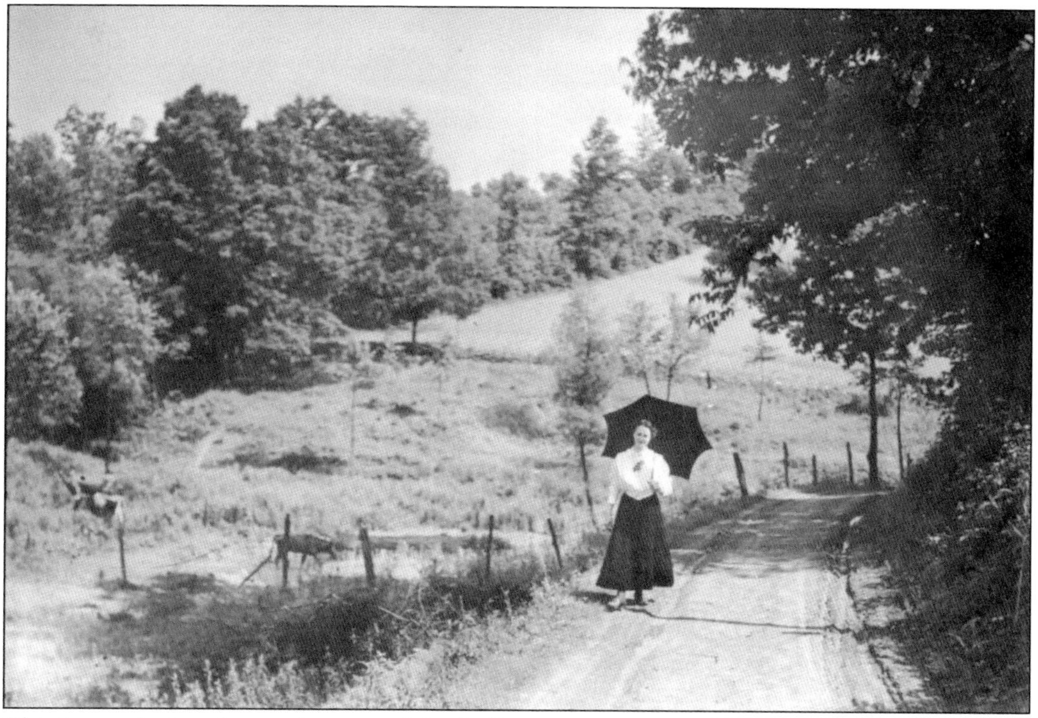

This image depicts the rural nature of the Dallastown area around the turn of the 20th century. Note the unpaved road marred with wagon wheel ruts on which the unidentified woman poses in the countryside of the Codorus Valley. Many of the dirt roads outside of the center of town were not paved until the 1940s and 1950s. (Courtesy of Cathy Bankoske.)

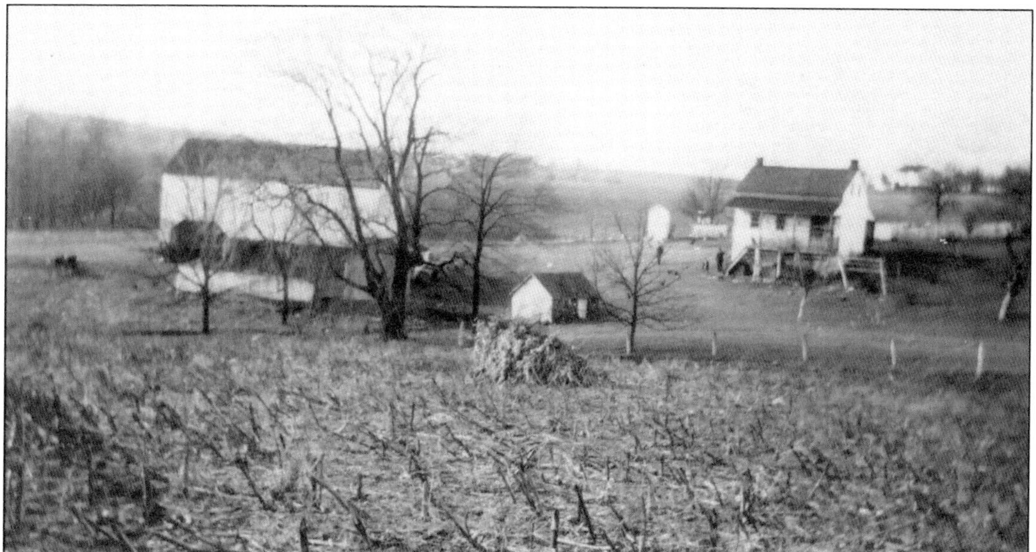

The Riedel (Reidel) farm near Dallastown is depicted on this postcard produced between 1918 and 1930. This farm is a good example of the many farmsteads located around this area in the early 20th century. It was located just outside of Dallastown in the Honey Valley area and was the residence of Michael Riedel and his wife, Margaret Snellbaker. Riedel was born in Germany in 1822 and immigrated to Pennsylvania in 1846. (Courtesy of Tom Taylor.)

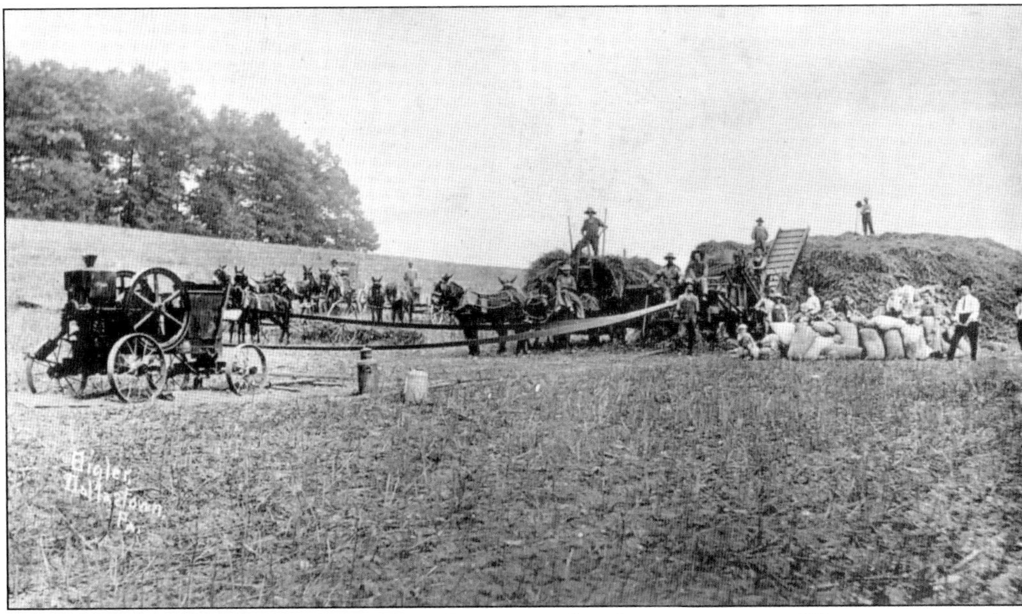

Dallastown-area farmers are depicted in this postcard gathering in a crop. The image was taken by Dallastown photographer William M. Bigler between 1904 and 1918. The scene shows a field of grain being harvested and bagged in the scenic Codorus Valley. It shows the relationship between manpower, horse- or donkey power, and machine power as the area's farming industry moves slowly towards more mechanization. (Courtesy of Tom Taylor.)

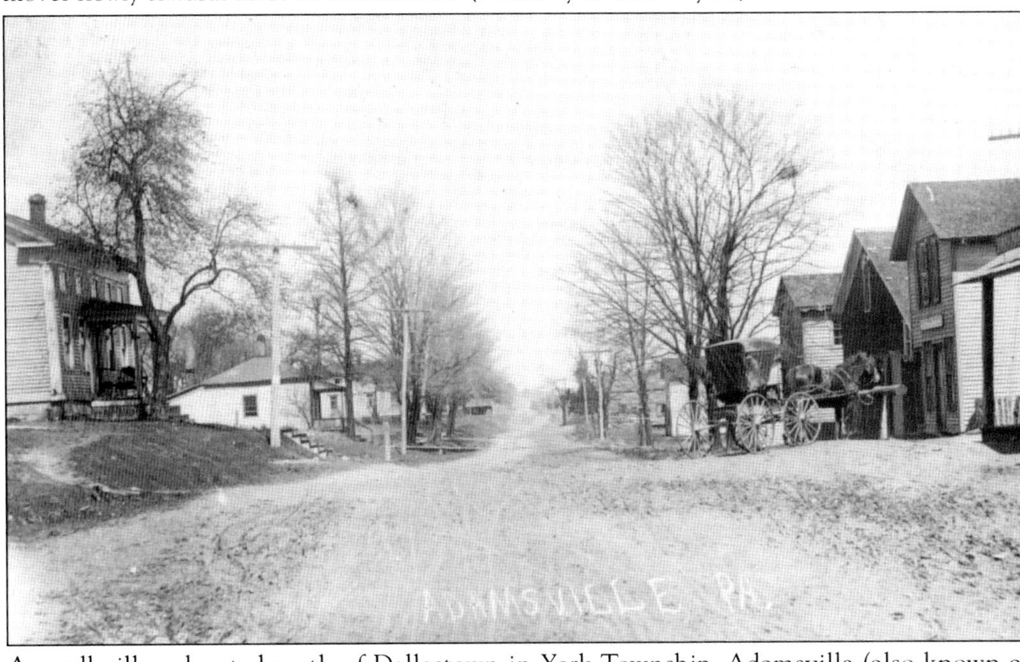

A small village located south of Dallastown in York Township, Adamsville (also known as Pinchgut or Arbor) is depicted on this postcard mailed in 1909. The view is of the main dirt road in the town and shows a one-horse buggy roped to a hitching post in front of a store. It is a crossroads town that is located near the intersection of South Duke and South Franklin Streets. (Courtesy of Tom Taylor.)

Two

Businesses

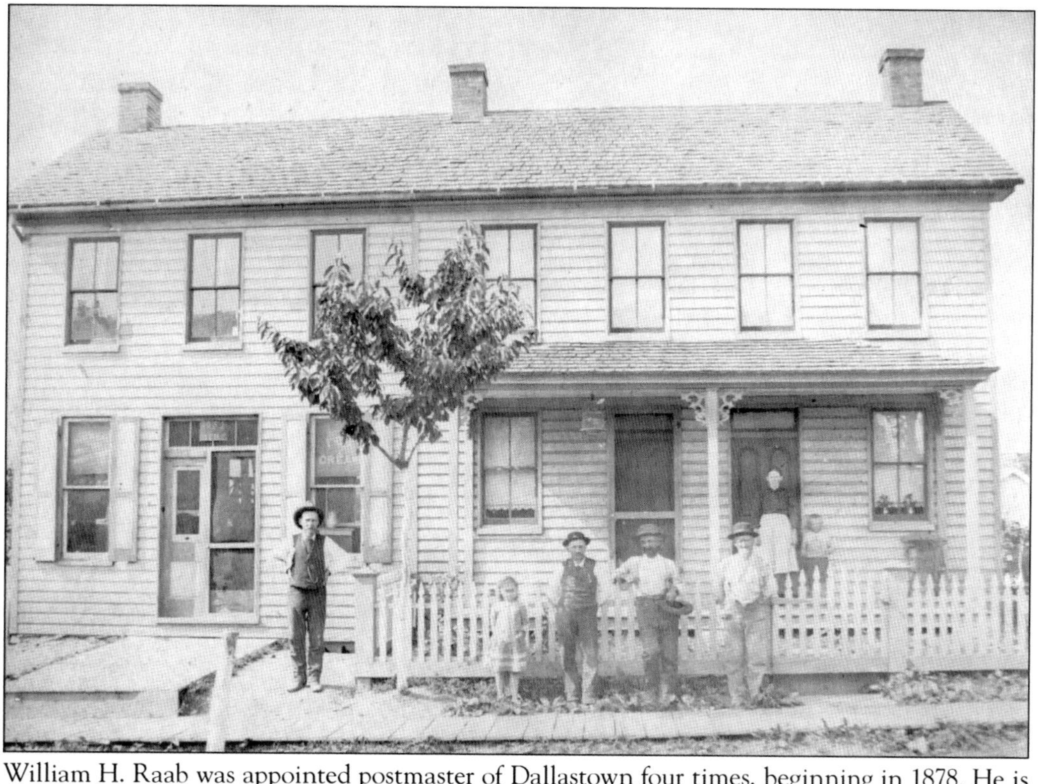

William H. Raab was appointed postmaster of Dallastown four times, beginning in 1878. He is also listed as a confectioner in an 1887 city directory. This photograph shows the post office in Dallastown and a store that sold Raab's confections around the 1880s. Three signs are visible in the windows on the first floor of the building—"Fancy Confections," "Post Office," and "Ice Cream." The building was located on East Maple Street.

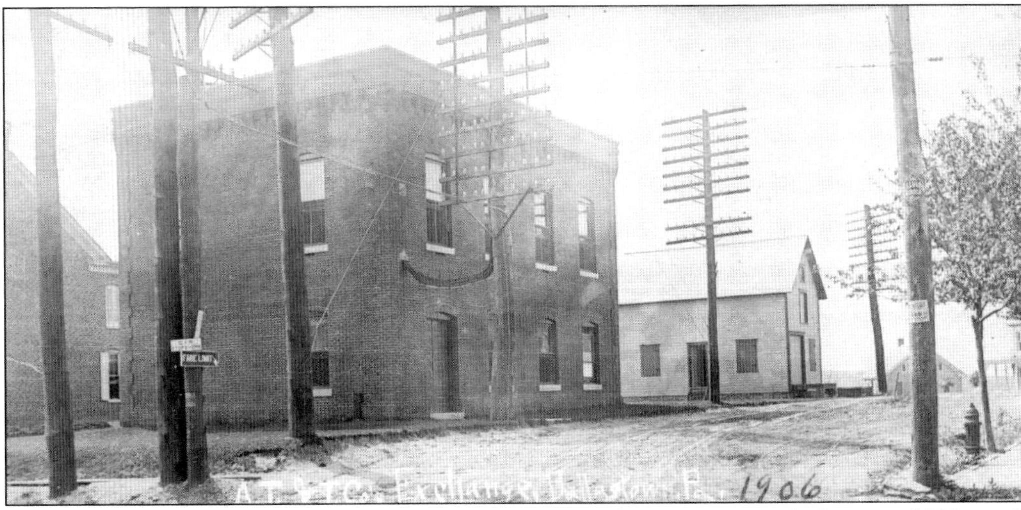

This 1906 postcard depicts the Dallastown test station for the American Telephone and Telegraph Company. Built in 1902, it was located on the southeast corner of South Park and East Main Streets. It was the company's most important testing station between Chicago and New York. In 1915, the Dallastown test station sent through the first transcontinental telephone message from New York to California. It was closed at the end of 1927. (Courtesy of Roger Fuller.)

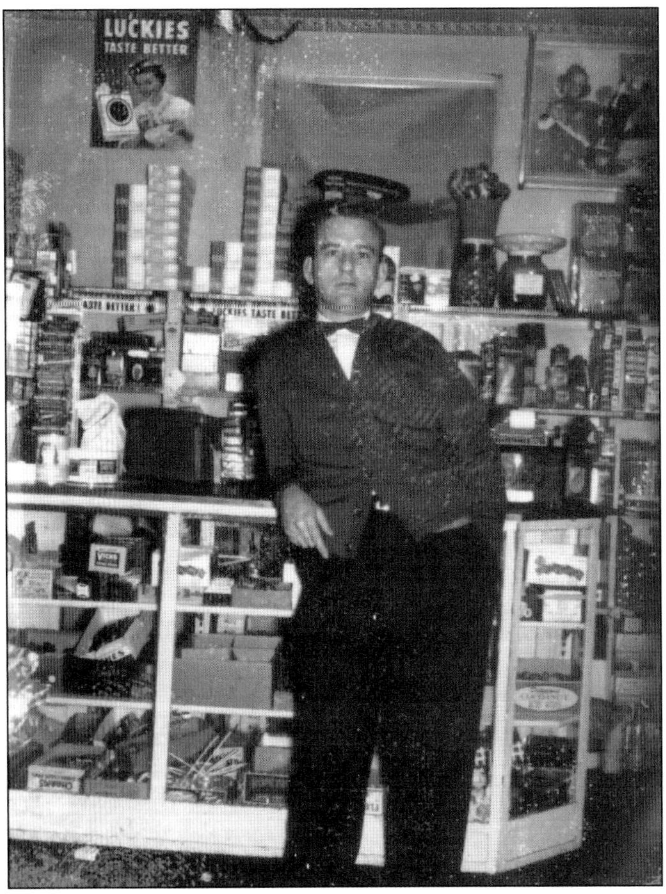

The interior view of the Community Pure Food Store, at 276 West Main Street in Dallastown, was taken in 1955. The man pictured in this photograph is the store's owner Harry Newman. He and his wife, Elsie Newman, lived above the store and were in business together there until 1958. (Courtesy of Cheryl Newman.)

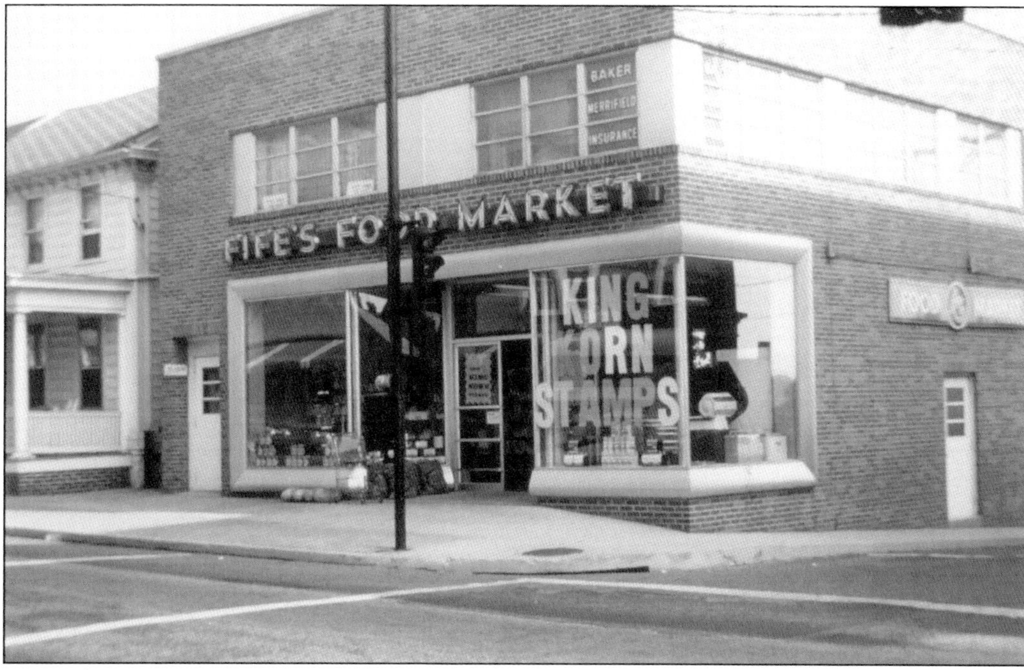

Located at 2 East Main Street, at the southeast corner of the square in Dallastown, this property was purchased in the early 1940s by Winfield R. Fife. Additions to the building were made in 1953 and 1954, as Fife's Food Market expanded. The Fife family ran this grocery store business from the 1940s until 1978. This photograph was taken in the early 1960s. The grocery store itself closed in 1986.

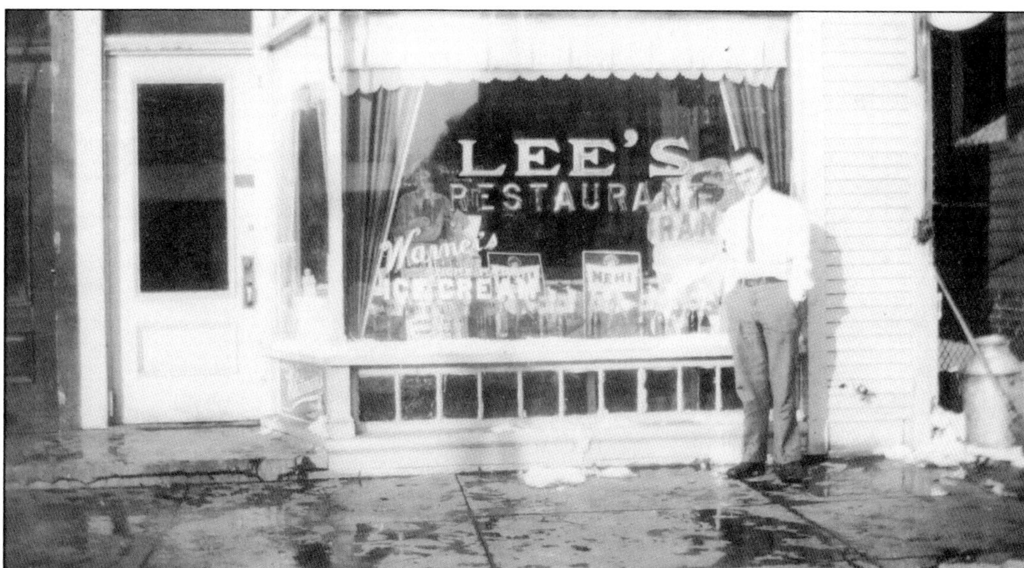

Lee L. Warner, the owner of Lee's Restaurant, is pictured in front of the eatery near the square around the 1940s. Note the old metal milk cans to the right of the building and the Warner's Ice Cream and Nehi advertisements in the restaurant's window. Warner operated a restaurant in Dallastown during the 1930s and 1940s. He and his wife, Edith, owned a home at 69 West Main Street.

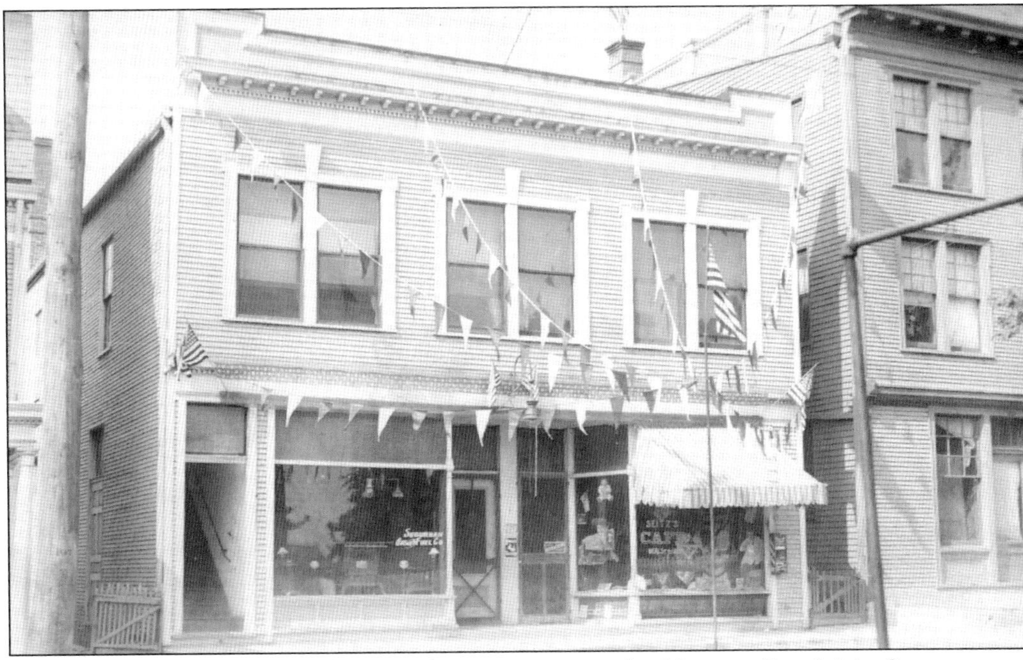

This postcard depicts two Dallastown businesses in one building on East Main Street around 1913. Suburban Gas & Fuel Company is on the left at 9 East Main Street, and Seitz's Café, run by Samuel F. Seitz, is on the right at 11 East Main Street. C.C. Grim was superintendent of Suburban Gas & Fuel Company. The image was shot near the town's square. (Courtesy of Tom Taylor.)

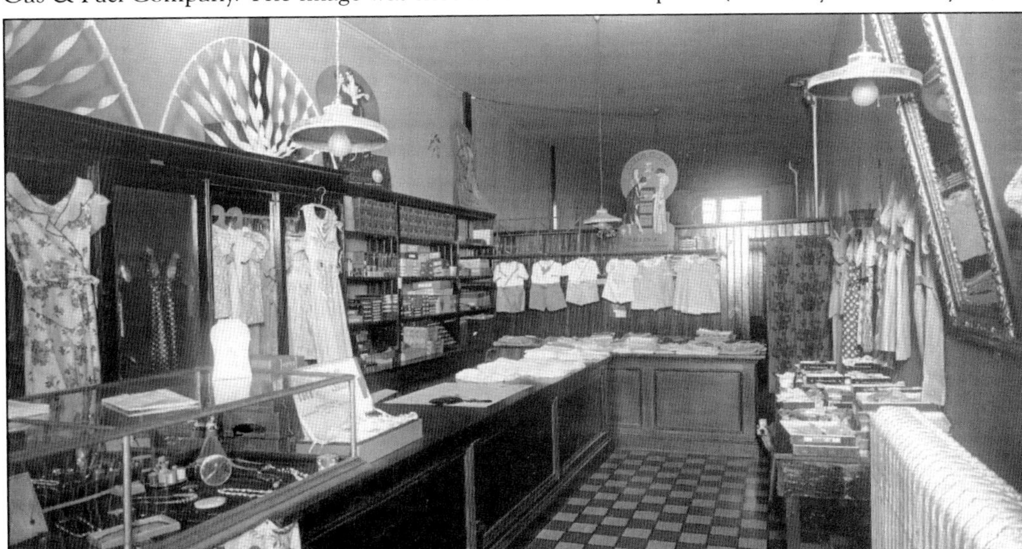

The interior of Lucretia's Specialty Shop located at 9–11 East Main Street is depicted in this photograph. The store was owned by Lucretia J. Barshinger McCleary. Ladies' and children's clothing, as well as jewelry, is displayed for sale in the store. Women's undergarments, hosiery, linens, and greetings cards were also sold at this shop. The building later housed Dick Snyder's television repair shop.

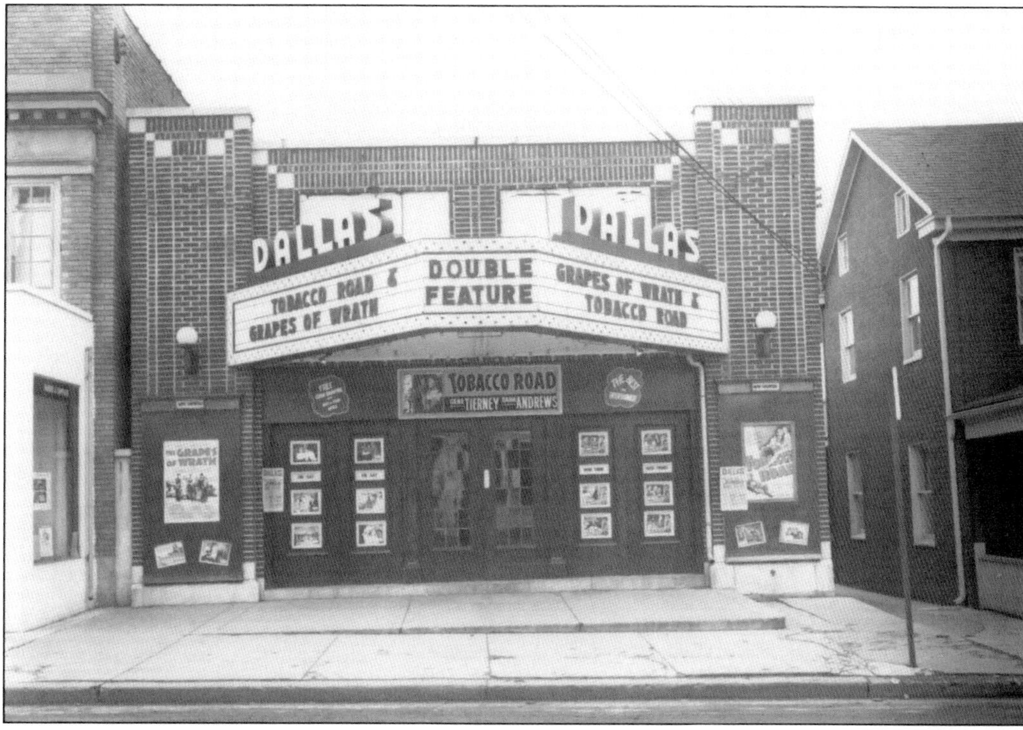

The Dallas Theatre, located at 16 East Main Street, is pictured in this image captured by Richard E. Gemmill in 1948. The movie theater was built in 1927 by Augustus Wagman. Note the movie posters and lobby cards advertising a special double feature showing of *The Grapes of Wrath* and *Tobacco Road*.

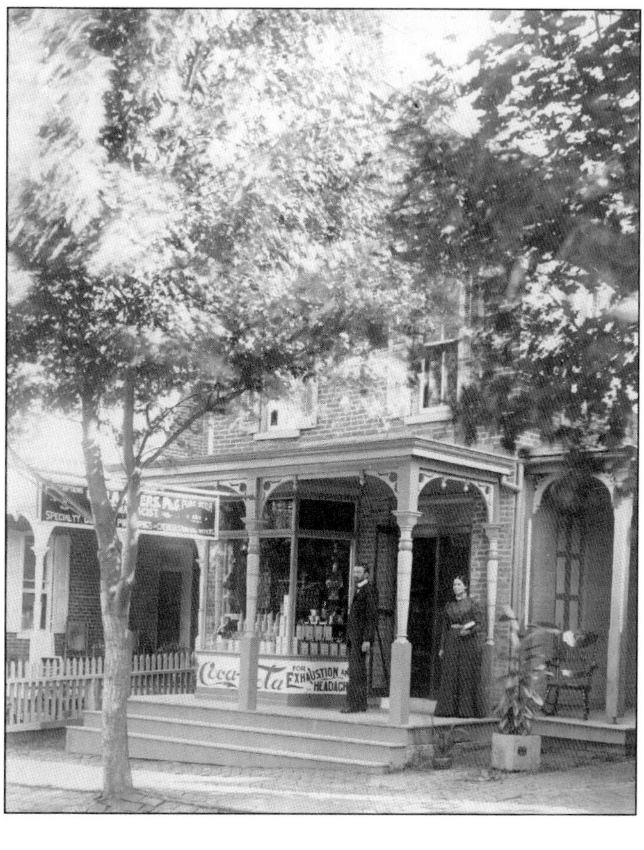

This image shows druggist George A. Meyers and his wife, Amanda, standing on the porch of their pharmacy and residence at 17 East Main Street in Dallastown around 1904. Coca-Cola advertising around the bottom of the pharmacy's bay window states, "Coca-Cola for Exhaustion and Headaches." At that time, Coca-Cola was advertised as having medicinal qualities, as well as being a drink, and cocaine was actually one of its ingredients. (Courtesy of Verdella Riedel's Estate.)

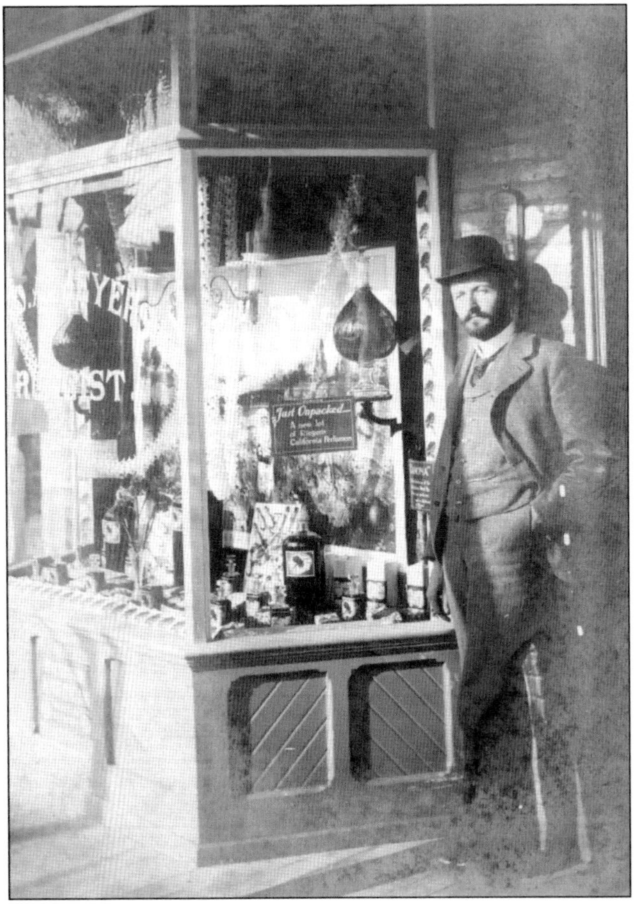

Druggist George A. Meyers is shown standing outside his drugstore at 17 East Main Street in Dallastown. A variety of Rieger's California Perfumes are displayed in the front show window of the pharmacy. A thermometer advertising Coca-Cola is attached to the wall of the building behind Meyers's head, as drugstores were popular places for soda fountains in this era. (Courtesy of Tom Taylor.)

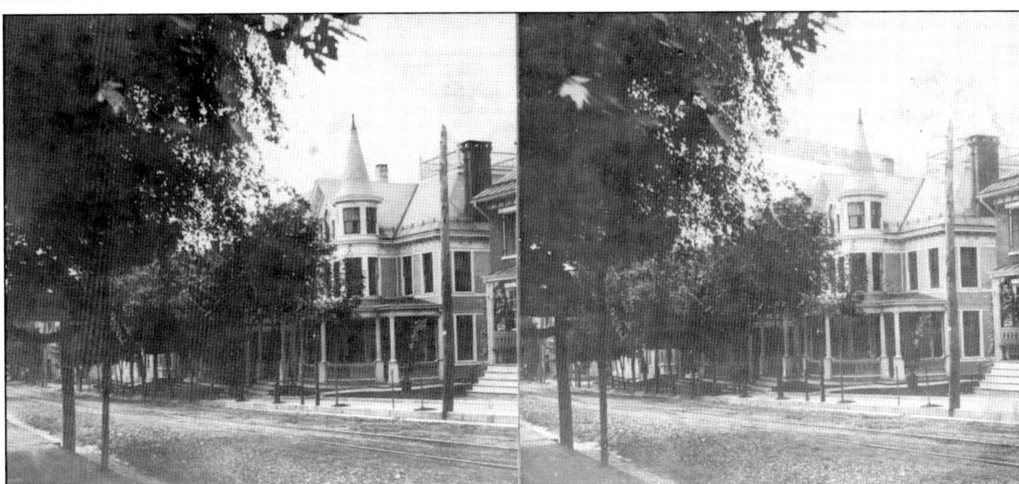

This stereograph depicts the cupola-topped residence of Michael Hose at 21 East Main Street. Born in 1853 in York Township, Hose married Adelaide Keesey in 1883. In 1884, they moved to Dallastown, where Hose began his cigar box–manufacturing business. Later, he started his own cigar manufacturing business, the Dallas Cigar Company. He was also a stockholder in many area banks and electric and water companies.

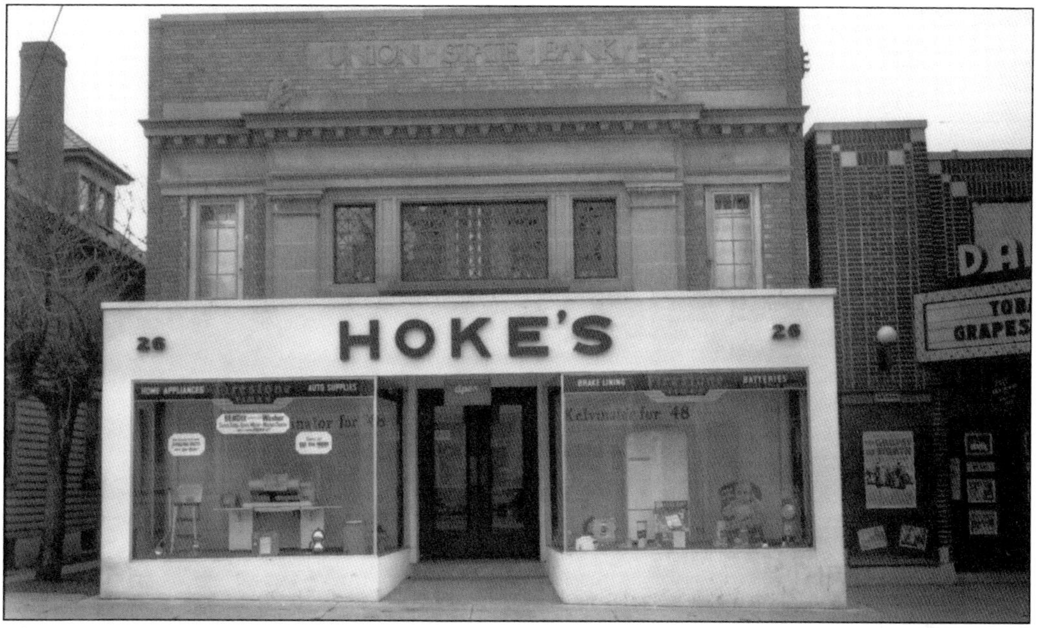

This photograph of Hoke's appliance store, taken in 1948 by Richard E. Gemmill, was located in the former Union State Bank building in Dallastown, next door to the Dallas Theatre. The bank was built in 1921 at 26 East Main Street. Later, the building housed a record store called Disk-A-Rama. Note the movie poster at right advertising the movie *The Grapes of Wrath*.

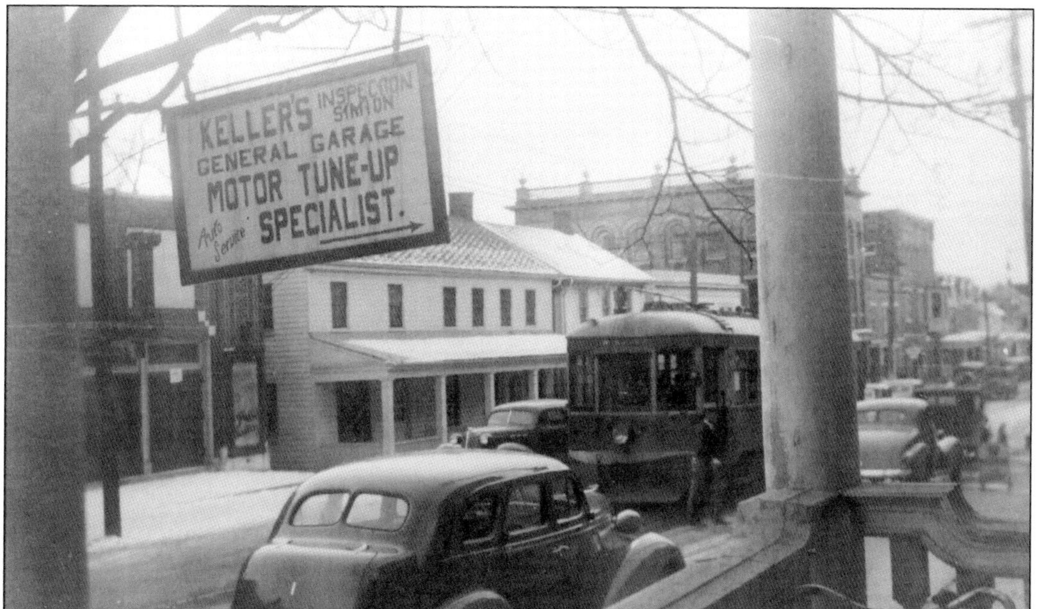

The image taken from the front porch of Harry E. Keller's auto service has a view looking west on East Main Street towards the square around 1939. The trolley is stopped a few houses west while discharging passengers. Across the street from Keller's, on the left side of the photograph, is Dallastown's movie theater, the Dallas. A movie poster can be seen to the right of the theater's entrance.

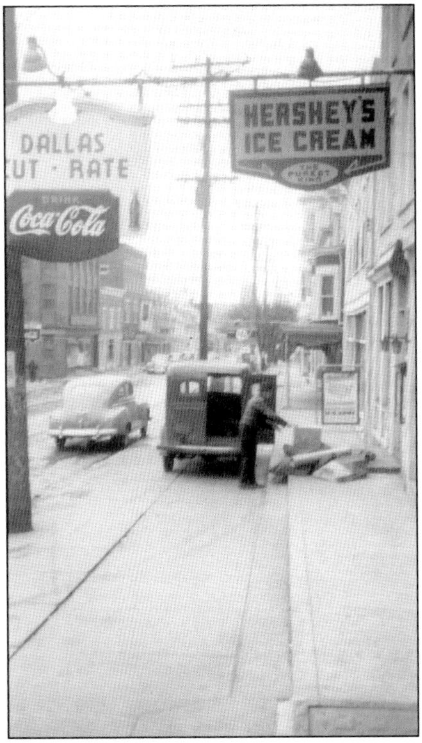

This outside view of the Dallas Cut-Rate, located at 19 East Main Street, looks west towards the town square, was taken by C.W. Simon Studios of York on June 1, 1948. A deliveryman unloads his truck onto a nearby sidewalk. Note the advertisements for Coca-Cola and Hershey's Ice Cream, both sold at the Dallas Cut-Rate, which also had a lunch counter.

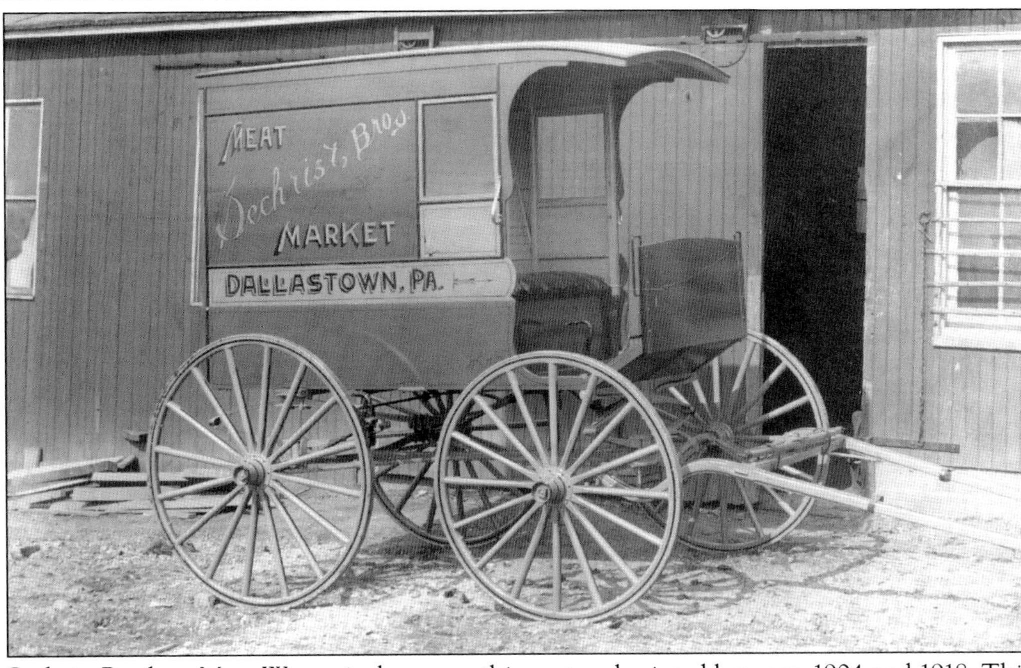

Sechrist Brothers Meat Wagon is shown on this postcard printed between 1904 and 1918. This horse-drawn wagon delivered meat to the residents of the Dallastown area. Located at 32 East Main Street, Sechrist Brothers has had a butcher shop at that location since 1877. The business, which is now run by the fourth generation of Sechrists, was established by Jacob Sechrist. It is well known for its national award-winning skinless franks. (Courtesy of Tom Taylor.)

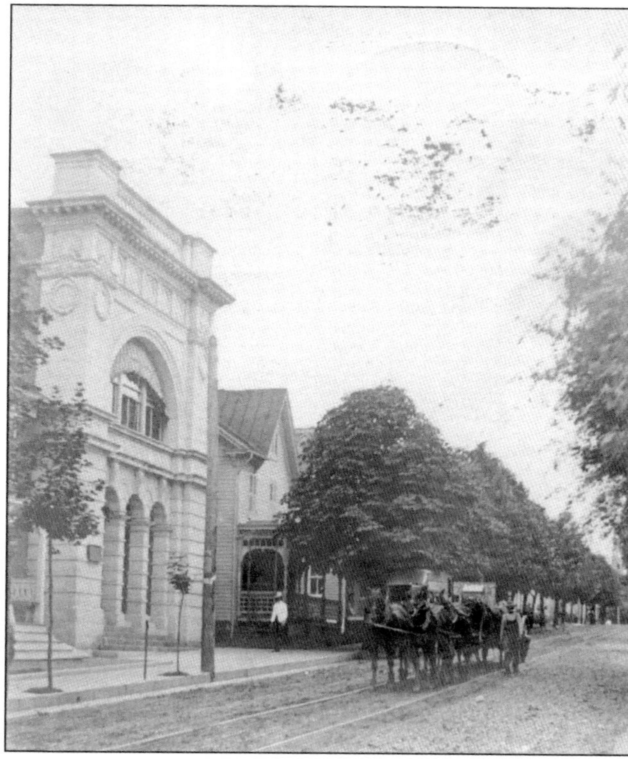

The large building on the left is Dallastown's First National Bank, built at 45 East Main Street and opened in 1904. John W. Minnich was elected its first president. This image shows a multi-horse-drawn cart heading west on East Main Street. A man in overalls walks next to the horse team on the unpaved road, which travels over the town's trolley tracks. (Courtesy of Tom Taylor.)

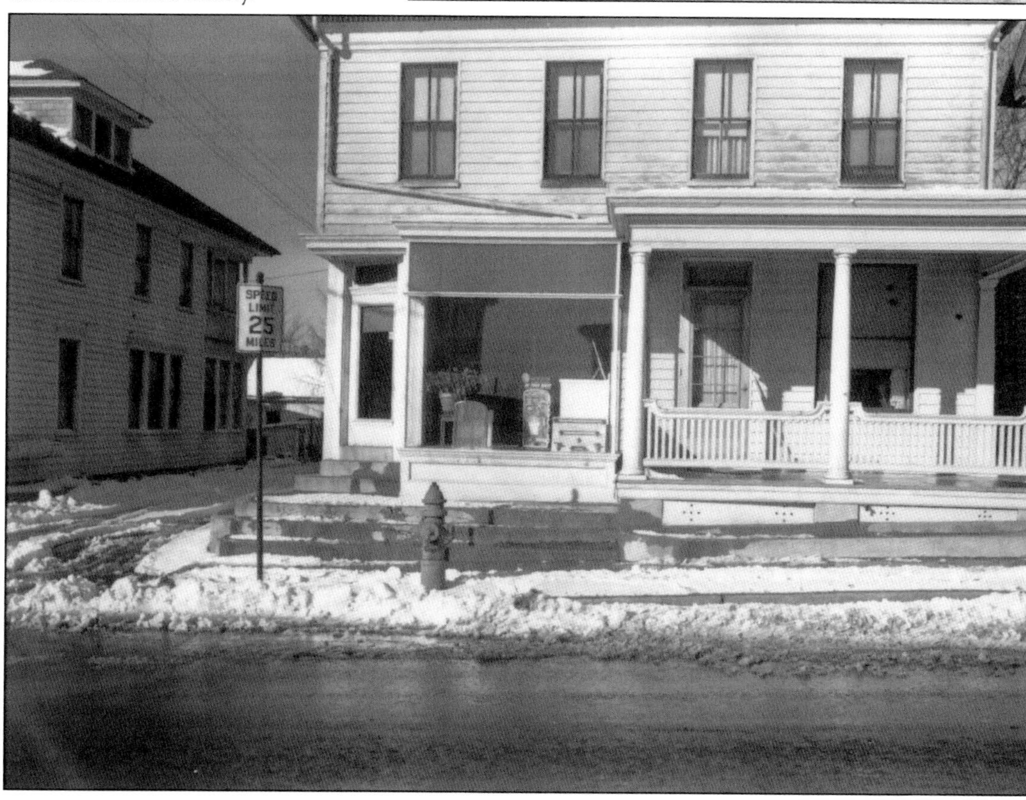

Harvey Zeigler's Plumbing Shop is depicted in this photograph taken by Richard E. Gemmill in 1948. Beginning in 1925, it was located at 55 East Main Street in the borough. According to city directories from 1923 to 1924, Zeigler's Plumbing was located at 29 East Main Street. This plumbing business was eventually acquired by the McWilliams family.

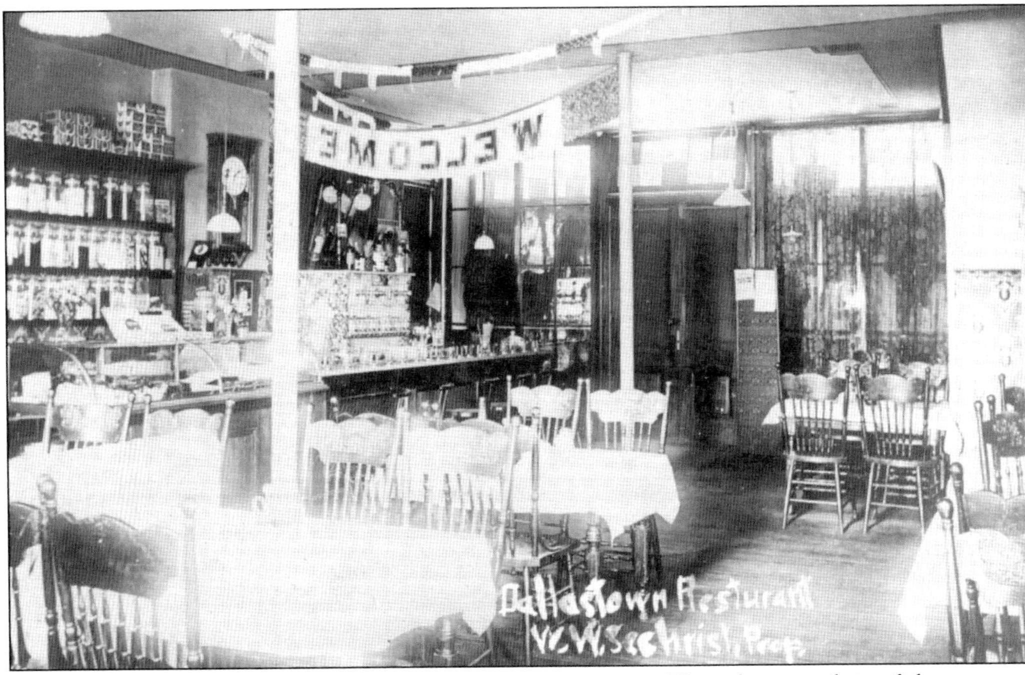

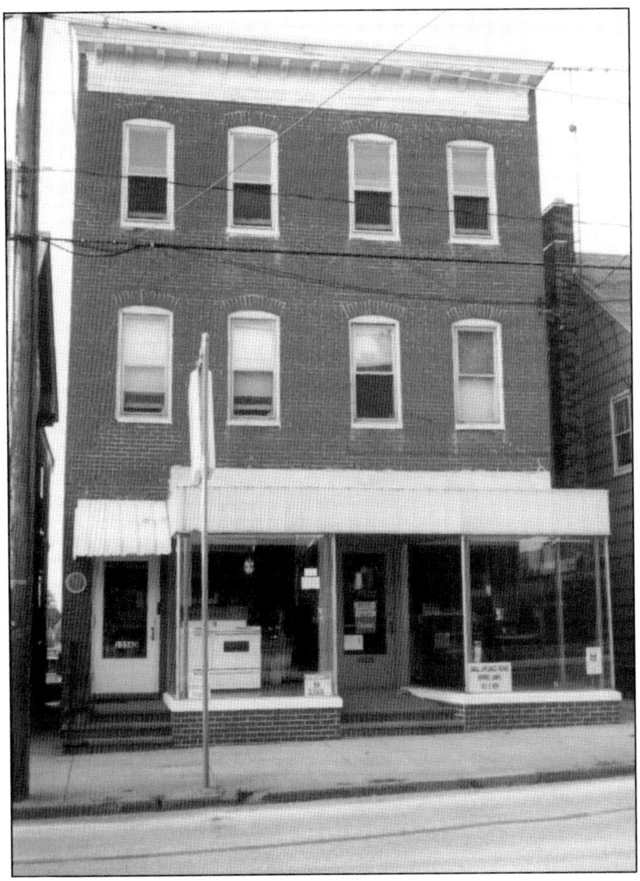

This photograph is of the interior of Wiley W. Sechrist's Restaurant, located at 67 East Main Street in Dallastown. The restaurant also had a soda fountain and bar. The address is listed in the city directory of 1905 as a restaurant and in 1907 as a restaurant and electrical supplies business. By 1910, the restaurant was closed and electrical supplies and accessories had become the sole business at that address.

Sechrist's appliance store at 135 East Main Street is depicted in this photograph. The ground floor was used as the appliance store. The second and third floors were used as apartments. In earlier days, the third floor served as the home of the Patriotic Order Sons of America, No. 607, a fraternal organization. The store was first owned and operated by Wiley W. Sechrist. The appliance store operated from around 1925 to 2000.

Glatfelter's furniture store has been a thriving part of the Dallastown business community throughout much of the borough's existence. It is located at 84 East Main Street at the southwest corner of East Main and South Charles Streets. This is an early image of Glatfelter's taken around 1890. Glatfelter's furniture store was established in 1884 by Wilson F. Glatfelter. Like many late-19th-century furniture companies, it was an undertaking business as well.

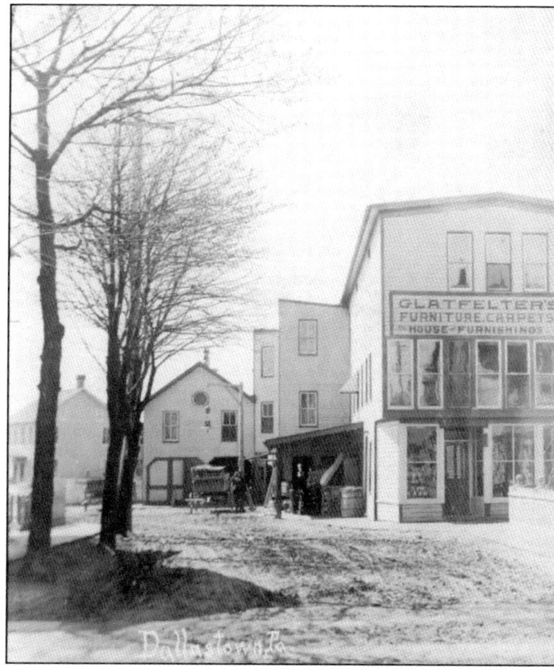

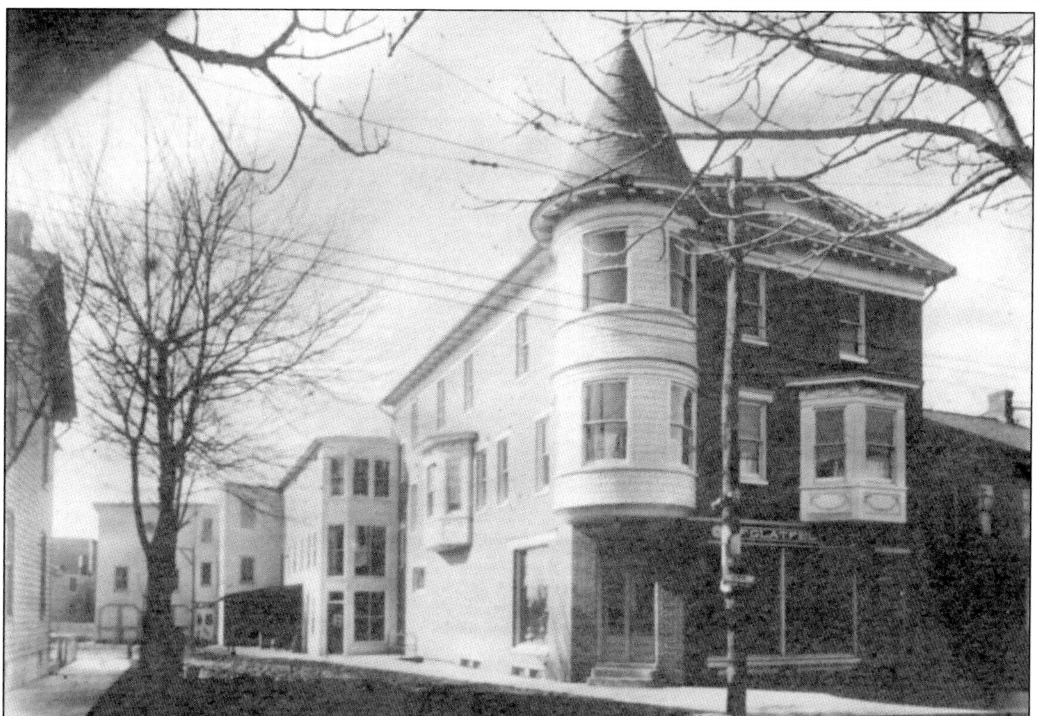

This postcard image of Glatfelter's furniture store was taken between 1907 and 1914, years after the image of the business in the previous photograph. A turret has been added to the second and third floors on the front left corner of the store. Children who grew up in the area will fondly remember the mechanical Santa Claus in the showroom's front window, looking out on East Main Street, which bowed to passersby. (Courtesy of Tom Taylor.)

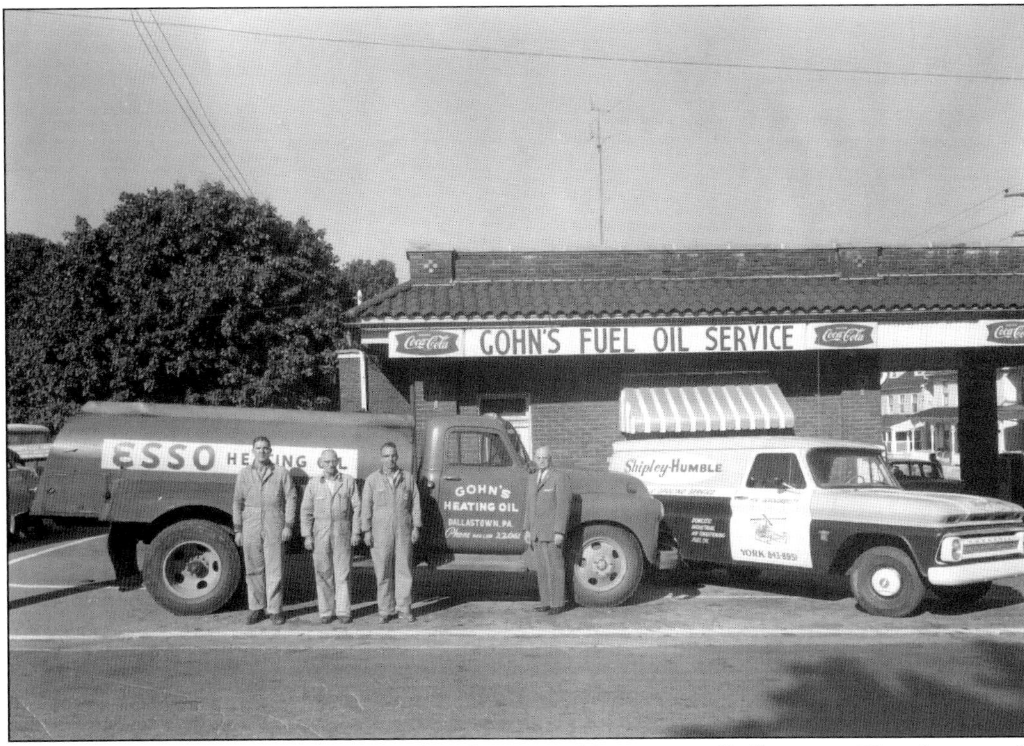

This 1966 image depicts Morris V. Gohn's heating oil business in Dallastown. The photograph shows the side of the station at the southwest corner of East Main Street and South Pleasant Avenue. Note the staff of Gohn's posing in front of their heating oil truck and the Shipley Humble vehicle. Gohn's was located at this address beginning around 1931. (Courtesy of Roger Fuller.)

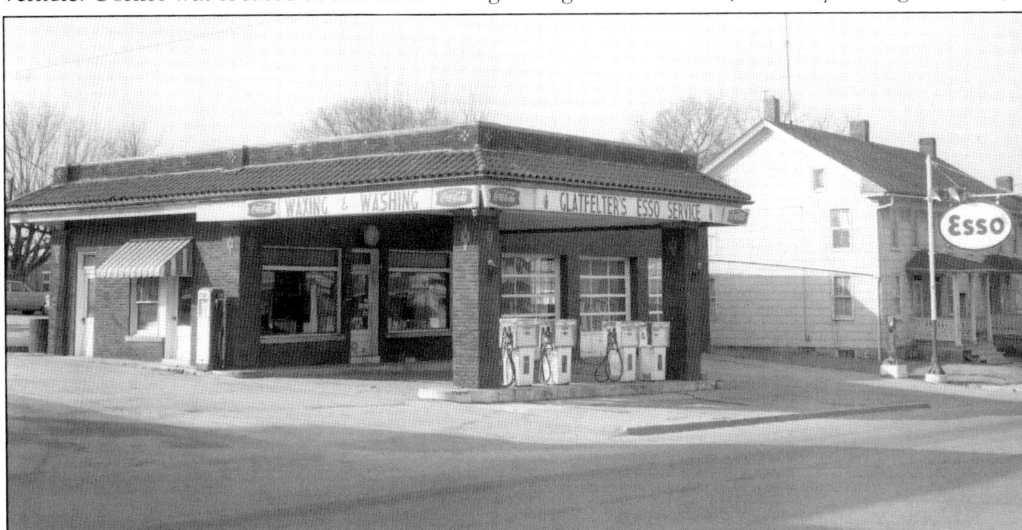

Glatfelter's Esso Service station is depicted in this photograph and was located at 150 East Main Street in Dallastown. The photograph shows the front and side of the station at the southwest corner of East Main Street and South Pleasant Avenue. Besides selling gasoline and oil, Glatfelter's also washed, waxed, and did basic servicing of automobiles. A service station of one type or another operated at this site until 2013.

Kieffer's was a local grocery store located at the corner of East Main and Locust Streets near St. Joseph Catholic Church in Dallastown. When this photograph was taken by Richard E. Gemmill in 1948, it was owned by Joseph Kieffer. After the grocery store closed, this building eventually became an antique store.

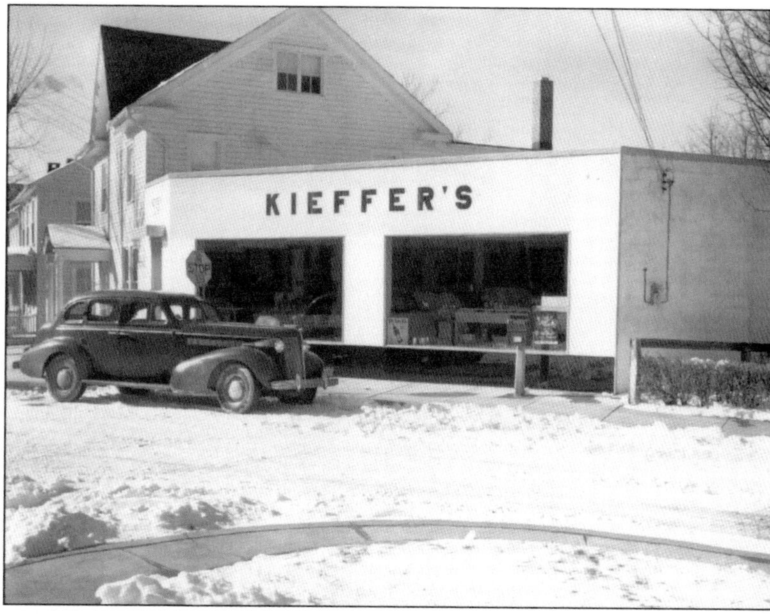

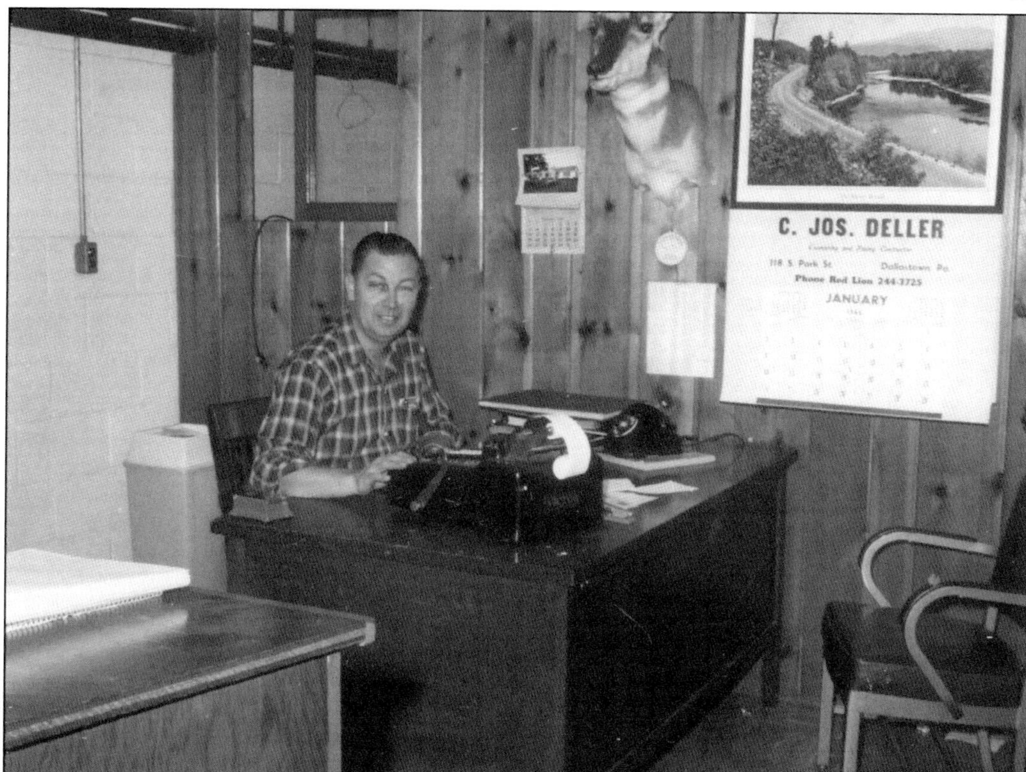

This photograph of the business office of C. Joseph Deller was taken when it was located in the basement of the Deller residence around 1966. Later, the office was moved to a new building at 30 South Park Street. Leroy Douglas is shown working at his desk as a bookkeeper for the business. The company was an excavating and paving business that operated from 1947 to 2013. (Courtesy of Michael L. Sentz Jr.)

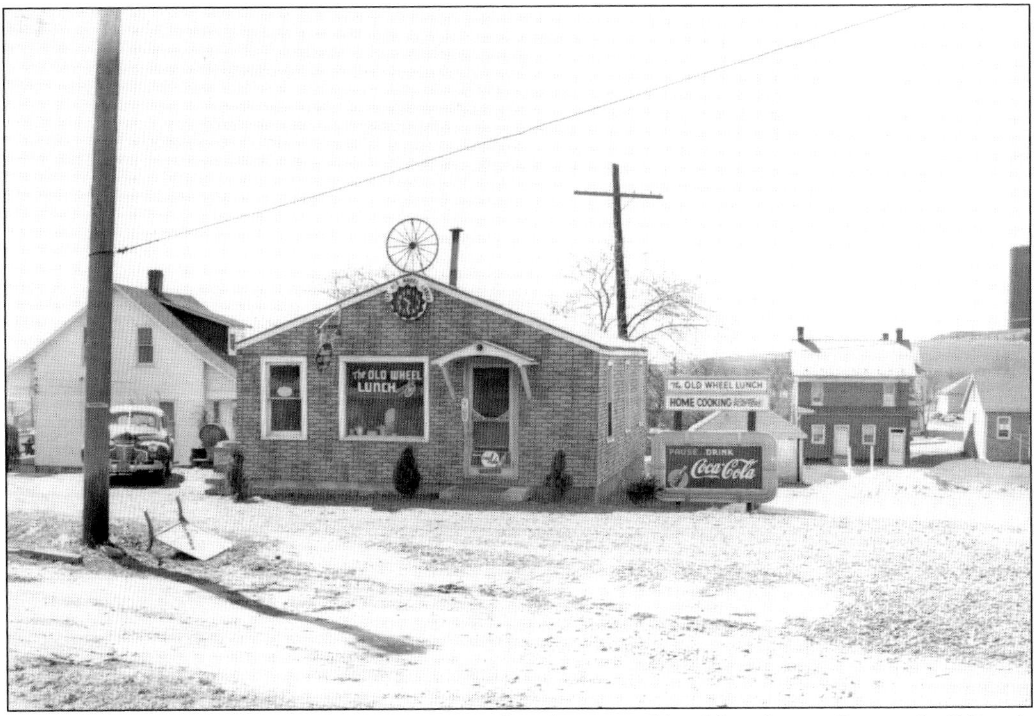

The Old Wheel Lunch was a restaurant owned and operated by Alice Lentz. Situated off South Duke Street in Dallastown, the restaurant featured home cooking and hamburgers. The car wash behind the gas station at the corner of East Main and South Duke Streets is currently on the spot where the Old Wheel Lunch was located. This image was taken by Richard E. Gemmill in 1948.

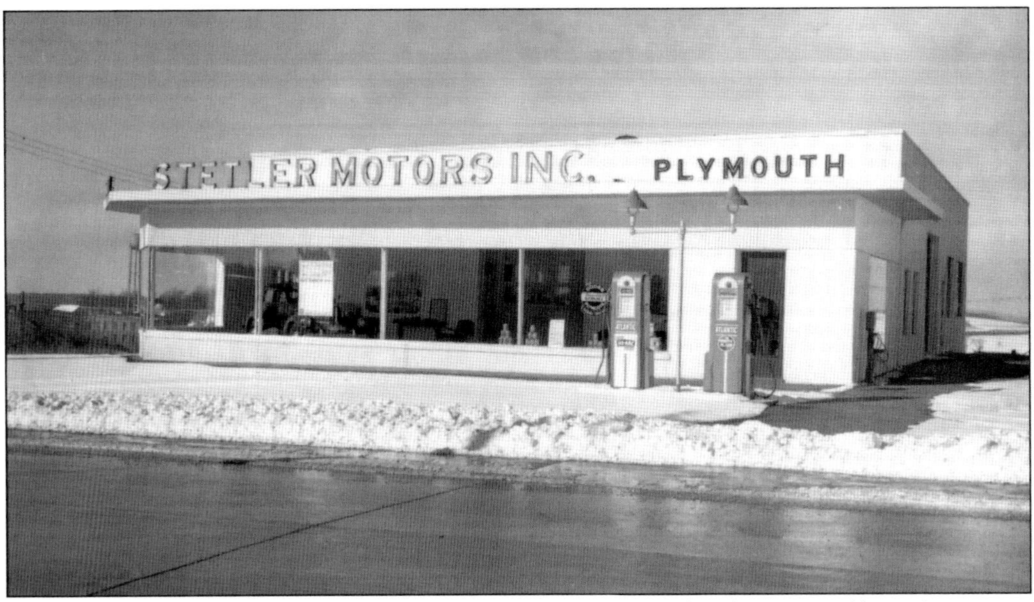

This photograph of Stetler Motors Inc. was taken in 1948 by Richard E. Gemmill. Stetler Motors was located at 515 East Main Street in Dallastown. It was a Plymouth dealership at the time this image was taken and also had a garage and gas pumps. The building now houses a plumbing and heating supply business.

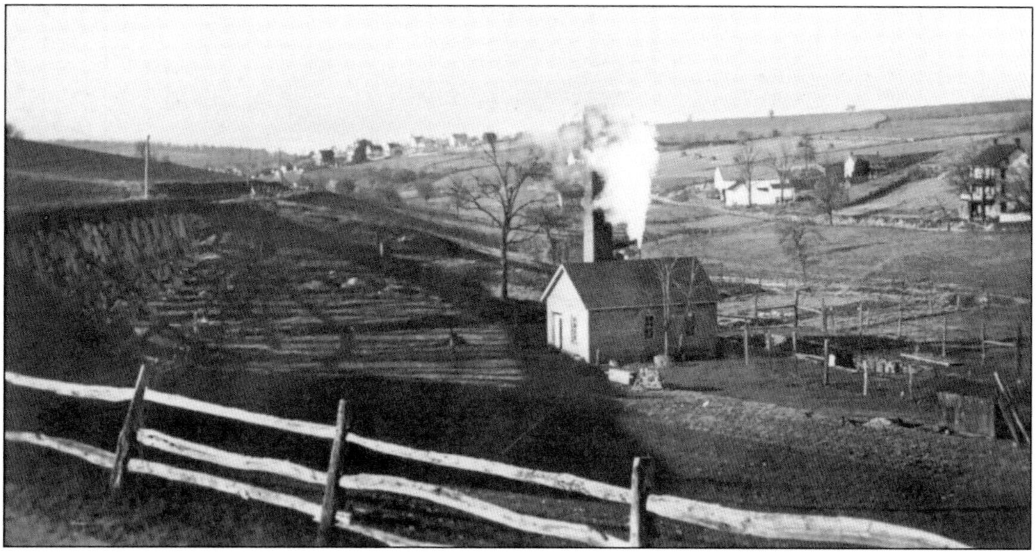

Dallastown Water Company's first pumping station is depicted in this photograph. Prior to its establishment in 1896, borough residents relied on wells for their water supply. This station was erected between Yoe and Red Lion at a spring owned by Jacob Taylor. It pumped water to a reservoir built at South Park Street. At left is a railroad trestle, and in the center background is the borough of Yoe. (Courtesy of Cathy Bankoske.)

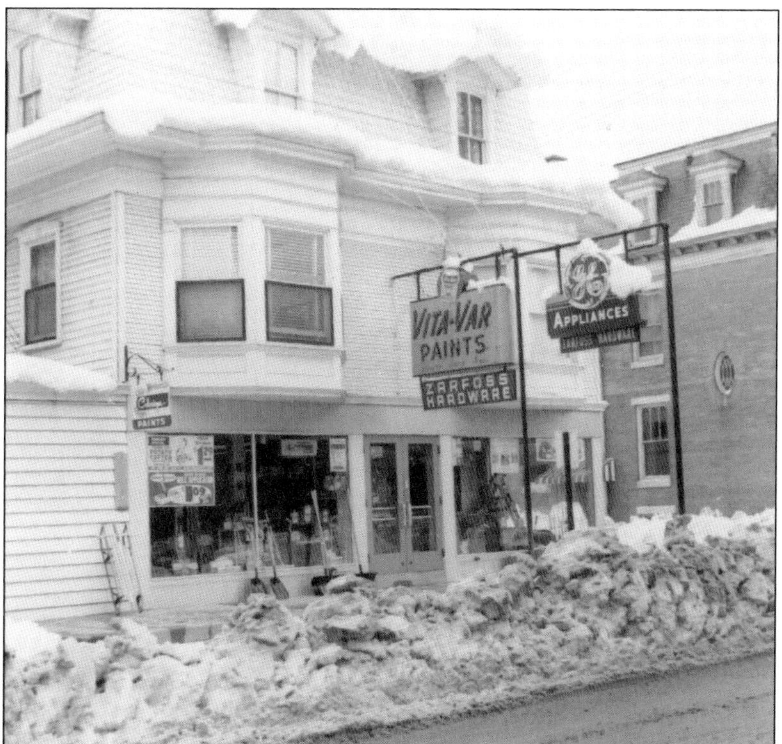

This photograph depicts Zarfoss Hardware store located at the northwest corner of the square of Dallastown, at West Main and North Walnut Streets. This is a winter scene where snow shovels and sleds were available, as well as the usual paint, hardware, and appliances. This building was eventually torn down and a Rite-Aid was built in its place. It later became the home of H & H Lighting.

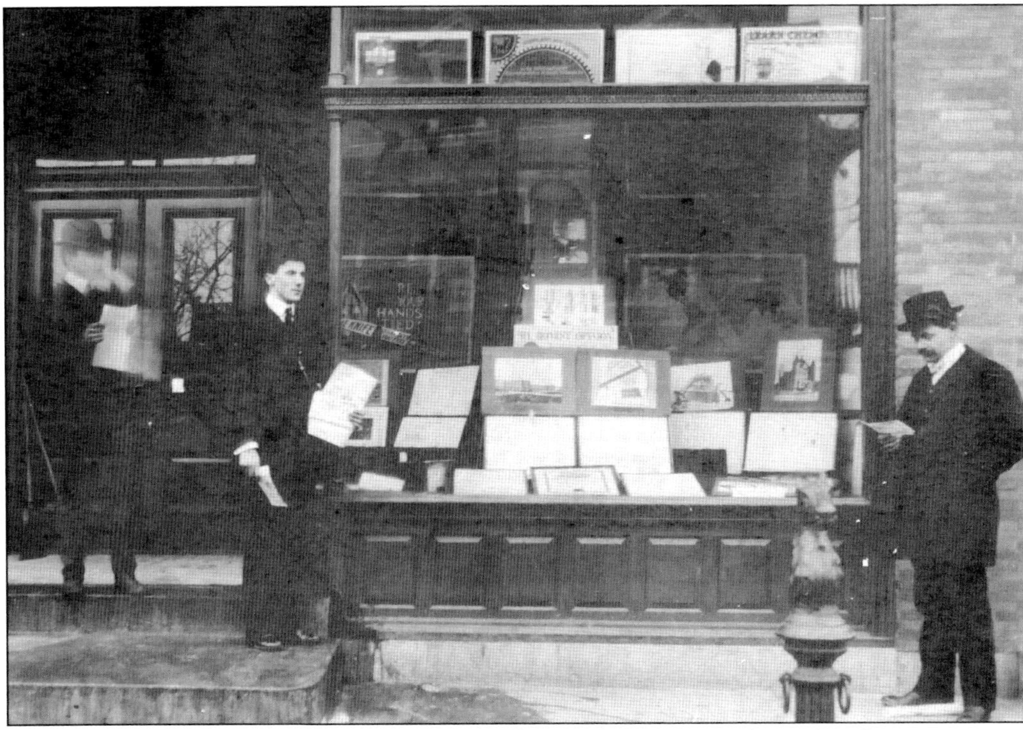

Shaw and Lau's general merchandise store in the Hose Building is pictured here. It was located at 2 West Main Street on the southwest corner of Main and Walnut Streets at the town square in Dallastown. John S. Shaw and Martin L. Lau were the proprietors of the store. This store was open around 1904 to 1909.

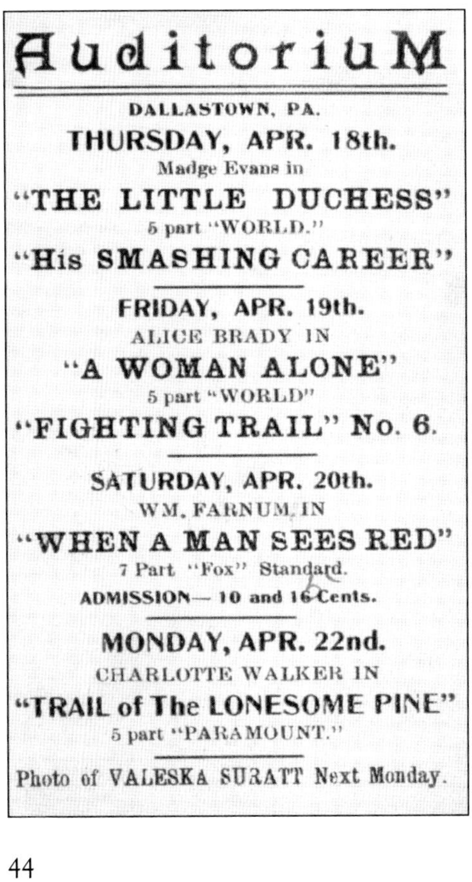

AuditoriuM

DALLASTOWN, PA.

THURSDAY, APR. 18th.

Madge Evans in

"THE LITTLE DUCHESS"

5 part "WORLD."

"His SMASHING CAREER"

FRIDAY, APR. 19th.

ALICE BRADY IN

"A WOMAN ALONE"

5 part "WORLD"

"FIGHTING TRAIL" No. 6.

SATURDAY, APR. 20th.

WM. FARNUM IN

"WHEN A MAN SEES RED"

7 Part "Fox" Standard.

ADMISSION— 10 and 16 Cents.

MONDAY, APR. 22nd.

CHARLOTTE WALKER IN

"TRAIL of The LONESOME PINE"

5 part "PARAMOUNT."

Photo of VALESKA SURATT Next Monday.

This advertising card for silent films played at the Lyric Theatre in Dallastown was issued in 1917. The Lyric was built at the corner of South Walnut and Howard Streets in 1906 as a 300-seat theater hall. It was used primarily to show silent films from 1906 to 1929 but also had a small stage used for live productions. The Dallastown Band Association played concerts in the Lyric's auditorium as well. (Courtesy of Tom Taylor.)

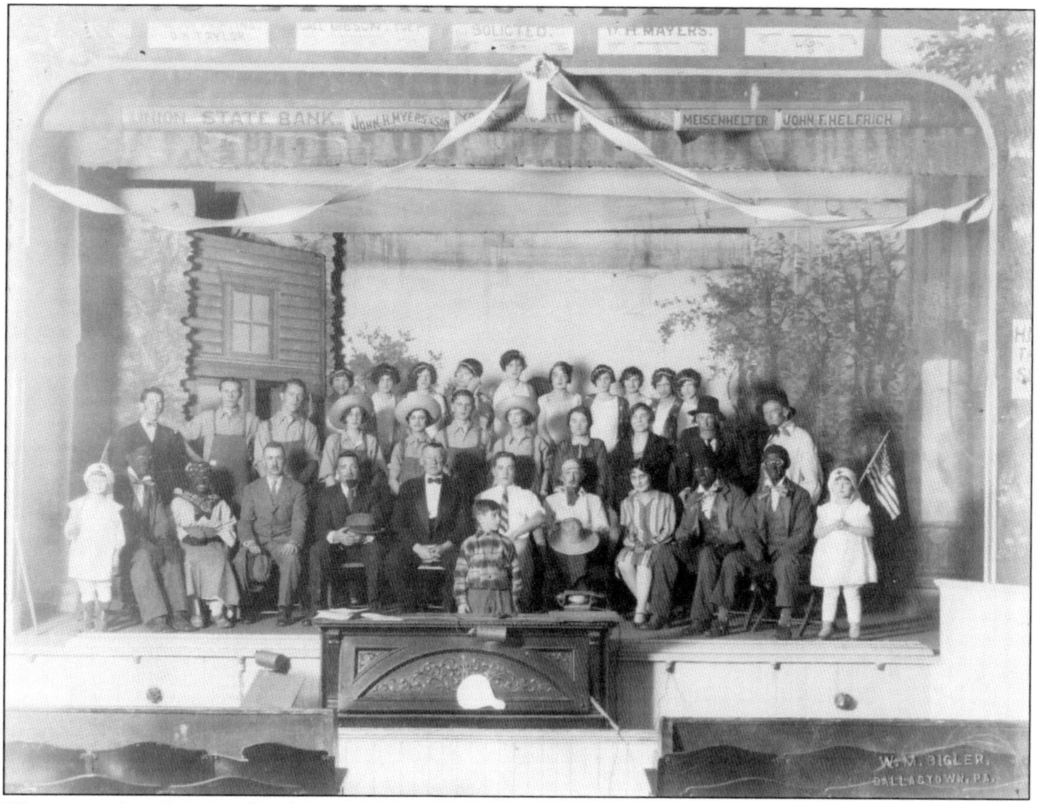

The cast of performers for the 1927 American Legion Show pose for this photograph. William M. Bigler took this image in the Lyric Theatre in Dallastown. Four of the performers are minstrels shown in theatrical makeup known as blackface. Numerous businesses advertised in support of the show and theater, including D.K. Taylor, Union State Bank, John H. Myers & Son, and John F. Helfrich. (Courtesy of Tom Taylor.)

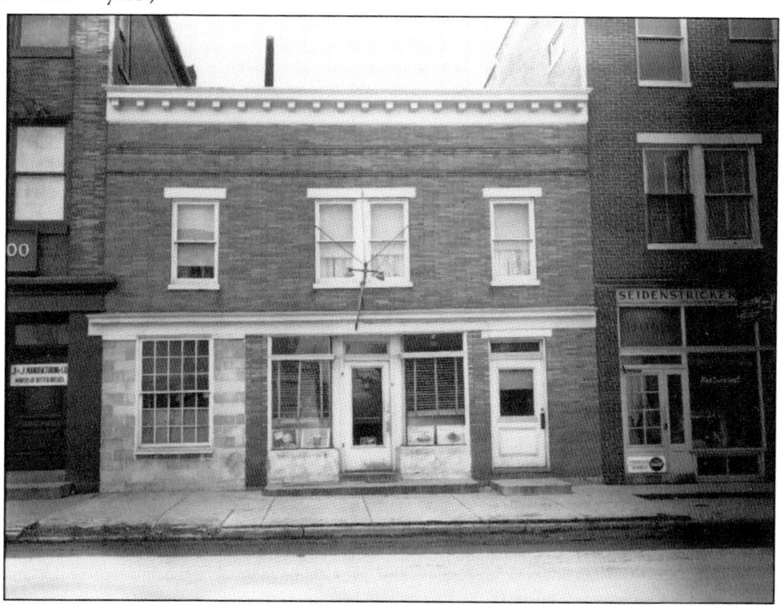

This photograph of the Dallas Bowling Alley building was taken in 1948 by Richard E. Gemmill. It was located at 6 West Main Street. It originally housed a barbershop owned by David Ness, then a movie theater, and was later turned into a bowling alley that was owned by Bill Eberly. At the time this image was taken, it was an insurance office. The building burned down in 1974.

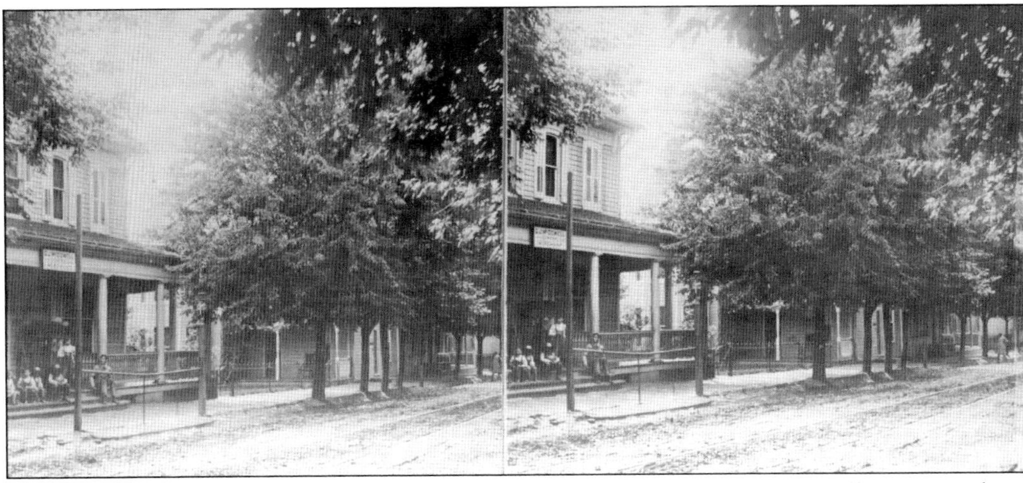

This stereograph is of George J. McDowell's General Merchandise store in Dallastown and was taken around 1907. General stores such as this were extremely prevalent throughout the United States in the 19th and early 20th centuries. The store was located at 22 West Main Street. To the right of the store is the home of Dr. William H. Bigler.

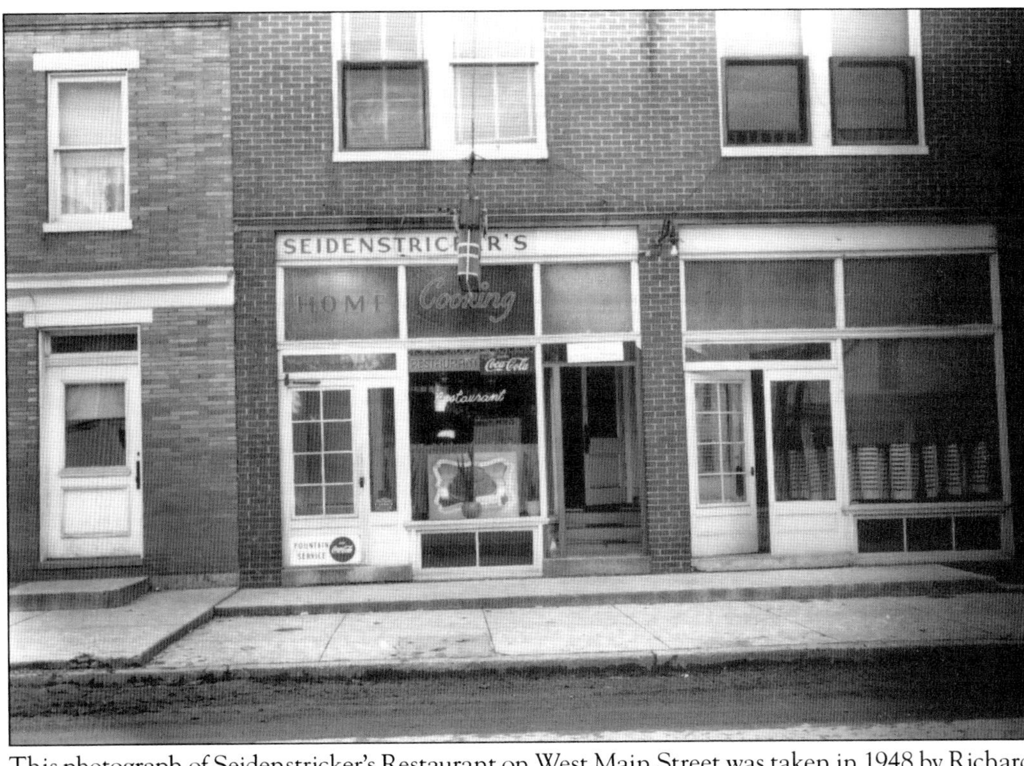

This photograph of Seidenstricker's Restaurant on West Main Street was taken in 1948 by Richard E. Gemmill. In the 1920s, this building housed an A&P store. Later, it became a Hershey's Ice Cream shop. In the 1940s, it was a restaurant run by Chauncey and Mable Seidenstricker and later by Jean Carman and Helena Waltermeyer. The building became Sal's Steak and Pizza Parlor in the 1970s.

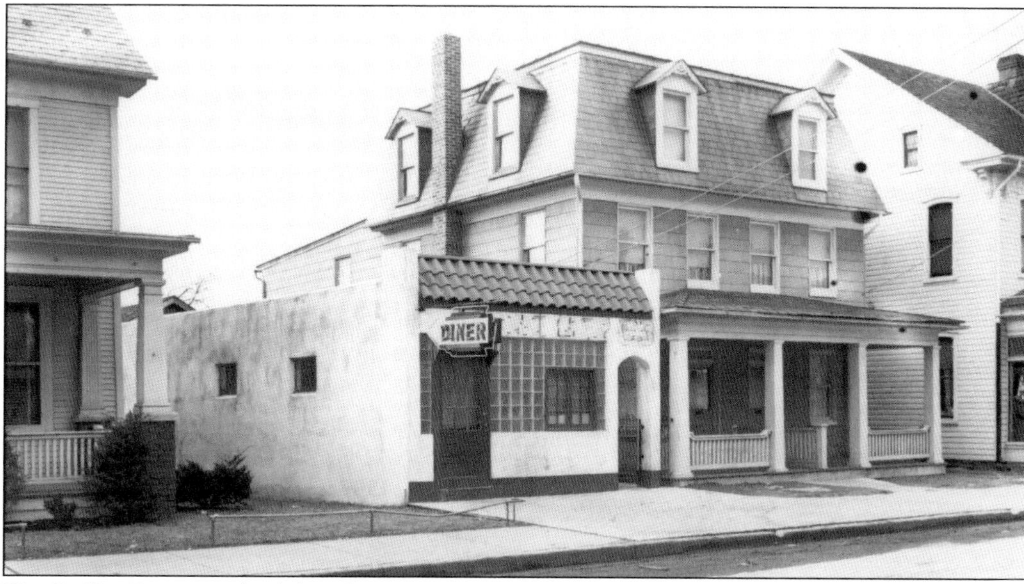

The Dallas Diner was built by Thomas Cox. Located at 40 West Main Street, and the restaurant was later owned by John and Betty Kell and later by Barry Jennings. In the 1970s, the diner was transformed into a Mexican eatery called Tia's Tacos. The building currently houses the Wandering Canvas Tattoo parlor. This photograph was taken by Richard E. Gemmill in 1948.

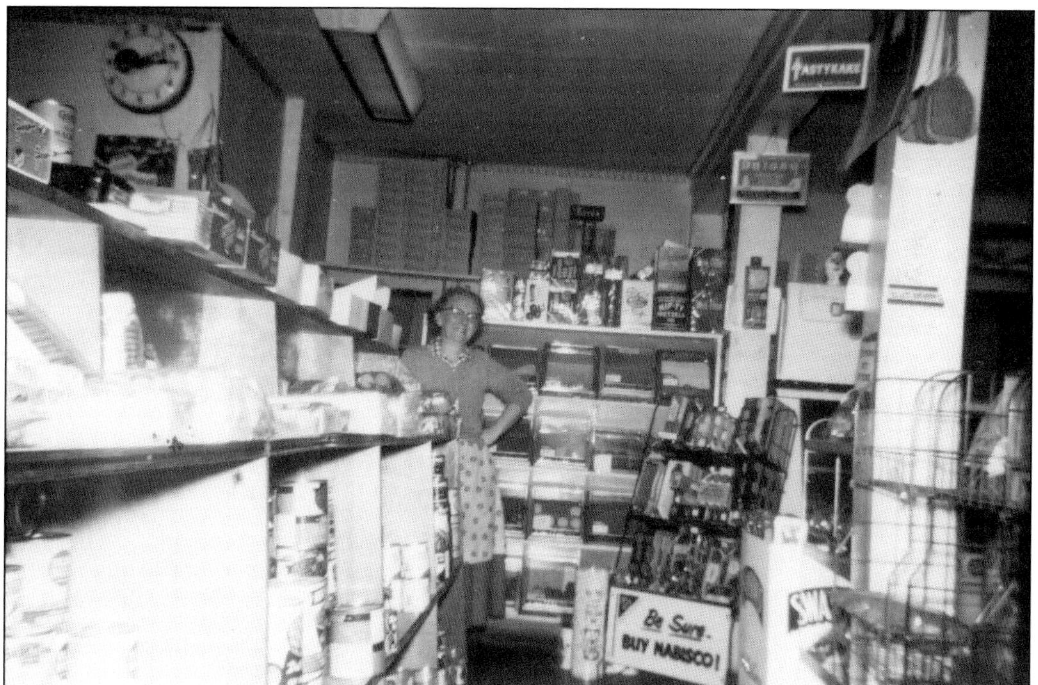

This photograph is of the interior of Community Pure Food store, one of the small grocery stores that once served Dallastown borough residents. Elsie Newman poses in the store that she ran with her husband, Harry, at 276 West Main Street. The town had a number of these privately owned grocery stores through the 1970s. Most were located on the ground floor of a multistory, single-family residence. (Courtesy of Cheryl Newman.)

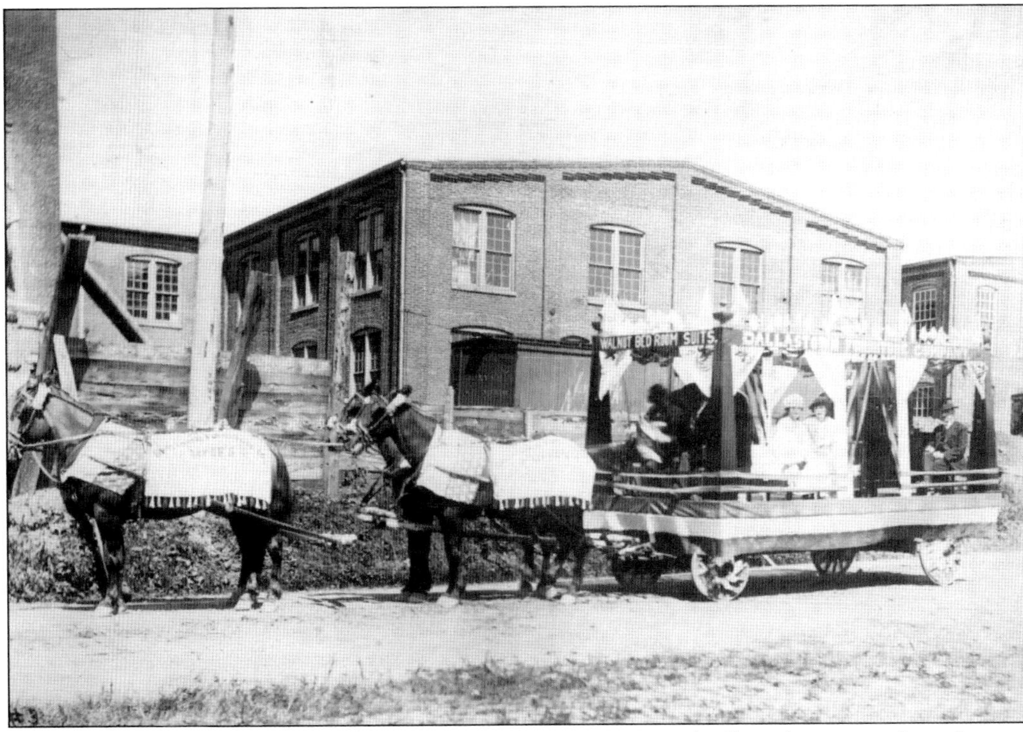

Pictured are employees of the Dallastown Furniture Company and a float they created to advertise the company. The float was drawn by a team of horses, likely in a local patriotic parade. The float advertised one of the company's chief products—walnut bedroom suites. This photograph was taken in 1919.

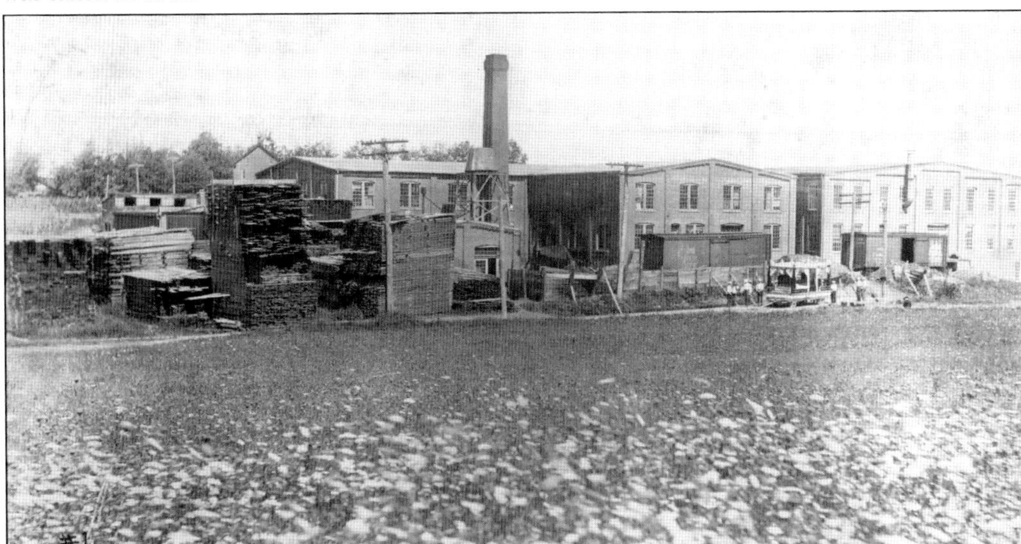

This photograph of the Dallastown Furniture Company was taken on September 13, 1919. Located at North Park Street and East Locust Street at the Maryland & Pennsylvania Railroad tracks, the company was incorporated in 1911. Alvin F. Fix was the organization's first president. Two railroad cars can be seen in front of the factory. In front of the railcars are employees of the company with their parade float.

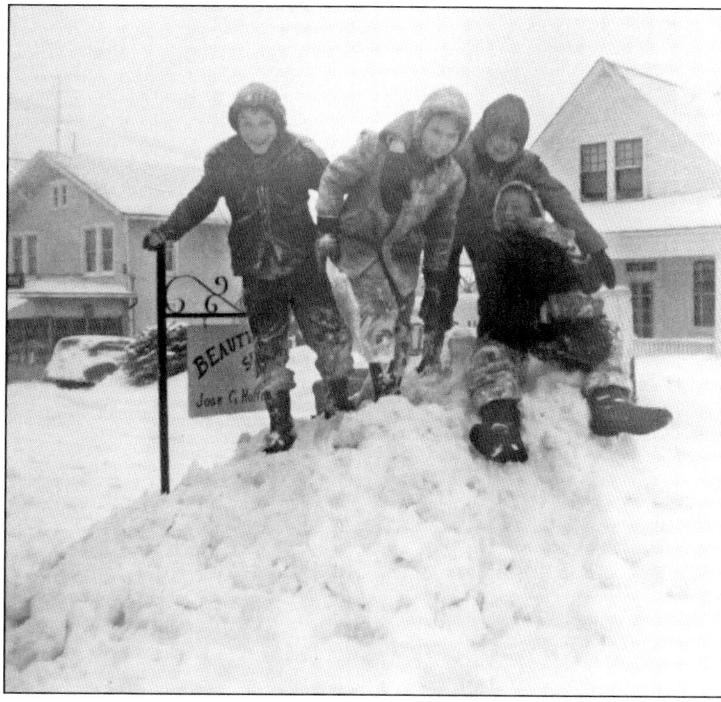

Winter fun is being enjoyed at 387 West Main Street in Dallastown around 1955. The children posing on the snowbank are, from left to right, (sitting) Priscilla Hoffman; (standing) Brian Dubs, Roger Holtzapple, and Jack Hoffman. In this photograph taken in the front yard of Joan Hoffman's beauty shop, West Main Street runs behind the kids. The building at far left is Harry and Elsie Newman's grocery store. (Courtesy of Priscilla Hoffman.)

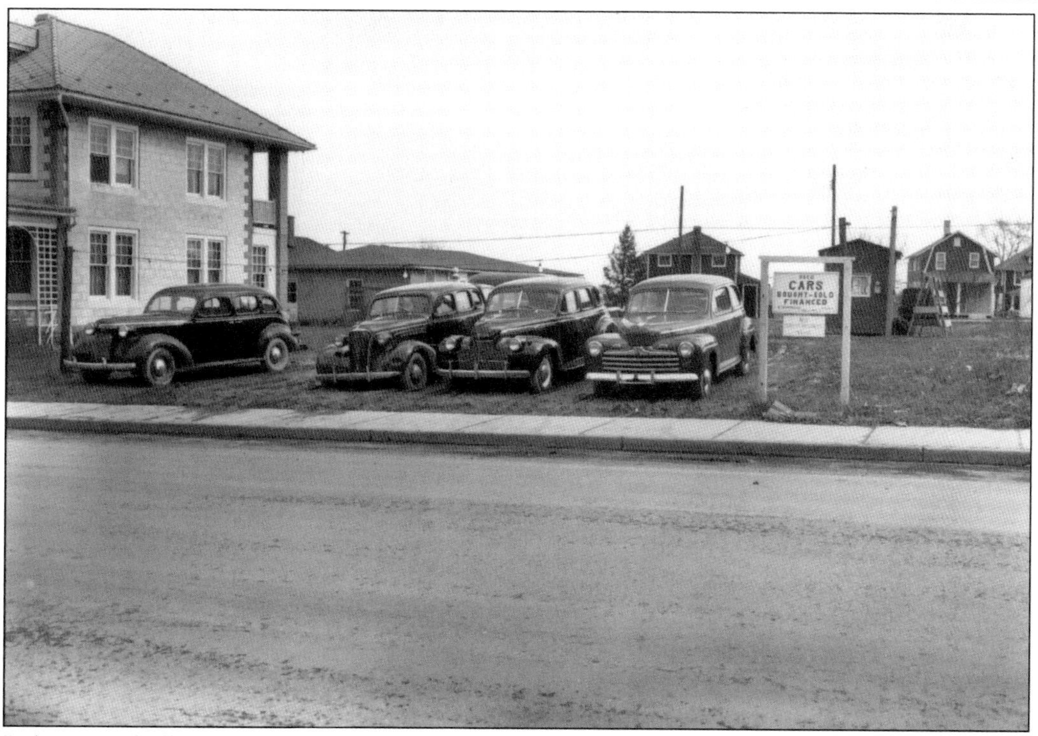

Robert Marshall's Used Cars was located next to his house at 432 West Maple Street in Dallastown. This car lot was situated to the left of Robert and Ruth Marshall's home. The large sign at the car lot reads, "Used Cars Bought—Sold Financed." The smaller sign below it states, "No Sunday Business Please." This photograph was taken by Richard E. Gemmill in 1948.

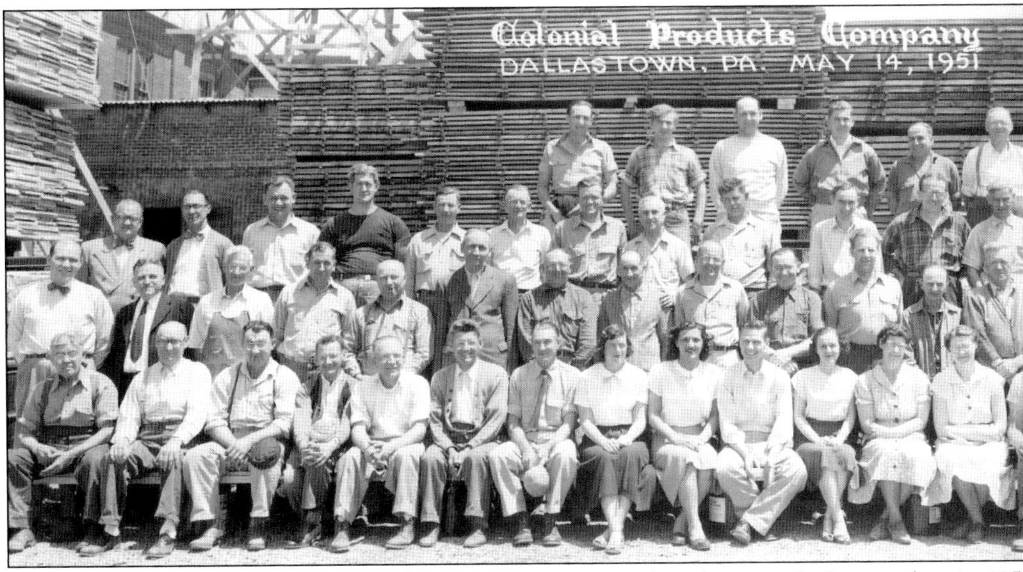

Employees of Colonial Products in Dallastown are posing in this photograph. It was taken in 1951 at the company's headquarters and plant at Broad and North Park Streets. Started in Dallastown in 1937, the company manufactured a variety of wood products but eventually specialized in producing kitchen cabinets. By 1966, Colonial Products employed more than 1,000 people in Dallastown, Glen Rock, Mifflinburg, Milton, Pottsville, Red Lion, and Stewartstown.

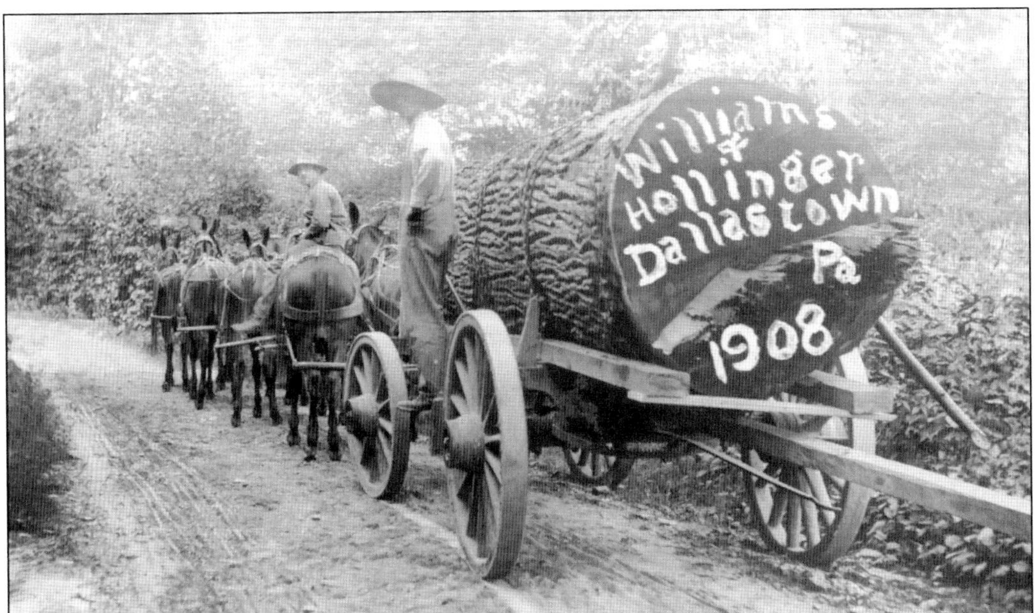

This postcard depicts an eight-horse team pulling a wagon that is hauling a large tree trunk to Williams & Hollinger's lumberyard in Dallastown. Two of the company's employees look back toward the camera in this image from 1908. Samuel Williams was one of the owners of this company and was listed in city directories as a lumberman. The other owner of the company was likely Leo Hollinger. (Courtesy of Tom Taylor.)

Three

Education and Religious Life

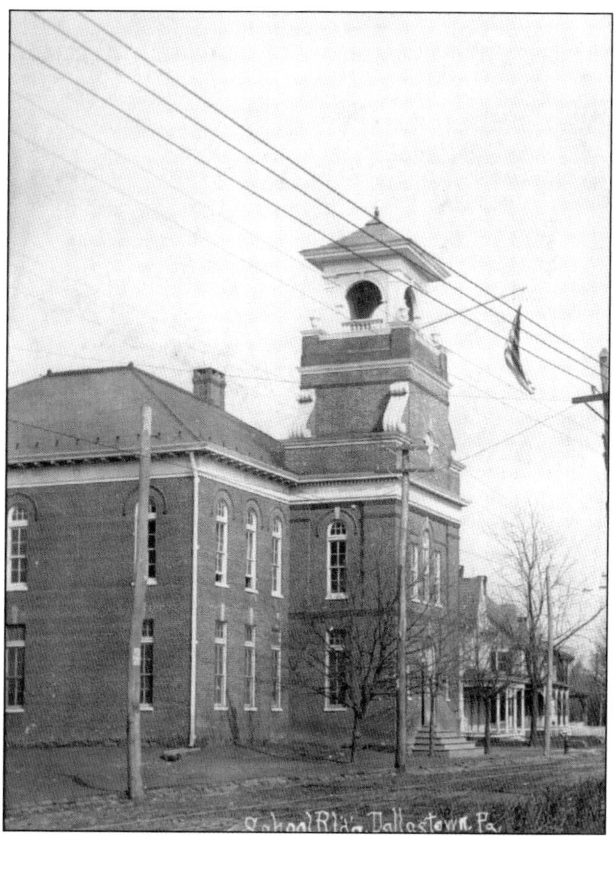

Located at the corner of West Main Street and School Place in Dallastown, this public school stood there from 1884 until 1959. Originally constructed as a one-story schoolhouse, it replaced three earlier school buildings on this site dating back to 1834. In 1900, a second-story addition was built. Elementary and high school students attended from 1884 until 1913. In February 1959, this elementary school was closed for good.

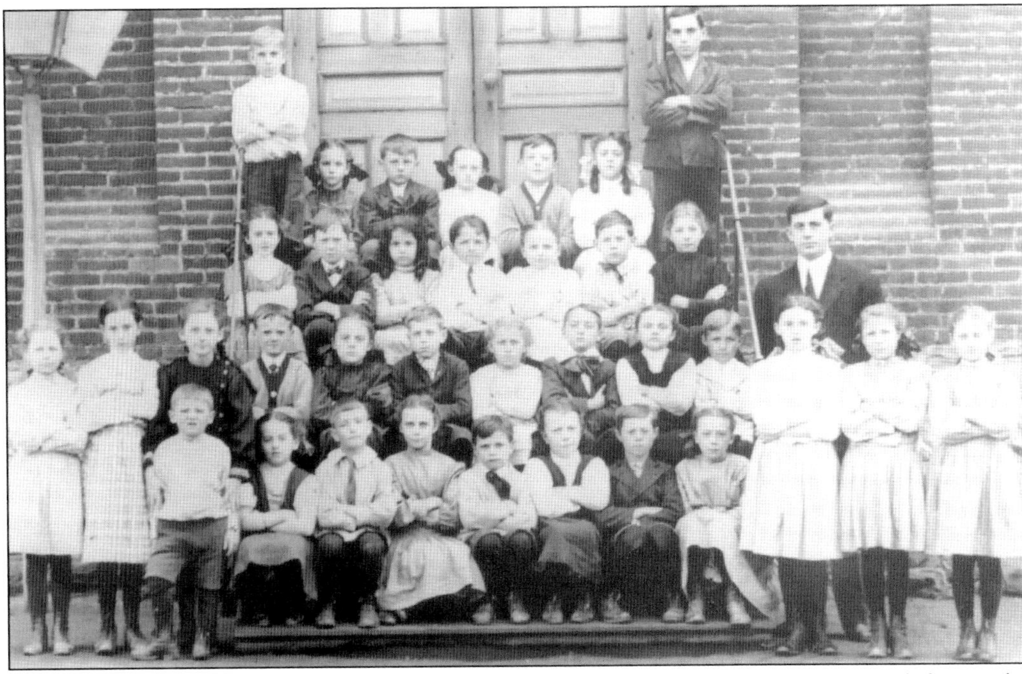

This photograph shows Dallastown's fourth-grade class in 1909. Pictured are, from left to right, (first row) Percy McDowell, Faye Workinger, Walter Geesey, Ida Noll, Robert Myers, Lydia Shue, Lloyd Eberly, Helen Reigart, Mabel McDowell, Martha Fry, Margaret Deller; (second row) Mary Hartman, Ethel Geesey, Mary McDowell, Rhodes Stabley, Marie Barnhart, Norman Kyle, Martha Leber, Spurgeon Peeler, Minnie Snyder, Myron Briggs, and teacher Isiah Rojahn; (third row) Phoebe Eberly, Raymond Butcher, Marie Ness, Earl Flinchbaugh, Clara Slenker, Robert Lutz, and Mary Minnich; (fourth row) Paul Stabley, Mary Flinchbaugh, Charles Ness, Aileen Snyder, Raymond Eberly, Isabelle McDowell, and Alfred Flory. (Courtesy of Roger Fuller.)

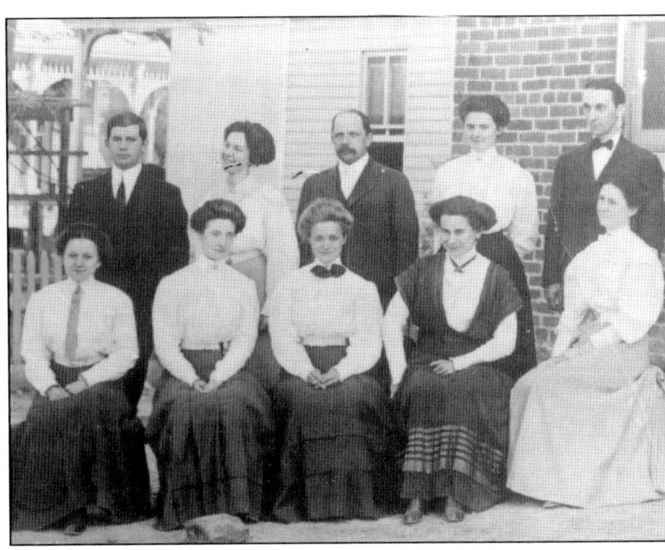

Teachers from Dallastown's public school, located at the corner of School Place and West Main Street, are pictured in this 1912 photograph. The school was used to teach both elementary and high school students from 1884 until 1913. From left to right are (first row) Mary Anderson, Blanche Manifold, Winifred Kauffman, Edna Mehring, and Elsie Grove; (second row) Isiah Rojahn, Mary Grove, John H. Meyers, Anna Norris, and Harry Stiles. (Courtesy of Roger Fuller.)

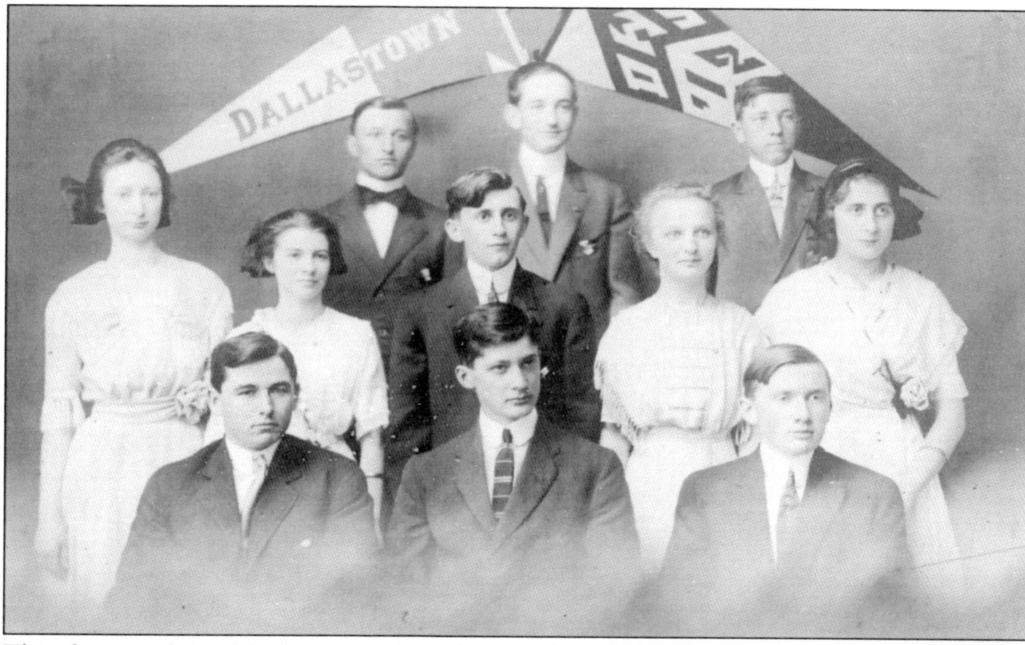

This photograph is of the high school graduating class of 1912 from Dallastown. These students graduated from the public school located at the corner of West Main Street and School Place. Class members included, in alphabetical order: Carl Anstine, Oran Flinchbaugh, Sarah Flory, Rachel Heckert, Walter Henry, Martin Keller, Clarence Ness, Newton Ness, Sallie Sechrist, Letha Shaw, Gerha Sheffer, and Roy Ziegler. (Courtesy of Tom Taylor.)

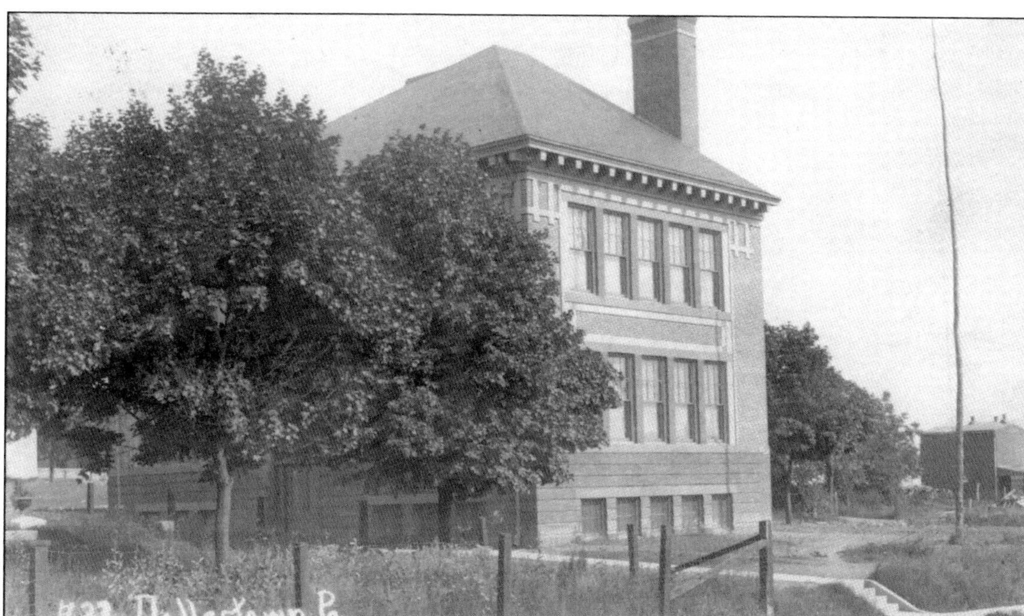

The postcard depicts Dallastown's school at 105 South Charles Street. It was originally built as Dallastown's public high school. When it opened in 1913, it had only four classrooms. Prof. John Myers was the first principal of the school. The building was constructed of brick. A large flagpole is visible in the front yard. (Courtesy of Tom Taylor.)

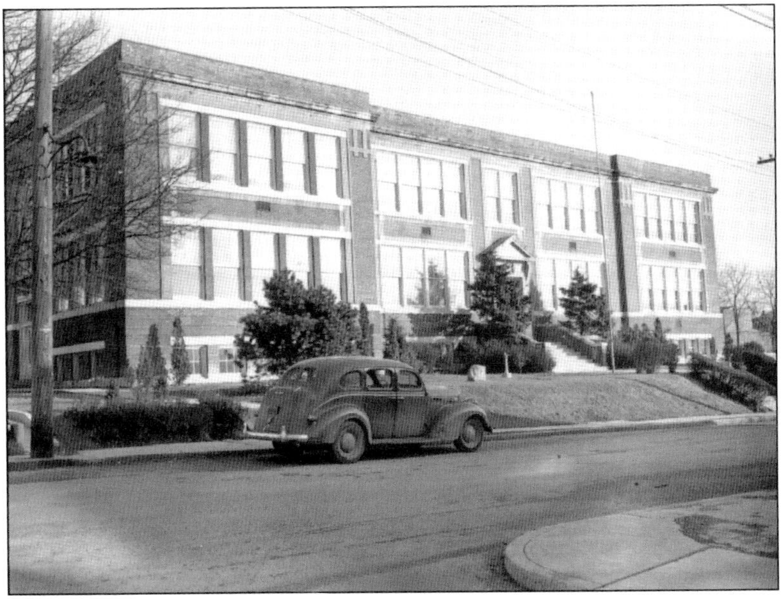

In 1929, the public high school on South Charles Street was expanded by an additional 10 rooms. Three more rooms were added in 1939. In February 1959, the building became the borough's public elementary school, after the new high school opened, and continues as such to the present. The image was taken by Richard E. Gemmill in 1948.

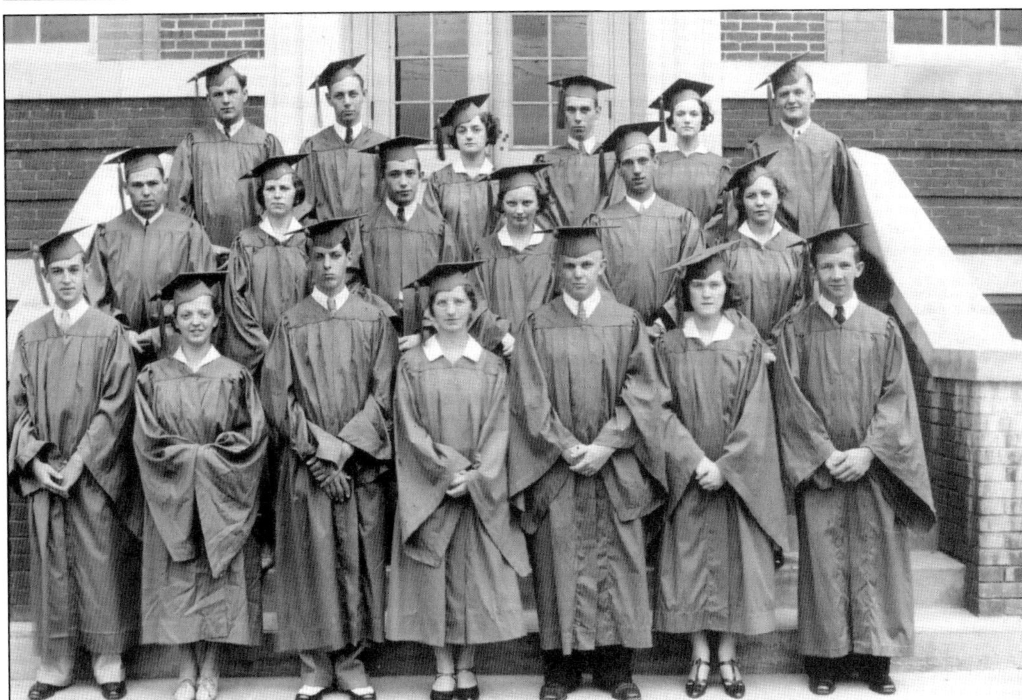

The graduating class of Dallastown Area High School in 1933 is depicted in this photograph. The class is shown posing on the front steps of the public high school at 105 South Charles Street. Class members, in alphabetical order, included Charlotte Barshinger, William Conaway, Melvin H. Deardorff, Mervin Deardorff, Violet Deardorff, Austin Eberly, Nevin Flinchbaugh, Selma P. Grim, Lois M. Guise, Lois Harbold, Philip Heisler, William Hench, Clair A. Holtzapple, Ruth Hose, Erdine Houser, Samuel Jamison, Lee E. Keener, Leo H. Keener, Mary McLaughlin, George Raab, Grace Riedel, Hildred Seitz, Marguerite Sheffer, Richard Eugene Snyder, Vernon Straub, Jessie E. Turner, and Woodrow W. Waltemyer.

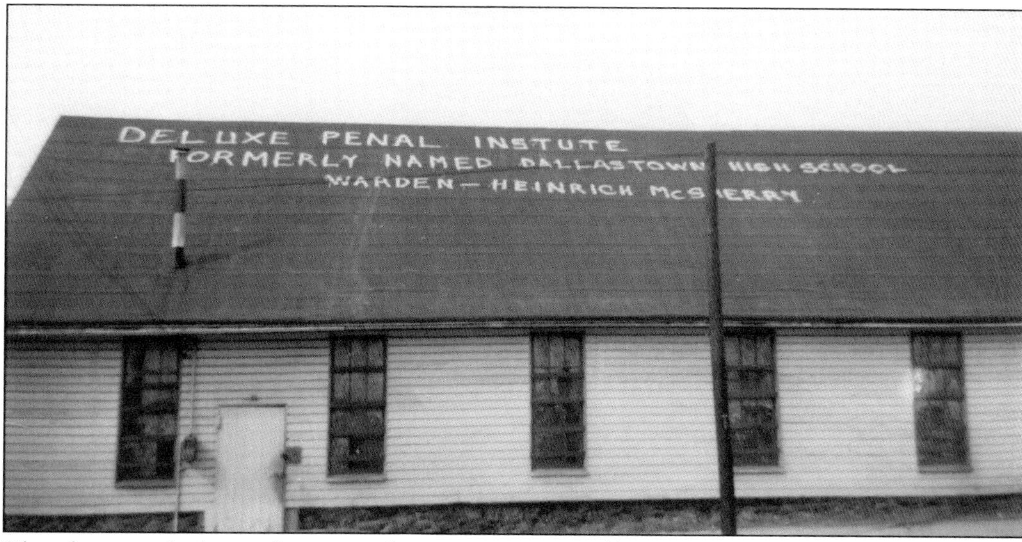

The photograph shows the original gymnasium in Dallastown, located at the corner of East Howard and South Charles Streets. Before it was converted into a gym, the building served as the borough's market house. School students painted words, including "Heinrich McSherry," on its roof. This references Ralph McSherry, who served as Dallastown's high school principal from 1938 to 1948. The students compared him to Heinrich Himmler, who oversaw Nazi concentration camps. (Courtesy of Jennifer Kinard.)

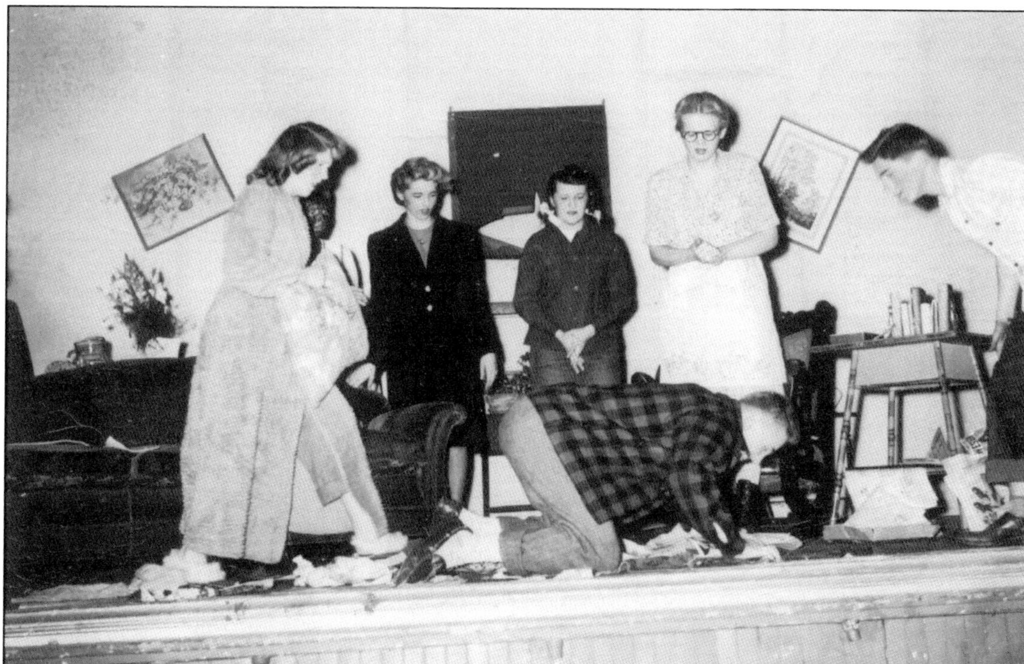
This is a photograph of Dallastown Area High School's junior-class play at the Lyric Theatre in 1947. The production was titled *The Duffy Dills*. The actress at far left is Joan Grim. The remaining performers are unidentified. Dallastown Area High School students put on their plays in the theater from the 1910s through 1948, before the school had its own auditorium. (Courtesy of Priscilla Hoffman.)

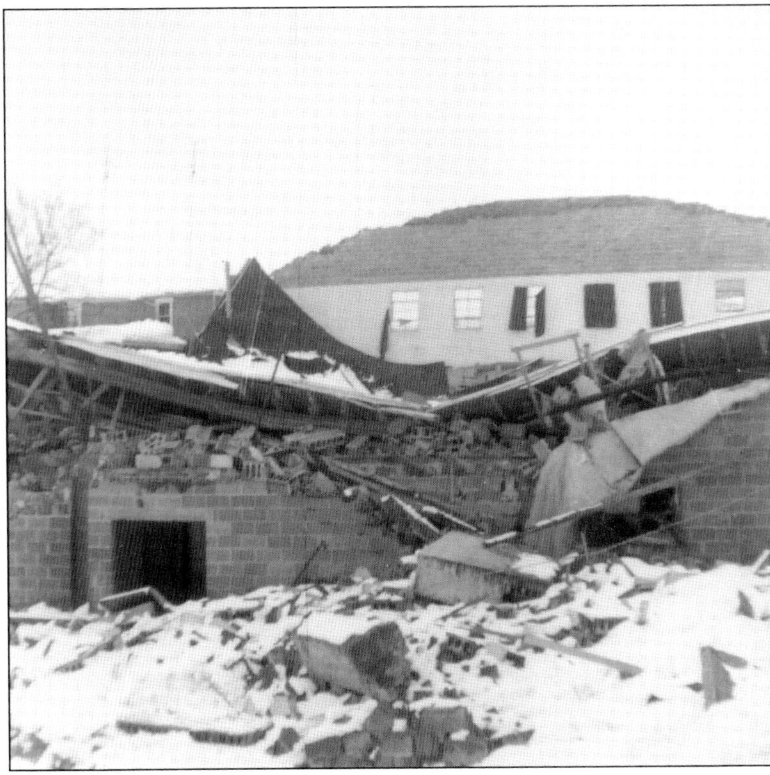

The aftermath of the collapse of the Charles Street Gymnasium and Auditorium due to the weight of four feet of snow on the roof can be seen in this image. This disaster occurred on March 20, 1958. School custodian Lloyd W. Behrensen was killed when the roof collapsed. This gymnasium/auditorium was originally built in 1948. Lance Wolf photographed this scene. (Courtesy of Lance Wolf.)

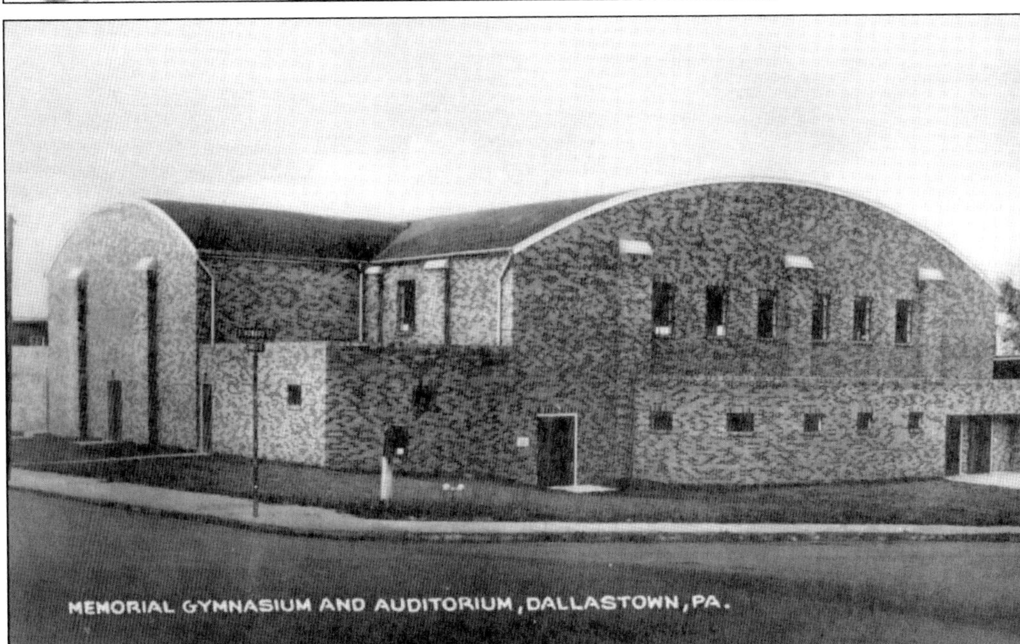

This postcard shows Memorial Gymnasium and Auditorium at the corner of South Charles Street and East Howard Street. The school gymnasium is directly across the street from Dallastown Elementary School. Part of the building also serves as a cafeteria for elementary school students. This new gym and cafeteria opened in 1961. (Courtesy of Cathy Bankoske.)

The image depicts the teachers and staff of Dallastown Elementary School around 1964–1965. From left to right are (first row) Ann Larkin, unidentified, Isabell Mansfield Sellers, Marion Hess, and Grace Benedict; (second row) unidentified, unidentified art teacher, Mary Jane Camponella (music teacher), Gayle Wiemeyer, Marguerite Martin, Armeda Eberly, and Violet Markey; (third row) George Tallman, Andrew Post, Robert Smith, and Fred Wilt (principal).

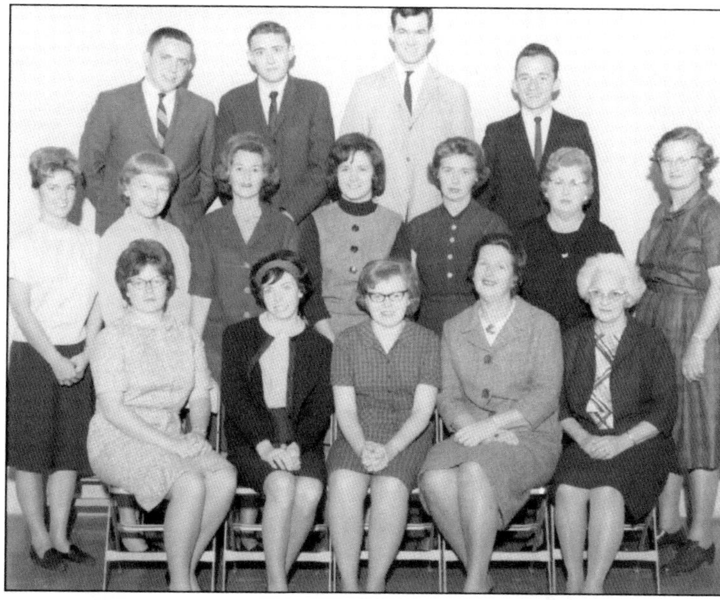

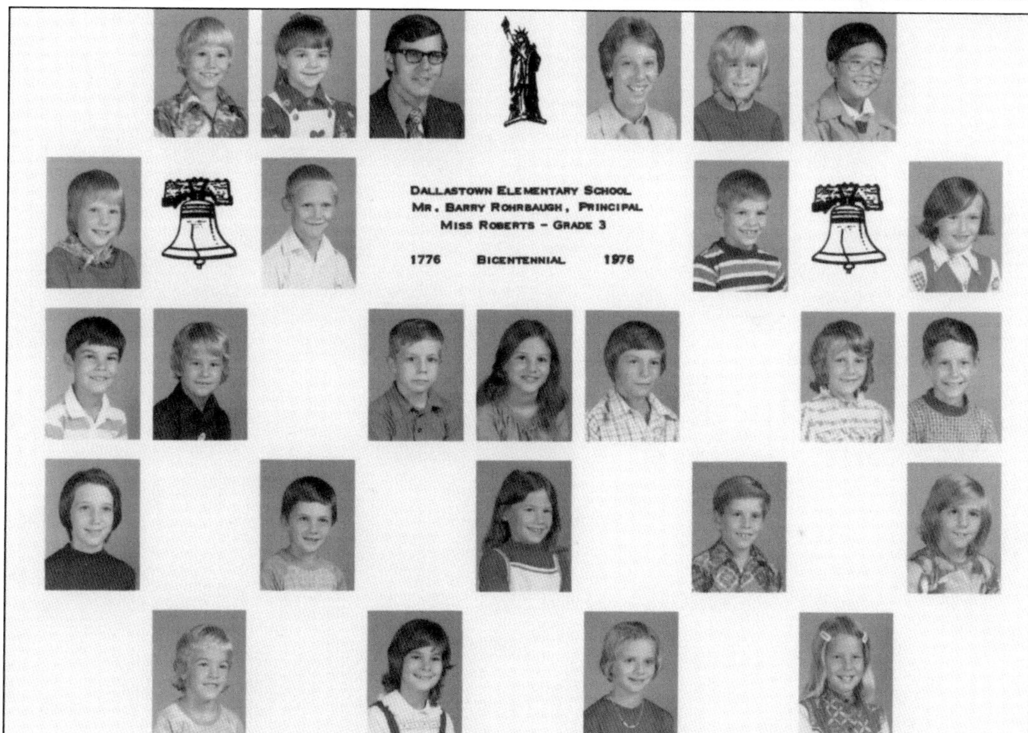

This photographic assemblage depicts one of Dallastown Elementary School's third-grade classes in the bicentennial year of 1976. From left to right are (first row) Tara Gemmill, Carin Campbell, Michelle Connor, and Laura Walker; (second row) unidentified, Richie Miller, Monika Kelkis, Brian Taylor, and Mike Ruth; (third row) Richie Saylor, Rusty Wilson, Wade Spiker, unidentified, Steve Whitsel, unidentified, and Scott Markle; (fourth row) Missy Bean, Billy Erdman, unidentified, and Missy Henry; (fifth row) Joe Miller, Krista Grove, Barry Rohrbaugh (principal), Sandra Roberts (teacher), Kevin Stough, and Eugene Suk. (Courtesy of Richard C. Saylor.)

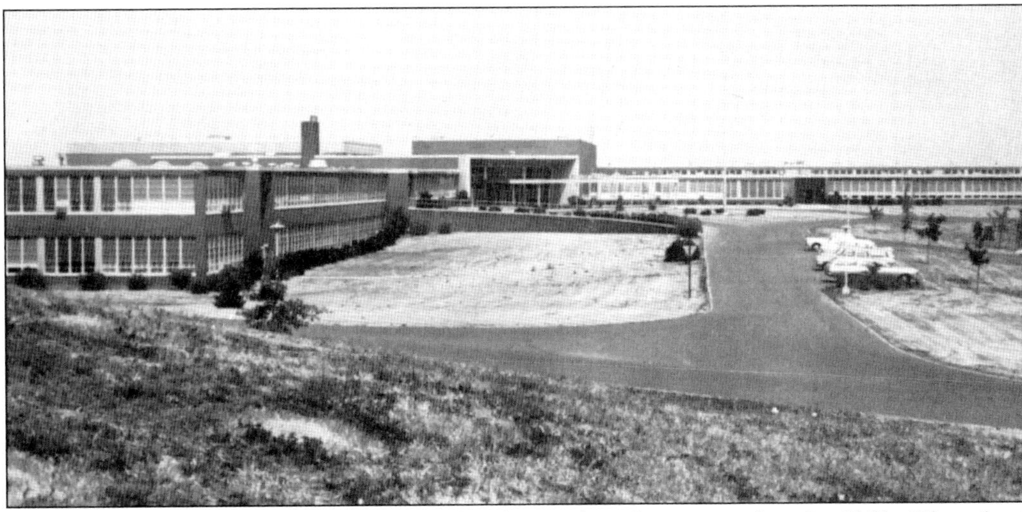

The modern Dallastown Area High School is depicted on this postcard in the 1960s. The school is located at 700 New School Lane and first opened in 1958. The first class to graduate from the school was the class of 1959. Later, a middle school for grades six through eight was built next to the high school and included a natatorium. (Courtesy of Tom Taylor.)

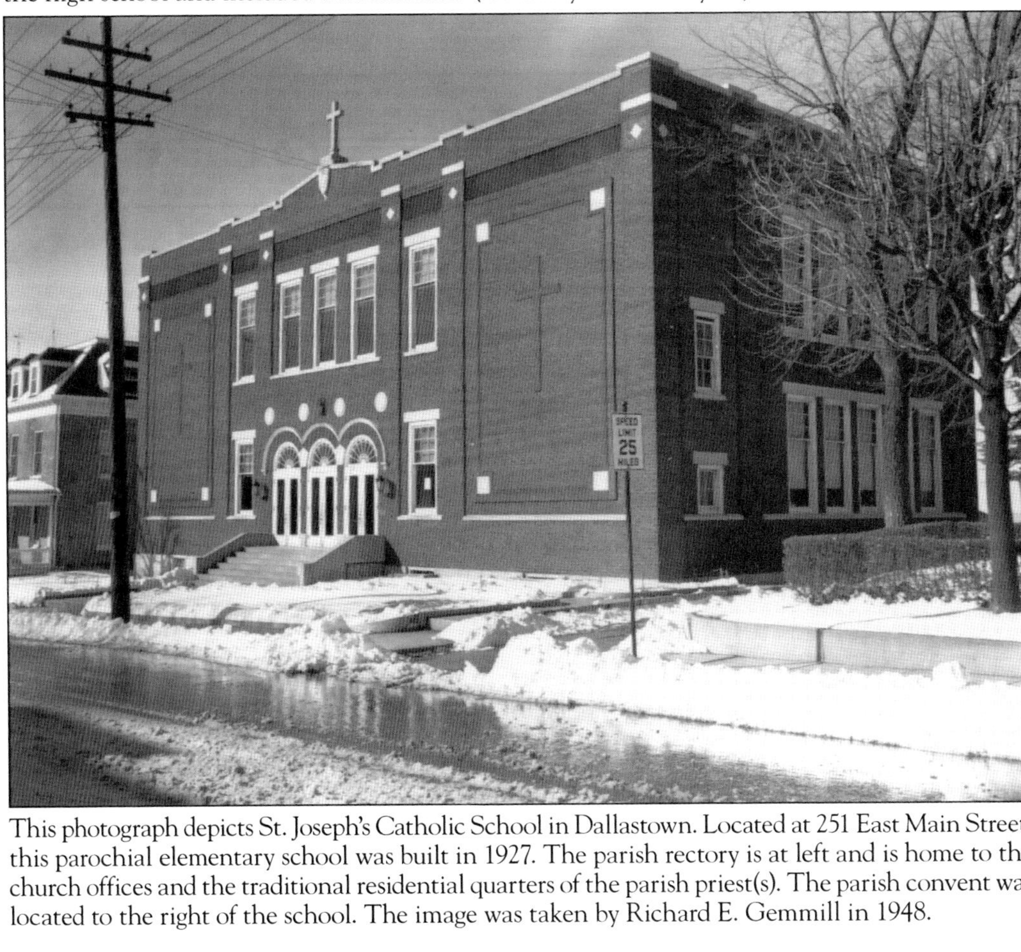

This photograph depicts St. Joseph's Catholic School in Dallastown. Located at 251 East Main Street, this parochial elementary school was built in 1927. The parish rectory is at left and is home to the church offices and the traditional residential quarters of the parish priest(s). The parish convent was located to the right of the school. The image was taken by Richard E. Gemmill in 1948.

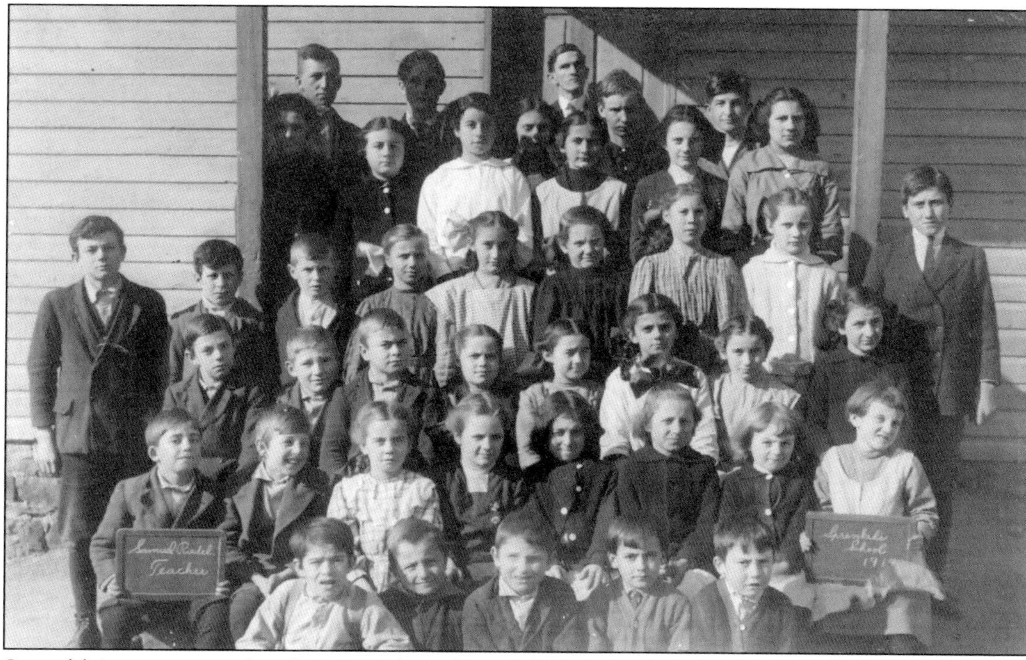

Sprenkle's one-room schoolhouse is the subject of this postcard. The school was located near the borough of Dallastown in York Township. This image of the students and their teacher, Samuel J. Riedel, was taken in 1914. Riedel was a resident of Dallastown, living at 21 West Main Street in 1915. He is located in the center of the back row, in front of the door. (Courtesy of Tom Taylor.)

Adamsville, also known as Pinchgut, is located just outside of Dallastown in York Township near the crossroads of South Duke and Franklin Streets. Adamsville School, as depicted here, was a two-room elementary school located on Arbor Drive. The school opened around 1909 and closed in 1949. The building was eventually converted into a two-family residence.

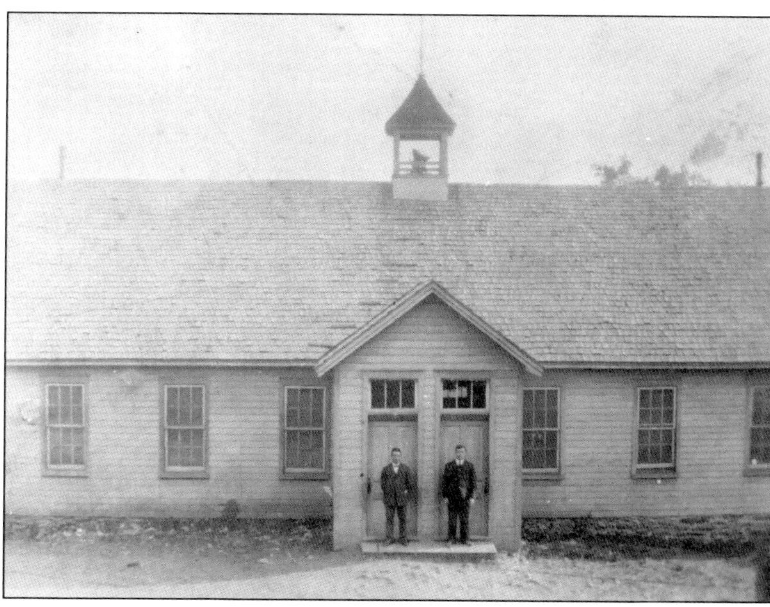

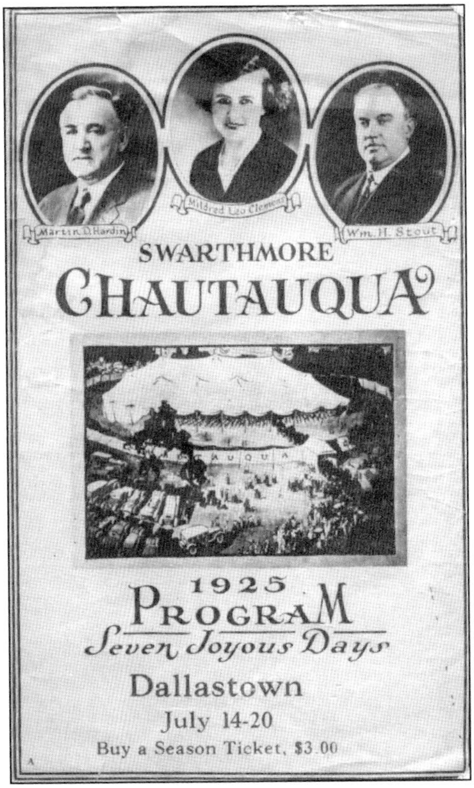

This program was created for the Chautauqua that was held in Dallastown from July 14 to 20, 1925. The weeklong educational events were held in a large tent that traveled along with the speakers from town to town. Lectures were the mainstays of Chautauquas, named for the lake in New York State where the event originated in 1874. Themes such as reform topics, Christianity, and current events were very popular.

William Jennings Bryan was the keynote speaker at Dallastown's Chautauqua on July 25, 1914. He is seated in the left rear of the automobile in this photograph, taken during his visit to Dallastown. He was the Democratic Party's presidential candidate in three separate general elections. From 1900 to 1925, Bryan engaged in speaking on the Chautauqua circuit across the United States, where he often talked about Christianity. (Courtesy of Cathy Bankoske.)

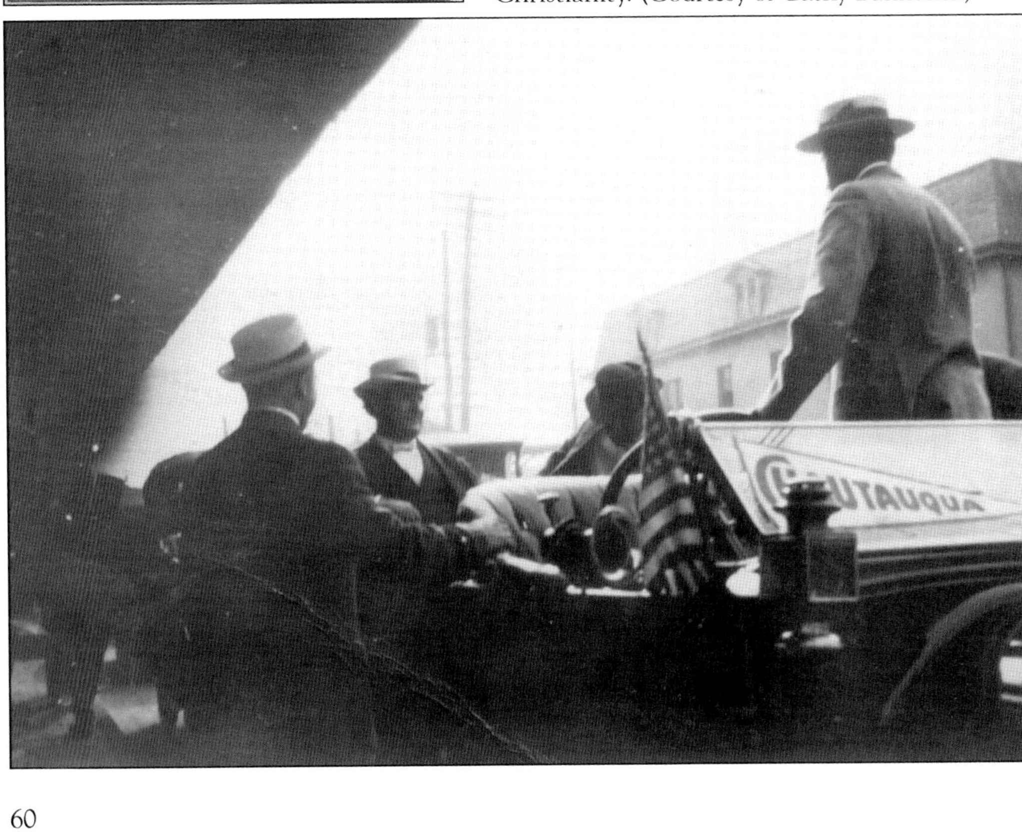

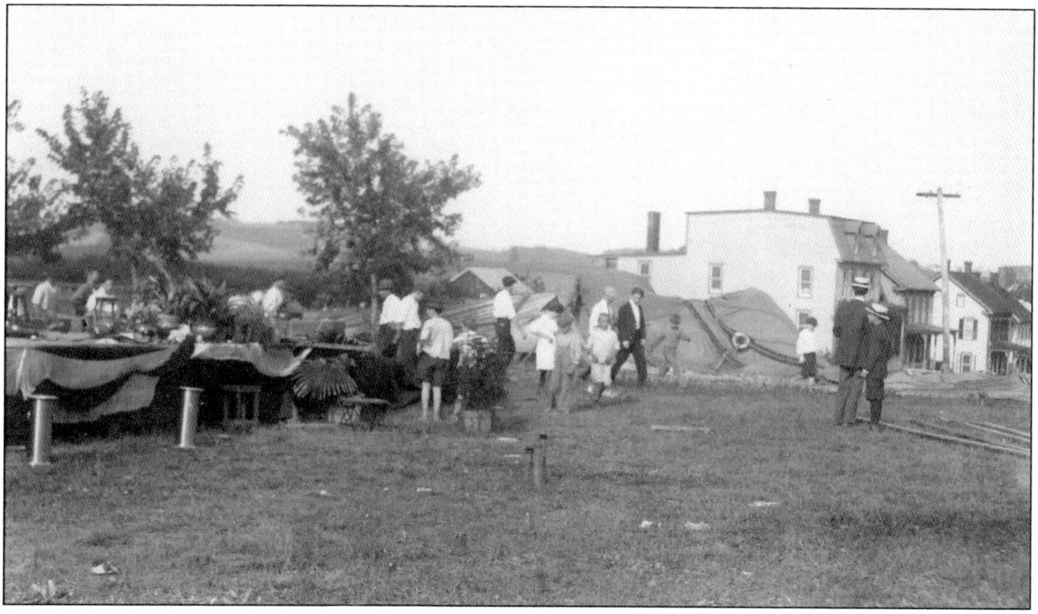

On July 19, 1915, a windstorm blew down the Dallastown Chautauqua's tent while 200 people were in attendance. Dr. Enos S. Mann and Robert Guy Hess were killed. Laura Barshinger, Grace Burk, Charles Conway, William Conway, Enos Eberly, Malinda Geesey, Charles Grim, John Heisler, Olinda Kauffman, Leo Keener, Annie M. Lau, Frances Lichtenberger, Anne Locke, Reba Lutz, Mattie Mellinger, John Reid, Ida Reidel, and William Snyder sustained injuries.

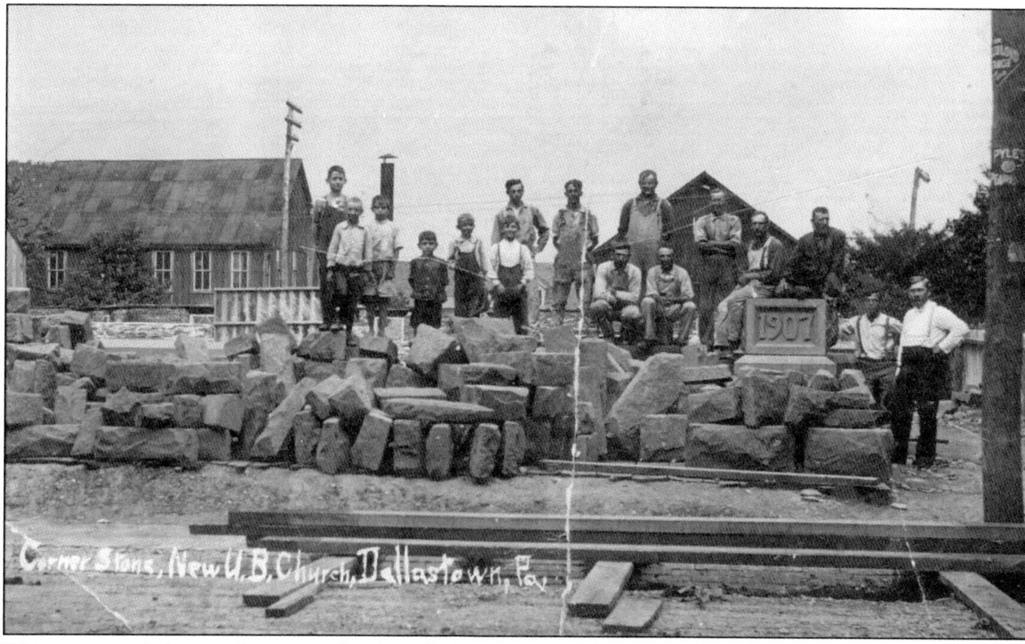

This postcard shows the recently placed cornerstone of the new Bethlehem Evangelical United Brethren Church in Dallastown. Children and workers pose on some of the brownstones that were used to build the church. Located at 109 East Main Street, the cornerstone was laid by Dr. W.H. Washinger on August 4, 1907, assisted by pastor Dr. L.W. Lutz. The photograph was taken by William M. Bigler. (Courtesy of Roger Fuller.)

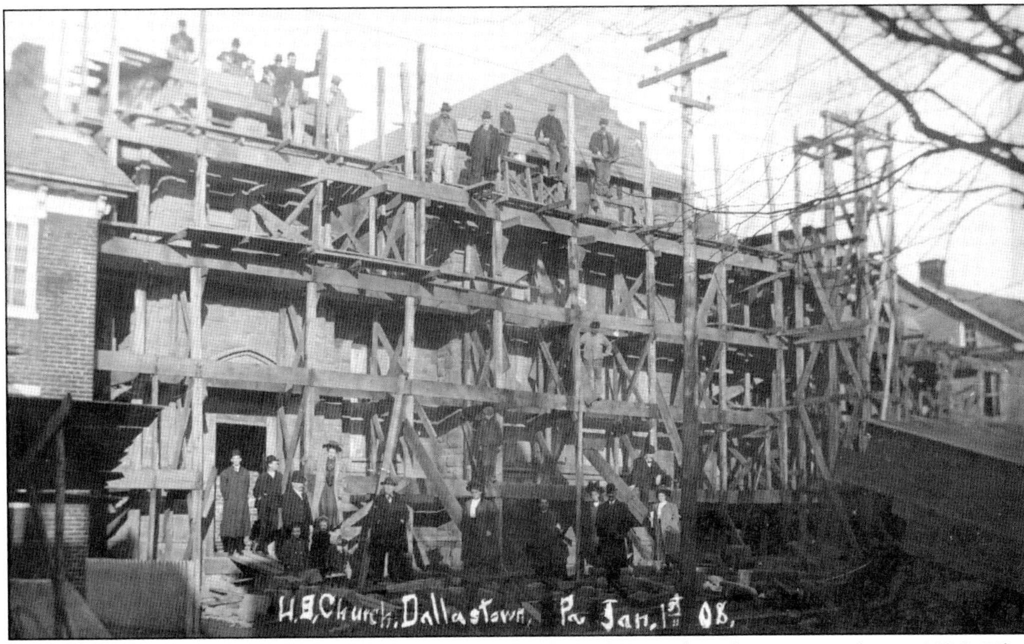

The construction of Bethlehem Evangelical United Brethren Church continued into 1908. This postcard depicts workers posing on the scaffolding at the front of the building on the north side of East Main Street. The structure originally measured 86 by 119 feet. The image was taken on January 1, 1908, by Dallastown photographer William M. Bigler.

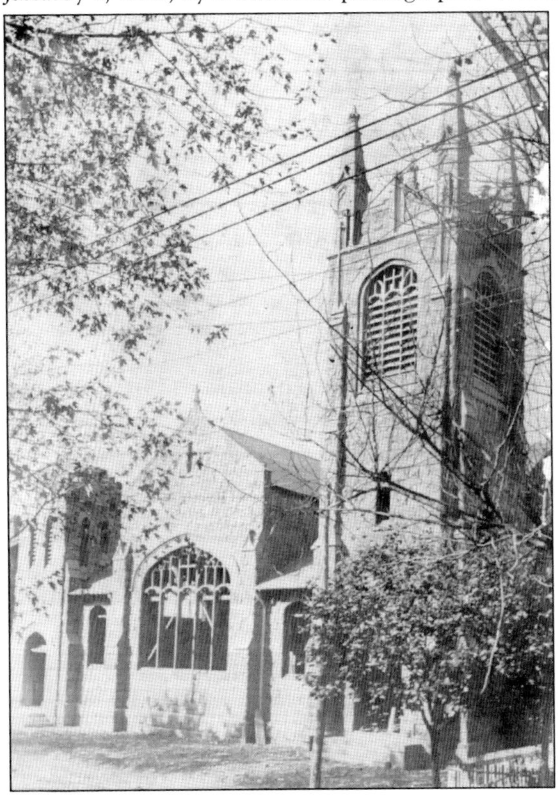

This postcard depicts Bethlehem Evangelical United Brethren Church almost completed. The window frames are in place, but the stained-glass windows have not yet been installed. The image was taken from a location on the south side of East Main Street in Dallastown. The card was mailed from Dallastown in 1909. (Courtesy of Tom Taylor.)

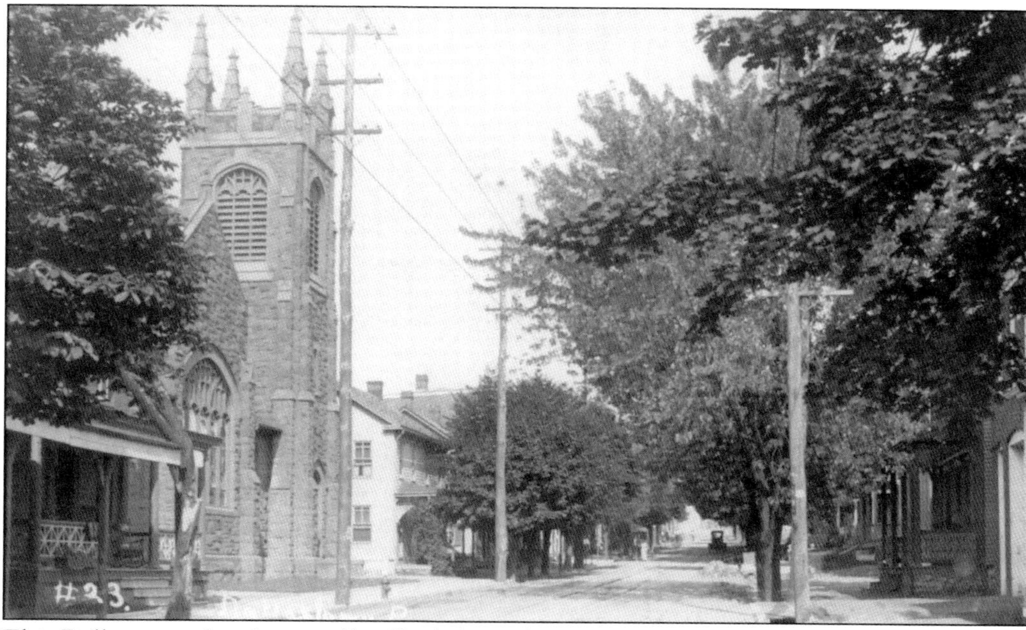

This Dallastown church was officially dedicated on May 15, 1910, by Bishop William M. Bell. Bethlehem Evangelical United Brethren Church is located on the north side of East Main Street. This view looks east along Main Street. Note the trolley tracks running down the street's center. In 1968, the church was renamed Bethlehem United Methodist Church following the merger of the Methodist Church and the Evangelical United Brethren Church.

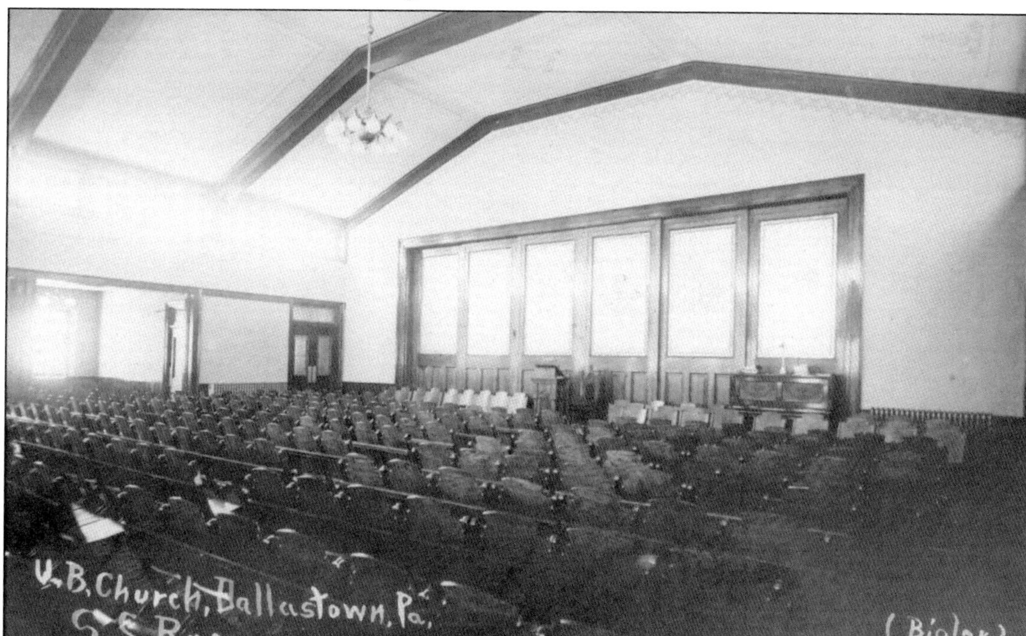

The photograph depicts the Sunday school room and auditorium inside Bethlehem Evangelical United Brethren Church, located at 109 East Main Street. It was taken by photographer William M. Bigler shortly after the church building was dedicated in 1910. The church was renamed Bethlehem United Methodist Church in 1968. (Courtesy of Roger Fuller.)

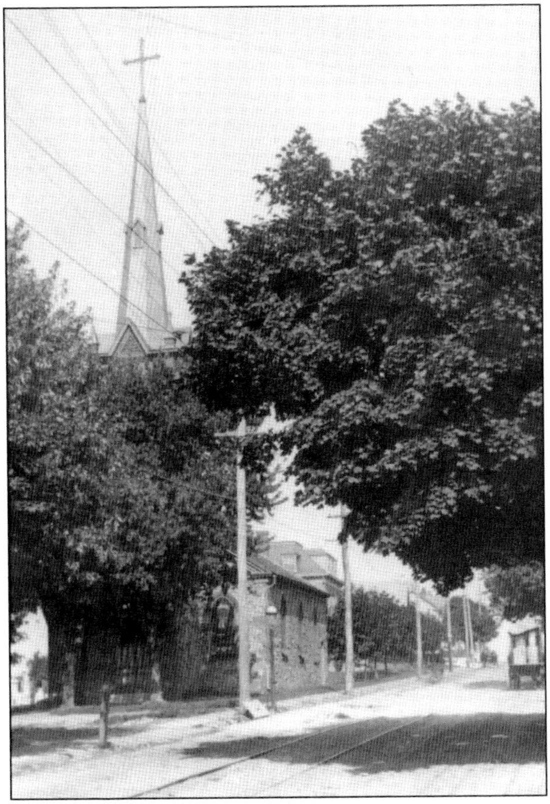

St. Joseph Catholic Church in Dallastown was established in 1850, predating the borough itself. The church land was purchased in February 1850, and the building's cornerstone was laid on May 20, 1850. This image, taken around the early 1900s, shows the original steeple of the church. The parish originally had a mostly Germanic congregation who had emigrated from the German principalities of Baden, Bavaria, Hannover, Hesse, Prussia, and Westphalia. (Courtesy of Roger Fuller.)

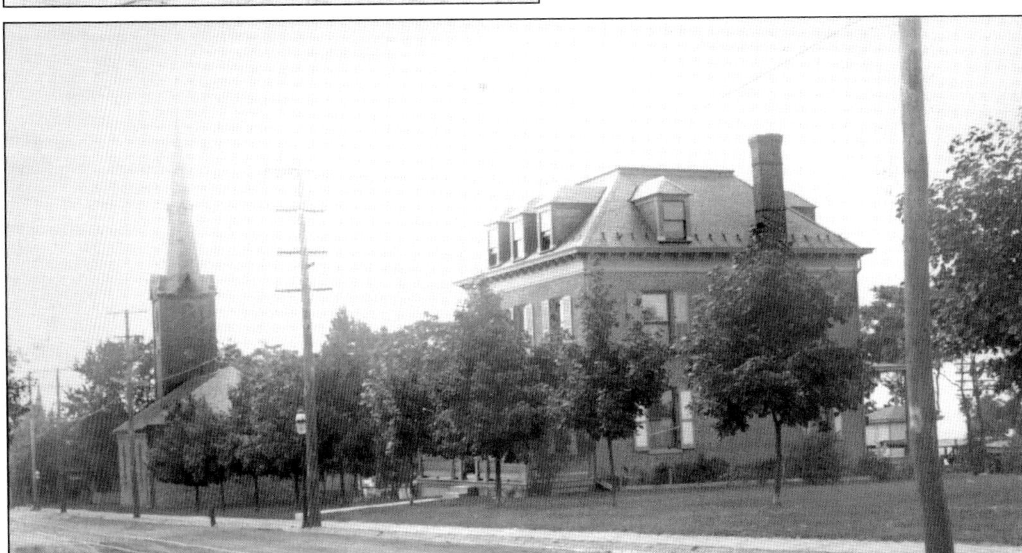

This postcard view looks west on East Main Street in Dallastown between 1904 and 1918. The building on the left is the original St. Joseph Catholic Church. The one on the right is the church rectory. The image predates the construction of the parish school. Trolley tracks are visible on the dirt road. (Courtesy of Tom Taylor.)

This image of the original stone St. Joseph Catholic Church was taken in 1948 by Richard E. Gemmill. Note that this was the second steeple to be placed on the church. To the right of the church is the rectory and to the right of that is the parish school. This church building served the parish from 1850 to May 1961.

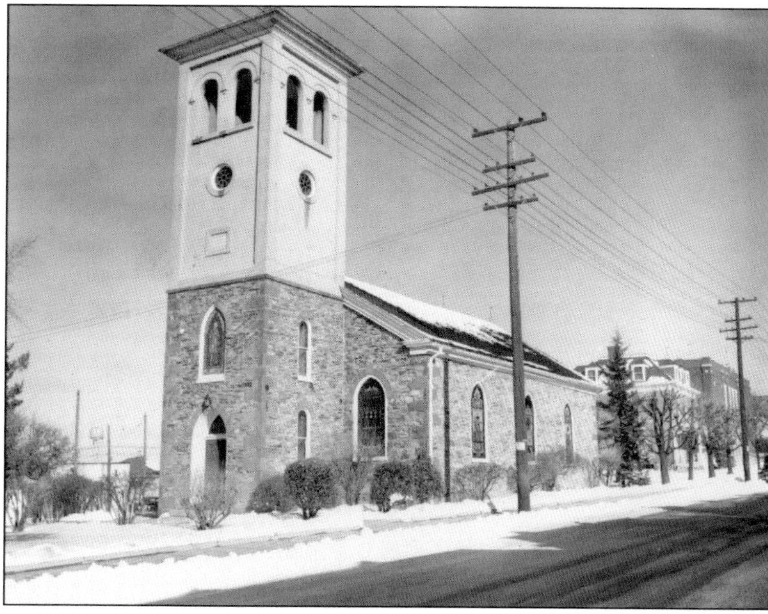

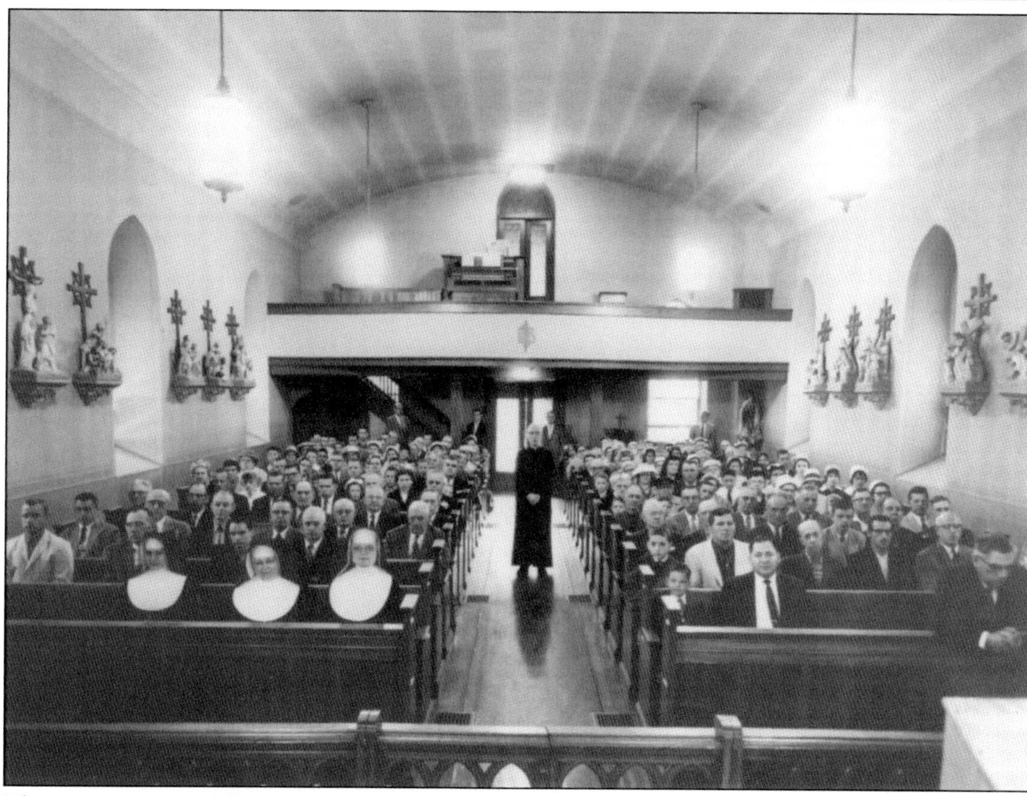

This interior view of the original St. Joseph Catholic Church dates from the 1950s. The photograph was taken from near the pulpit, with a view looking back toward the faithful in the pews, with Rev. Edward J. Gerrity standing in the aisle. Father Gerrity was the pastor of the church from 1957 to 1962. The three sisters of St. Francis sitting in the front left pew were teachers at the parish school. (Courtesy of Cathy Bankoske.)

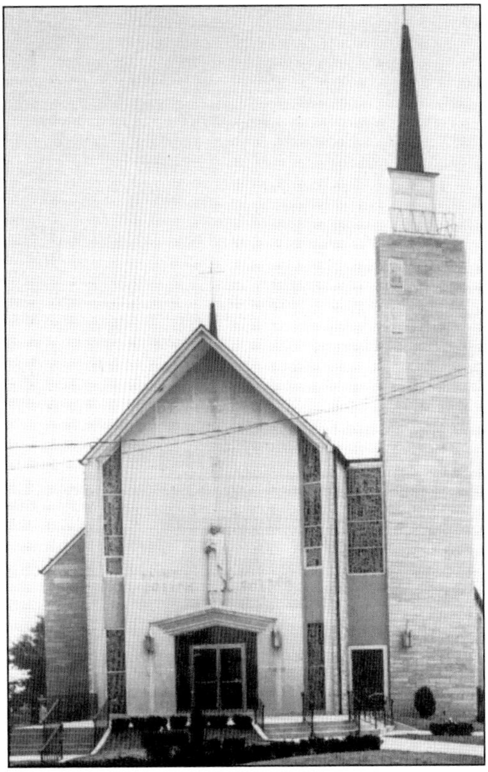

St. Joseph Catholic Church's second church building is depicted on this postcard. The building was opened in 1963, taking the place of the original 1850 church, and Dallastown parishioners have called this church home ever since. The image, taken from Locust Street, shows the front of the edifice and the main entrance. (Courtesy of Tom Taylor.)

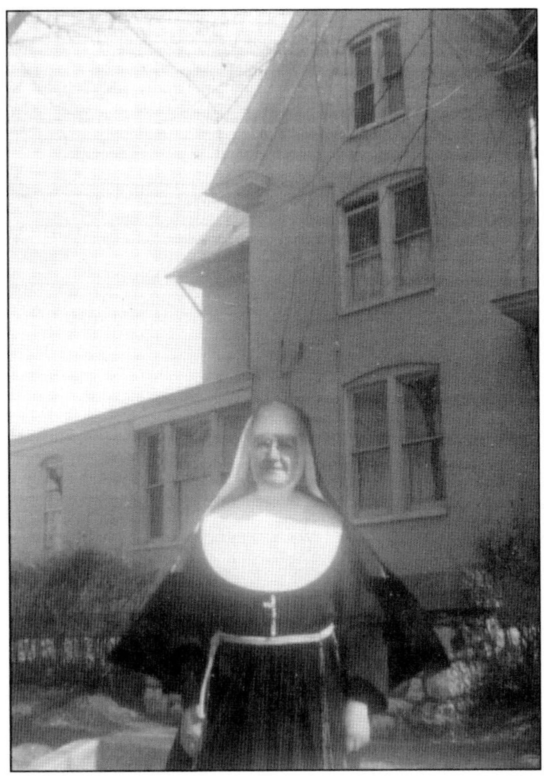

An unidentified Franciscan nun is shown here standing near the side of St. Joseph's convent. The convent was located on the north side of East Main Street in Dallastown, to the right of the parish school. The convent was purchased for the sisters before they arrived to teach at the new parochial school in 1927. Prior to that, the building had been the home of the Bartenslager family.

This photograph shows Christ Evangelical Lutheran Church and its parsonage at left. The church was located at 54 West Main Street and was dedicated in August 1888. This image was taken during the ministry of the Reverend S.H. Greenhoe, who served from 1904 to 1912. Services were held at this building until a new church was completed for the congregation in 1932.

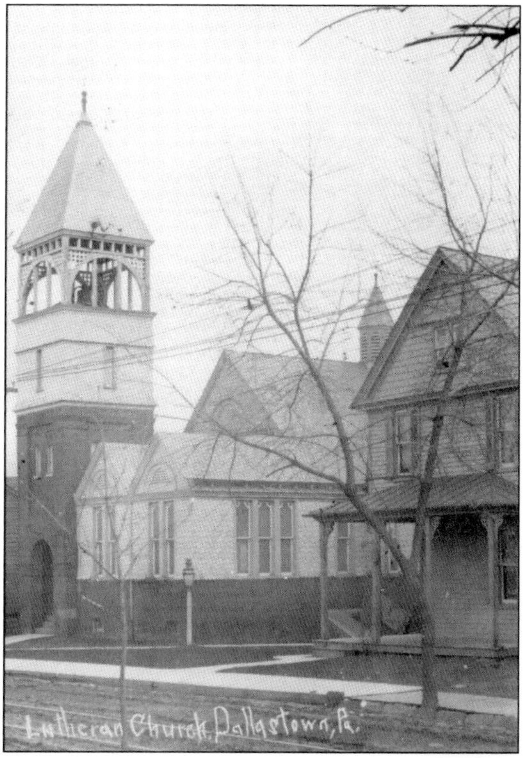

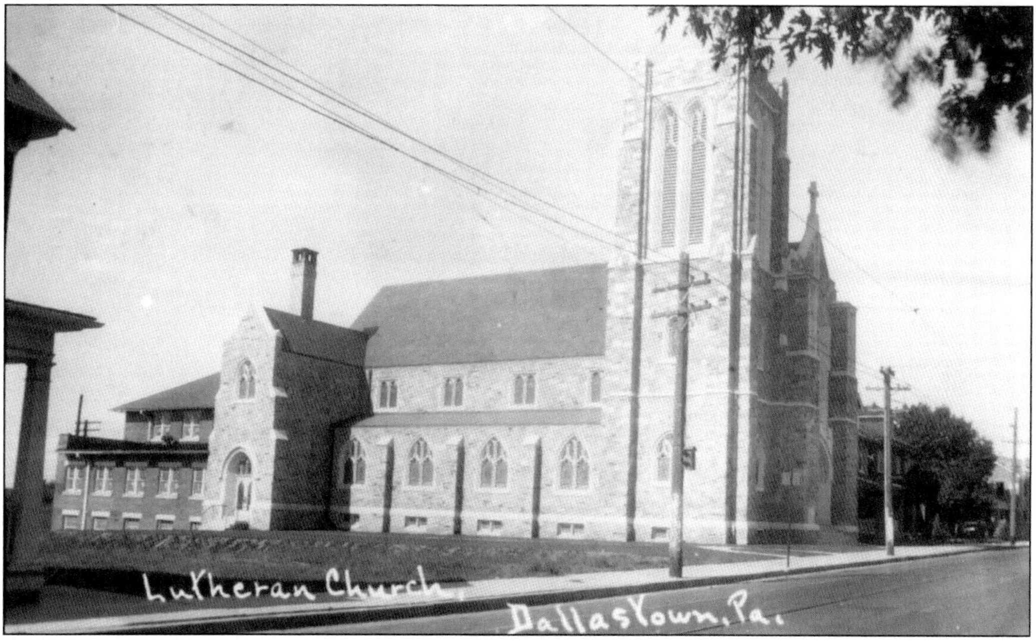

This c. 1937 postcard of Christ Evangelical Lutheran Church at 126 West Main Street depicts the second church building for this congregation. Construction on this church began on March 29, 1931, while the cornerstone was laid on June 14 of the same year. The dedication of the new church was held on June 12, 1932, and was presided over by the Reverend H.D. Hoover of Gettysburg's Lutheran Theological Seminary.

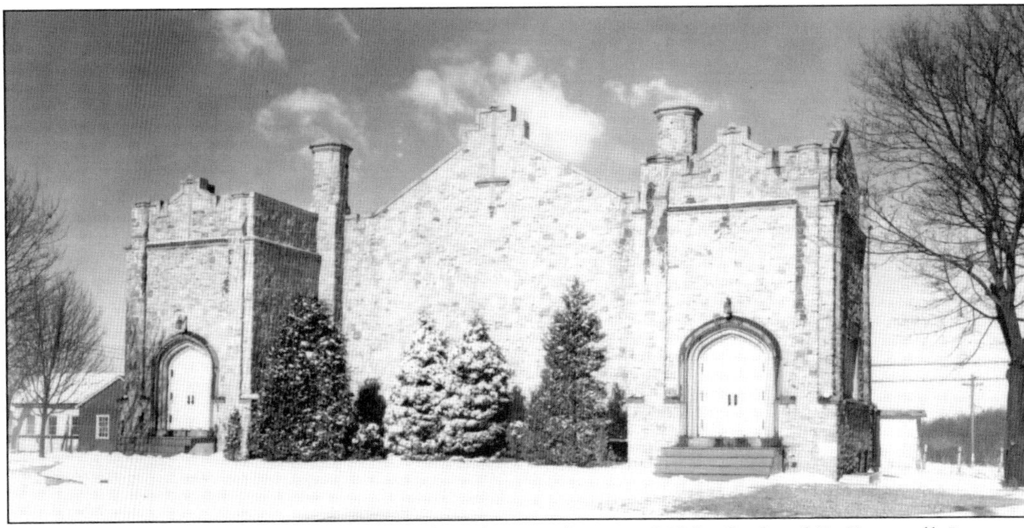

The photograph of St. Paul's Reformed Church was taken in 1948 by Richard E. Gemmill. Located at 205 West Main Street, it was the second church at this address. The original 1855 church at this location was made of brick, while the one depicted in this image was made of stone. The present St. Paul's United Church of Christ was built at this site in 1964.

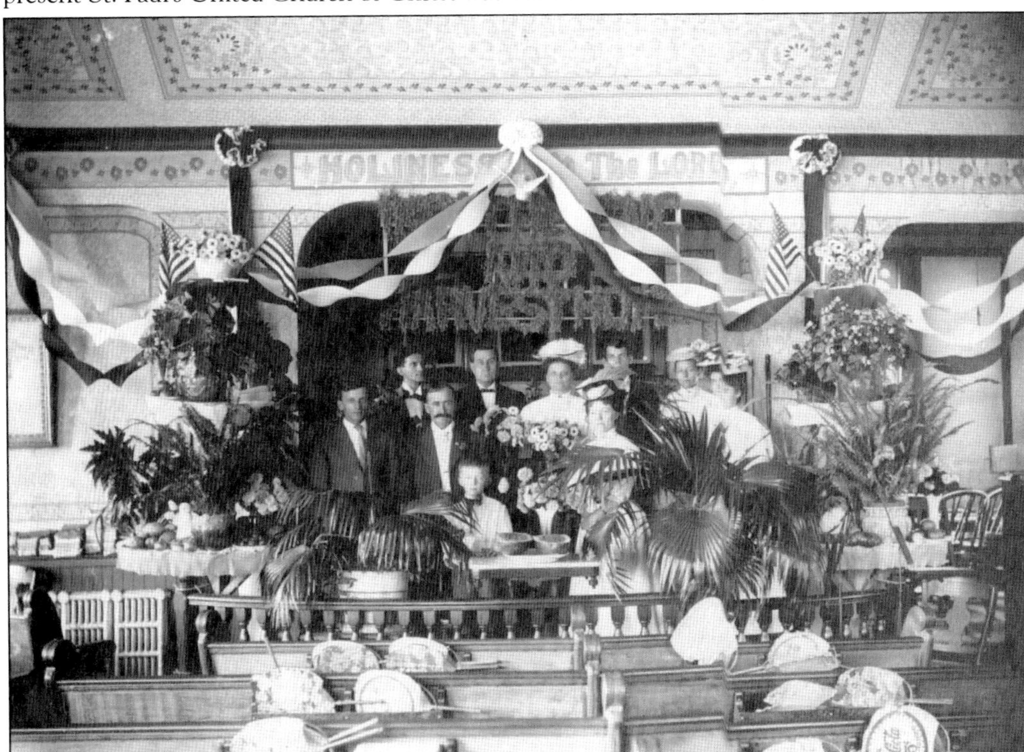

This harvest-themed Dallastown church scene shows flowers, plants, fruits, and vegetables related to the produce season in Pennsylvania. Some of the hand fans in the pews of the church were provided by the Coca-Cola Company as an advertising premium for its 5¢ bottles of soda. Many churchgoers used fans like these to keep cool during an era where air-conditioning did not exist in local churches.

Four

Tobacco Industry

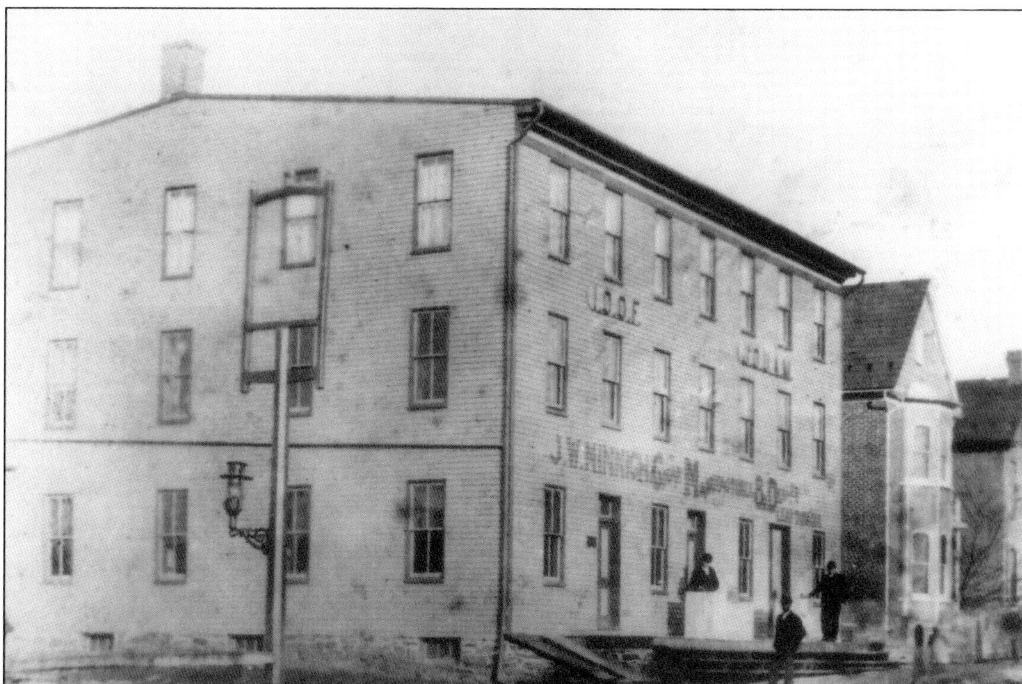

Minnich's Cigar Manufacturer's building was located at 13 East Main Street in Dallastown. The cigar factory was owned by John W. Minnich, who began manufacturing cigars in 1882. The "I.O.O.F." sign on the upper floor indicates that the Independent Order of Odd Fellows met there. This was the Dallas Lodge, No. 1017. The "J.O.U.A.M." sign signifies that the Junior Order of United American Mechanics also met in this building. (Courtesy of Roger Fuller.)

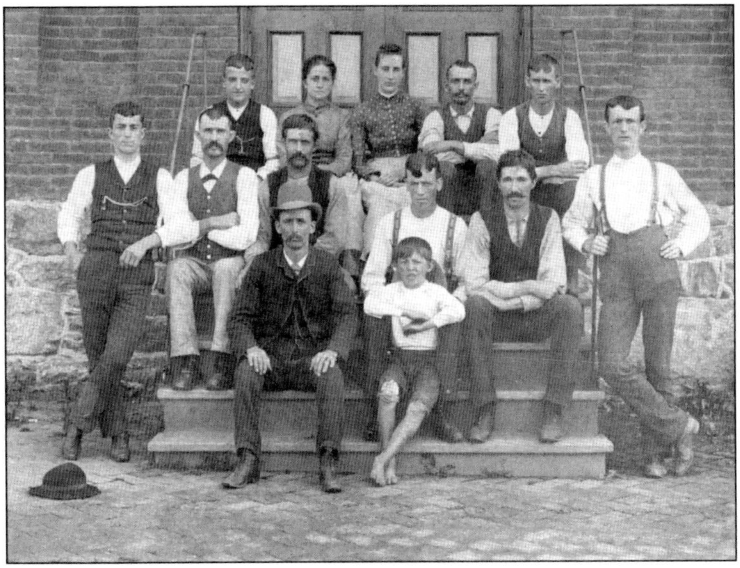

John W. Minnich's cigar factory employees and family are shown posing in front of the old United Brethren church in Dallastown in the 1890s. The location of this building is where the Dallastown Area Historical Society now resides. People depicted in the image include Annie M. Taylor, Cinny Smith, Little Fred Spotz, Uncle John ?, Pop ?, Dr. William H. Minnich, and Henry ? (Courtesy of Roger Fuller.)

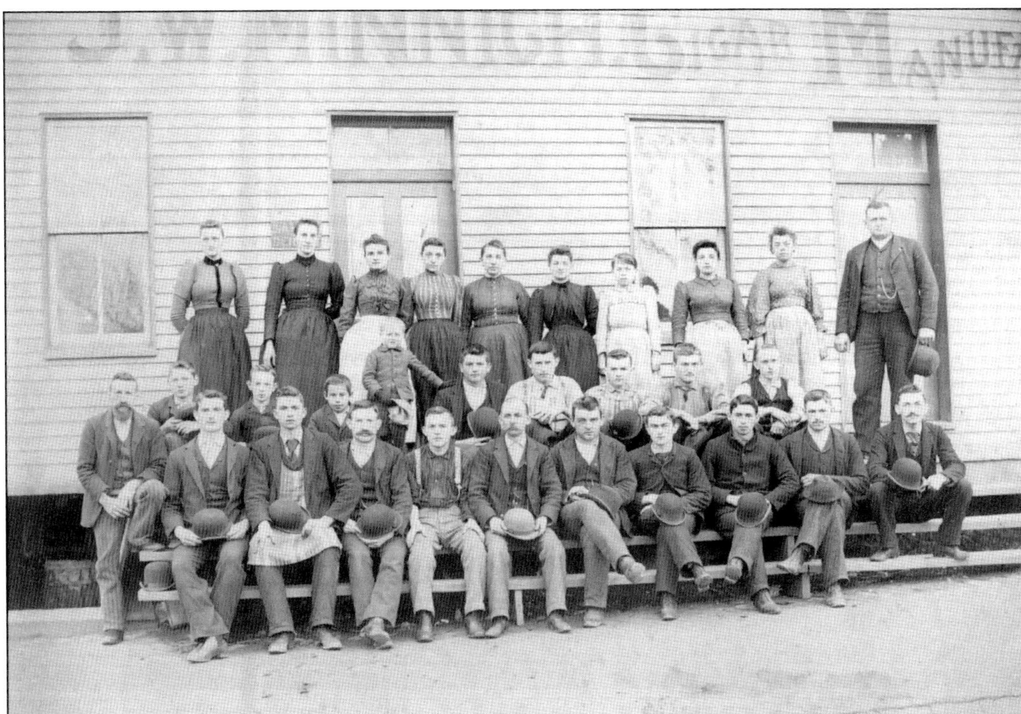

Employees of J.W. Minnich's cigar company are shown posing in front of the cigar factory in Dallastown. John W. Minnich began working in the cigar industry in 1879. By 1882, Minnich had three employees. In 1907, Minnich employed an average of 125 workers, and the company's output was the largest of all cigar factories in York County, with annual production of over 12 million cigars.

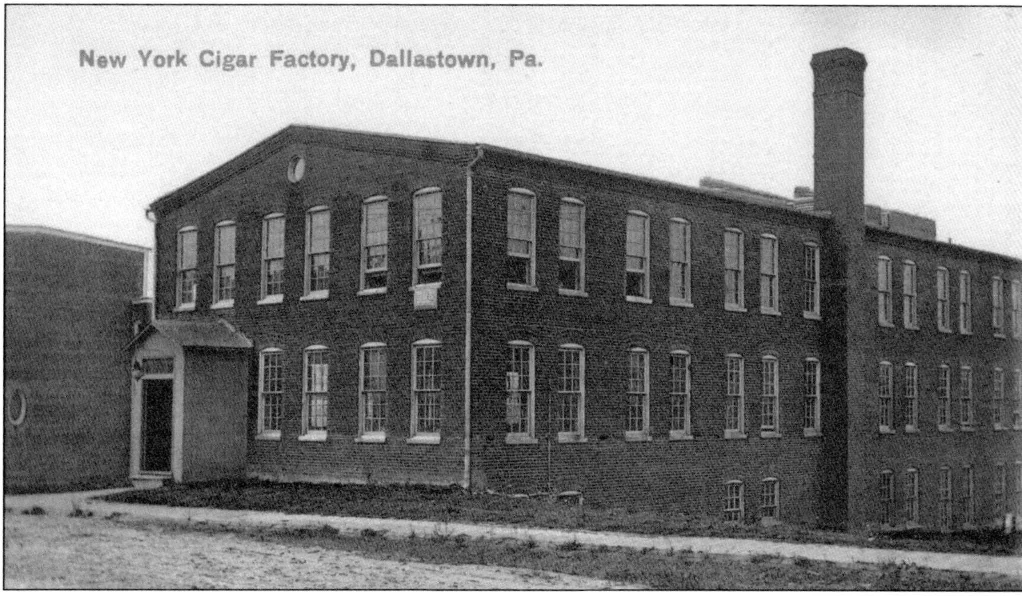

Dallastown's New York Cigar company is depicted on this postcard. The factory was located on South Walnut Street. The company also had factories in York, Red Lion, Windsor, and Yoe. After the Dallastown factory closed, the facility became a sewing factory, for many years being operated by Standard Garment Company. After the sewing business left, the building became home to a storage facility. (Courtesy of Cathy Bankoske.)

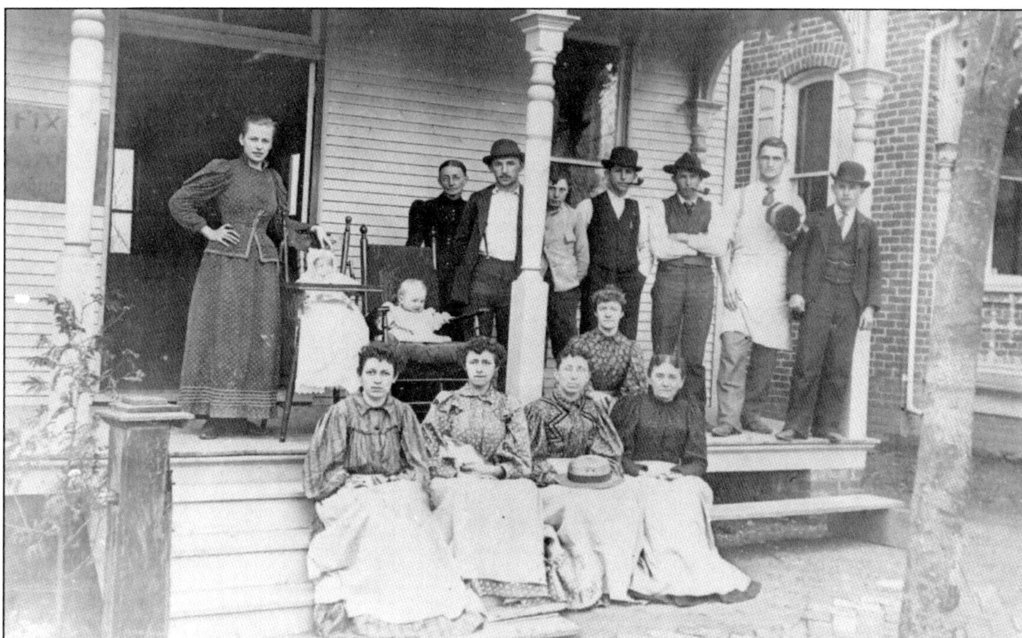

Originally owned by Frederick Fix, who was born in Frankfurt, Germany, this cigar factory was in operation by 1881. By 1904, the factory was run by Frederick's son Alvin F. Fix at 7 West Main Street. In 1921, A.F. Fix & Company was located at 13 West Main Street and was managed by Isaiah H. Rojahn. By 1927, the factory was listed as being located at 17 West Main Street. (Courtesy of Roger Fuller.)

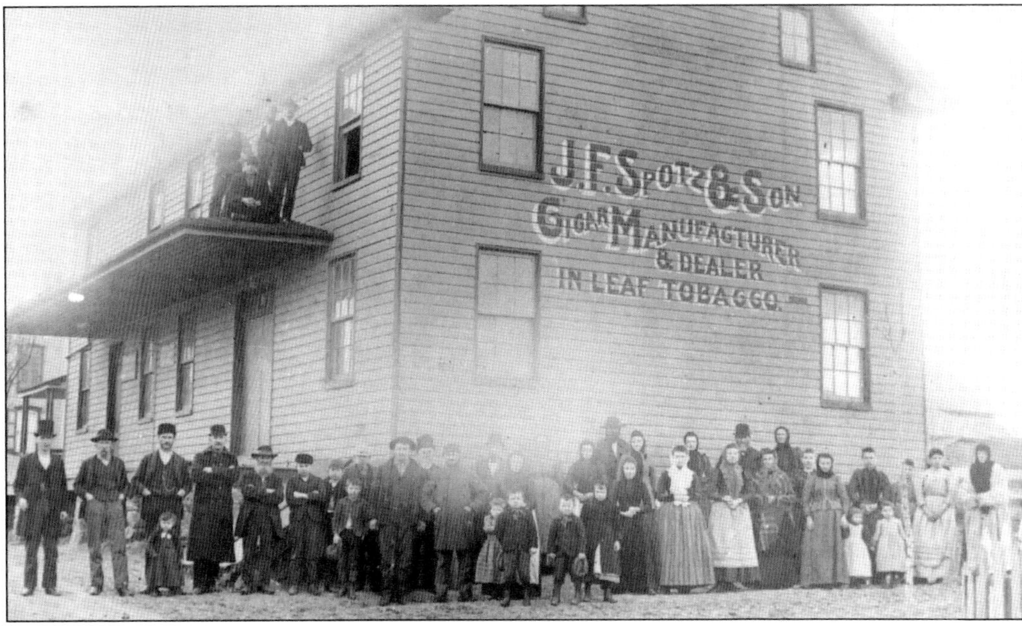

Jacob F. Spotz (sometimes spelled Spatz) was manufacturing cigars in Dallastown by 1877. J.F. Spotz Cigar factory was located at the southeast corner of East Main Street and Pleasant Avenue. By 1904, the company had changed its name to J.F. Spotz & Son and was located at 86–88 East Main Street. In this image, Spotz company employees are posing at the side of the factory building. (Courtesy of Roger Fuller.)

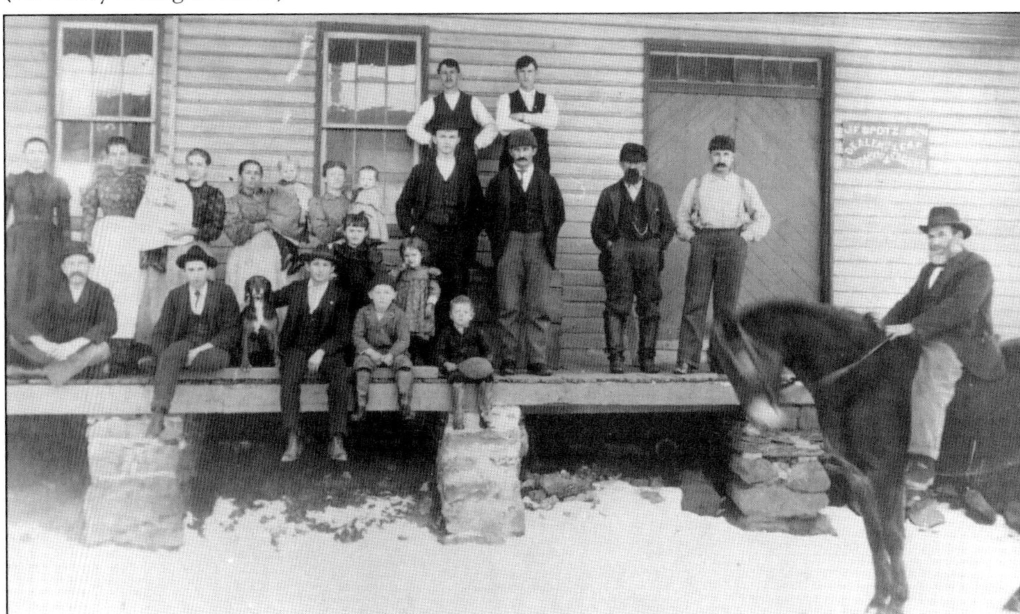

J.F. Spotz cigar company employees are pictured in the front of the factory building. By 1885, Dallastown had 85 cigar factories, while the neighboring town of Red Lion had 55. J.F. Spotz's son Henry L. Spotz joined the company by 1904. According to city directories, J.F. Spotz & Son was located at 204 East Main Street beginning in 1925. By 1927, the company was out of business. (Courtesy of Roger Fuller.)

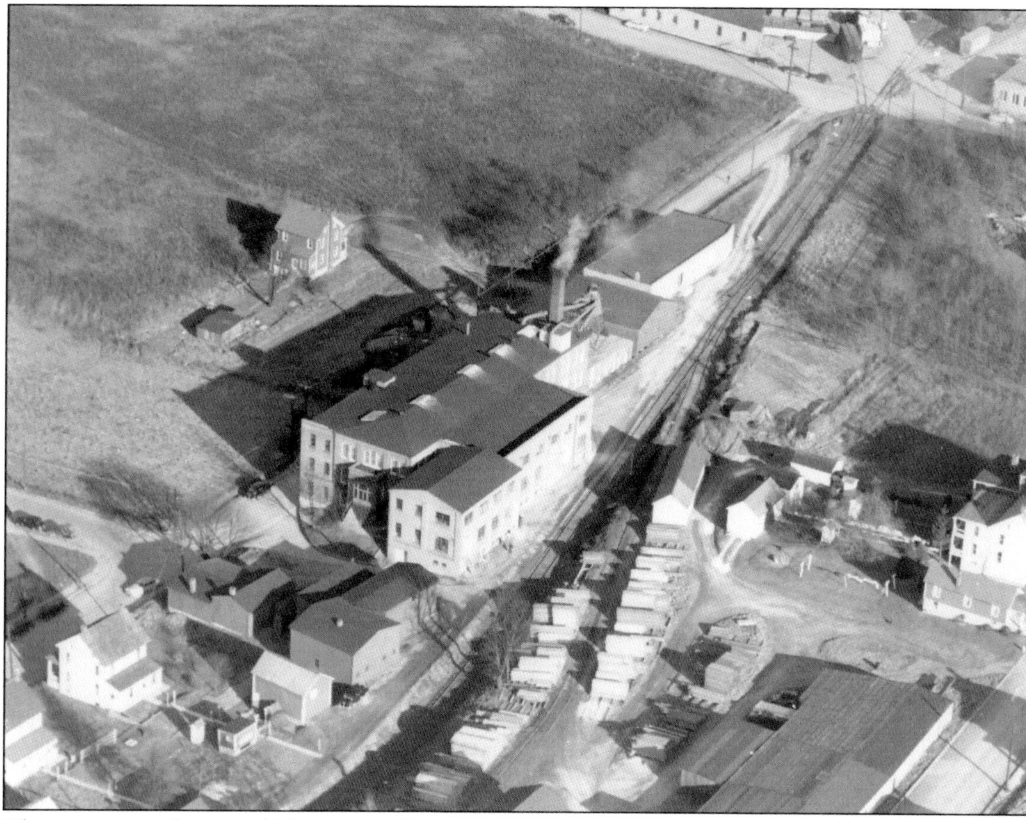

This is an aerial view of Merchants Cigar Box Company around 1949. From 1900 to 1932, the company only produced cigar boxes. The factory was located at the southeast corner of Broad and Lombard Streets near the Maryland & Pennsylvania Railroad tracks. From 1932 until 1959, the company continued to produce cigar boxes but also began producing miniature cedar chests and various custom-made boxes of all varieties.

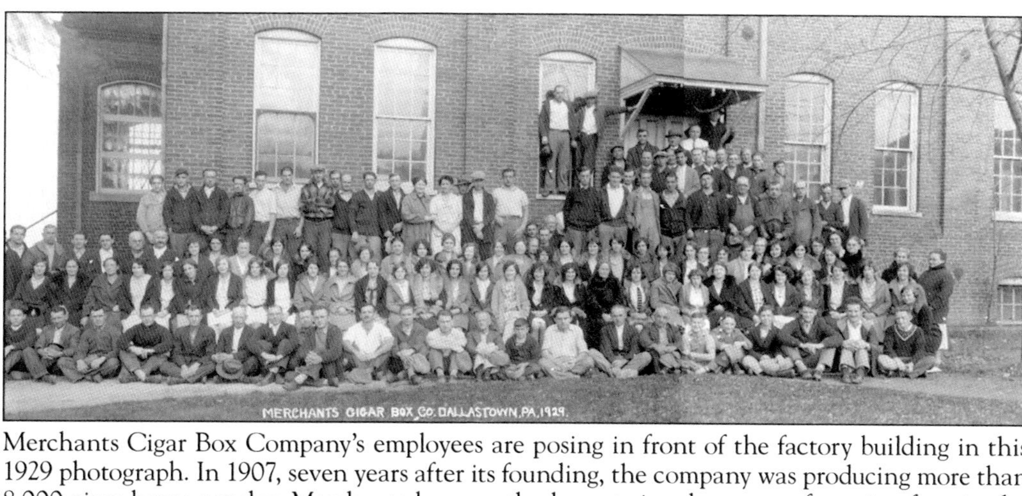

Merchants Cigar Box Company's employees are posing in front of the factory building in this 1929 photograph. In 1907, seven years after its founding, the company was producing more than 8,000 cigar boxes per day. Merchants became the largest cigar box–manufacturing firm in the Dallastown area, although it had strong competition from other firms.

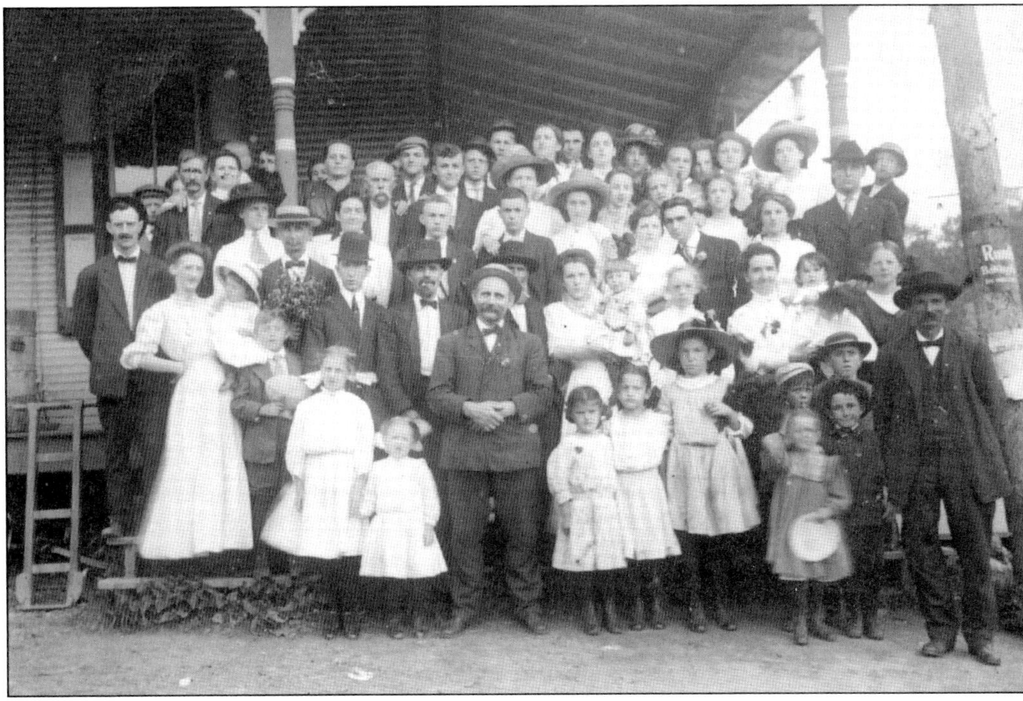

Merchants Cigar Box Company employees pose for this postcard image on the day of a company picnic, sometime between 1904 and 1918. Company picnics were an annual tradition for many local community businesses during this time period. Merchants Cigar Box Company was organized in 1900 for the manufacture of cigar boxes. George A. Kohler was the president of the company during this era. (Courtesy of Tom Taylor.)

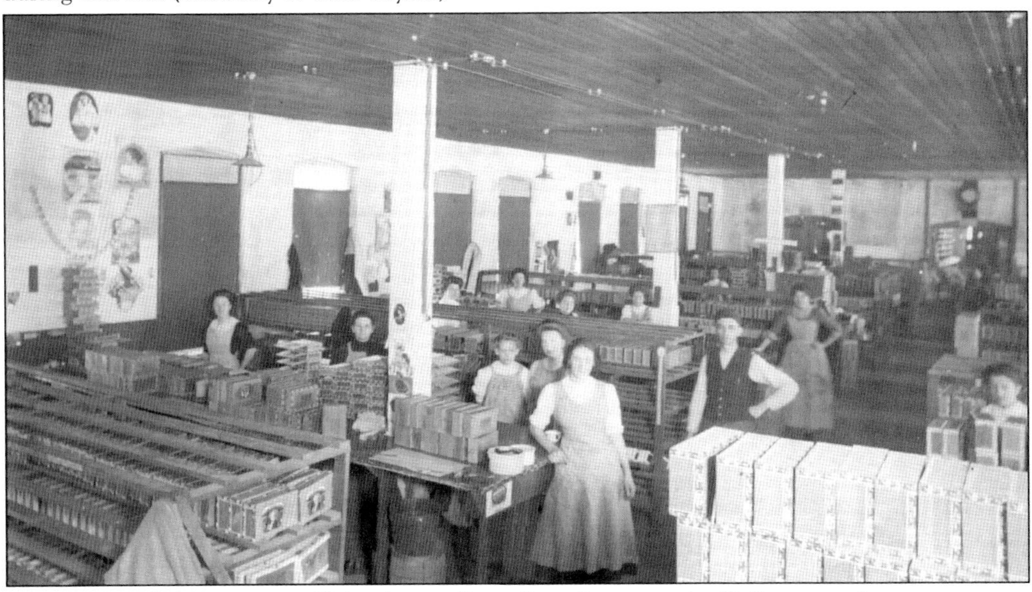

This image of the interior of Merchants Cigar Box Company in Dallastown shows numerous women and girls posing at their work stations where they made and labeled a variety of different brand cigar boxes around 1905. The male in the photograph appears to be a supervisor. There were about 100 people employed by the company by 1966.

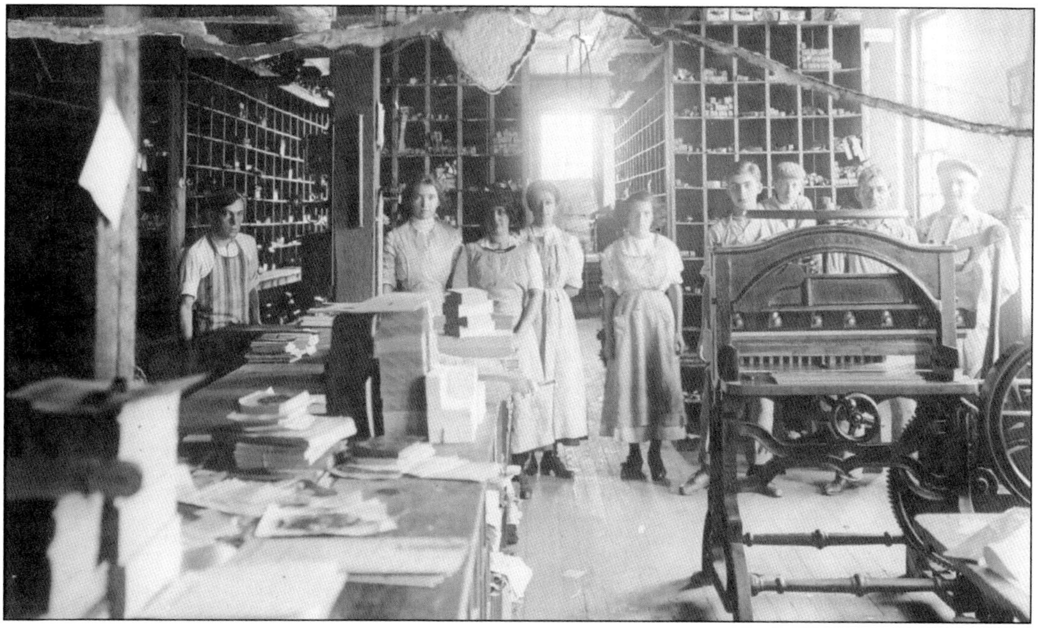

Dallastown boasted a number of cigar box factories, including Merchants Cigar Box Company, Dallastown Steam Box Company, and Pioneer Steam Box Factory. This is an image from the interior of Merchants Cigar Box Company. The left side of the photograph shows stacks of labels that are to be applied to cigar boxes. Towards the right side of the image is an Alsen printing press used to print cigar box labels.

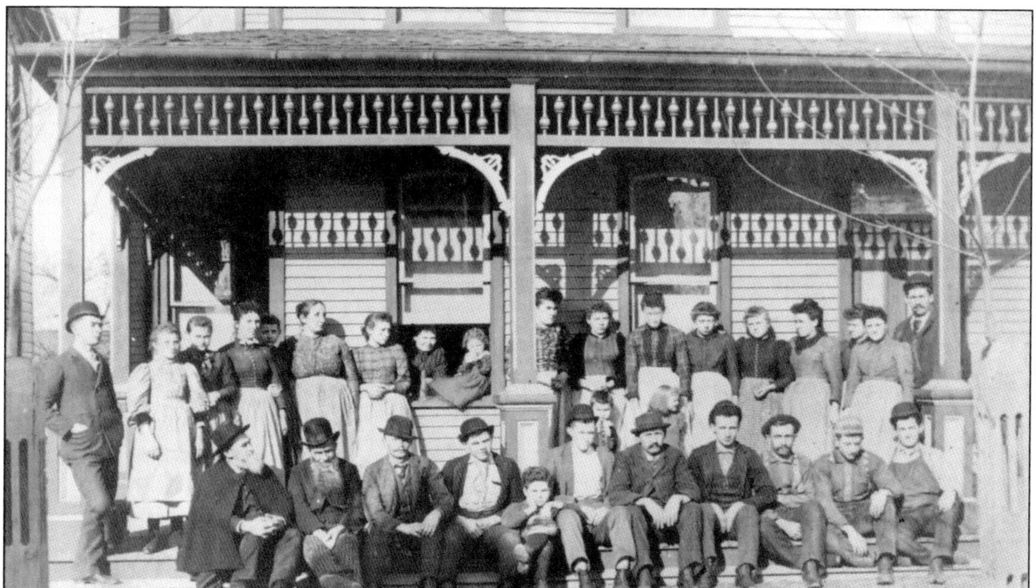

Kauffman Cigar factory employees pose in front of the plant in this c. 1909 image. Solomon D. and Hamilton D. Kauffman were the owners. The factory was located on West Maple Street near the Maryland & Pennsylvania Railroad depot from 1909 through 1915. Later, the company moved to 41 West Main Street, where it remained in business through 1933. Hamilton died in April 1927, and Solomon followed in December 1933. (Courtesy of Roger Fuller.)

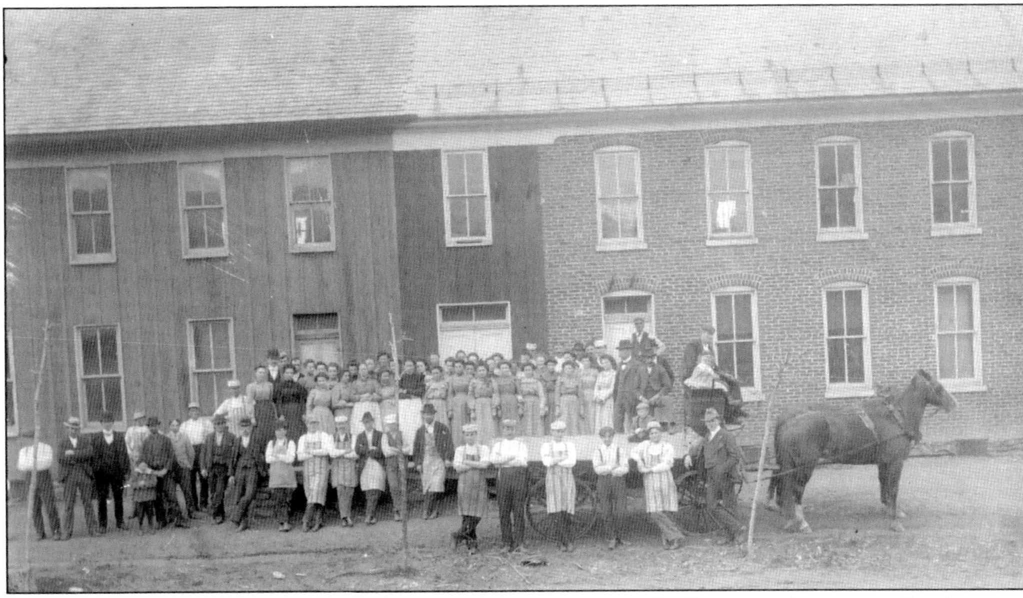

William H. Raab was one of the early cigar manufacturers in Dallastown, beginning his business in 1874. This photograph of his factory and employees on East Maple Street also shows Raab standing in the far right doorway. In 1904, six Dallastown cigar manufacturers exhibited at the world's fair in St. Louis, Missouri, where William H. Raab & Son was awarded a bronze medal for the quality of its cigars. (Courtesy of Tom Taylor.)

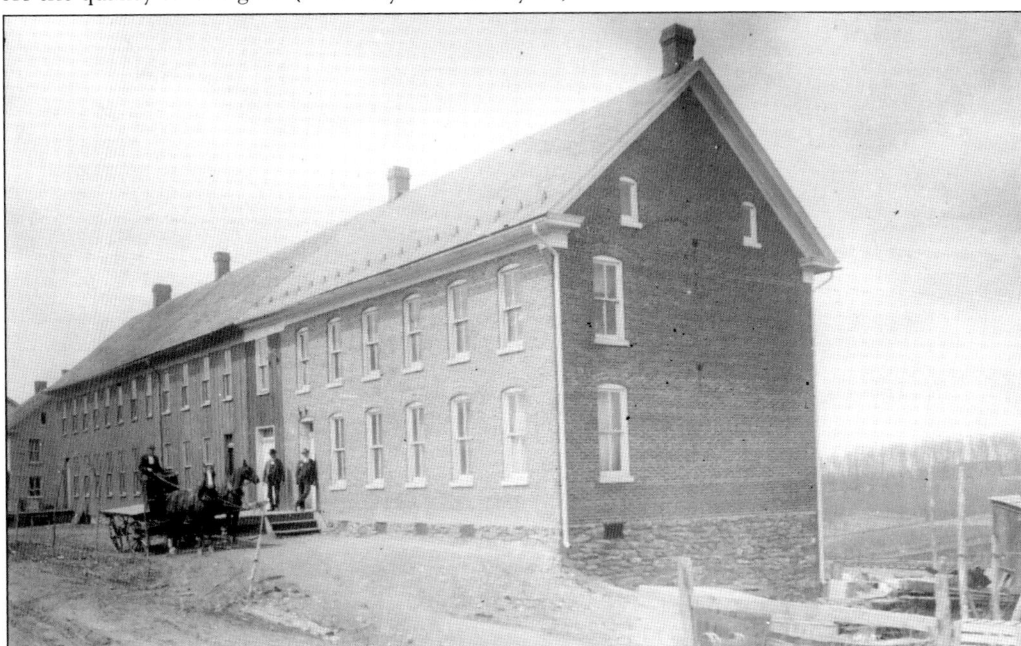

This photograph depicts William H. Rabb's cigar factory in Dallastown around 1900. The horse-drawn wagon in front of the building was likely used to transport goods to and from the factory. The dirt road in front of the factory is East Maple Street. It is interesting to note that the left half of the factory's exterior is made of wood while the right side is made of brick. (Courtesy of Tom Taylor.)

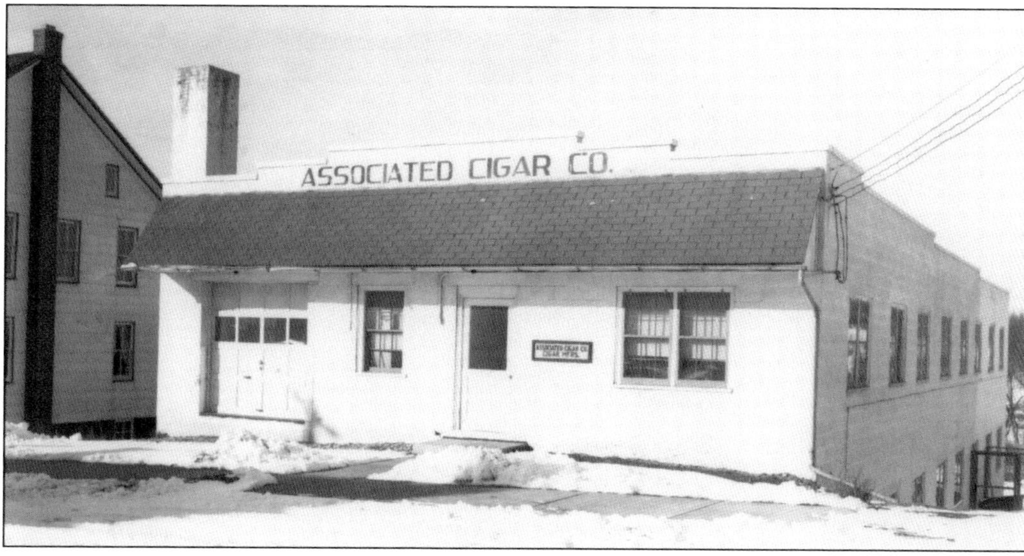

The Associated Cigar Company in Dallastown was built by Joe Klinefelter in the 1940s. This photograph was taken at the cigar business at 33 West Maple Street in 1948 by Richard E. Gemmill. The building was later bought by Philip Rojahn around 1957. Rojahn transformed the cigar factory building into a kitchen cabinet manufacturing business. Today, Rojahn Custom Cabinetry is still in business at this location.

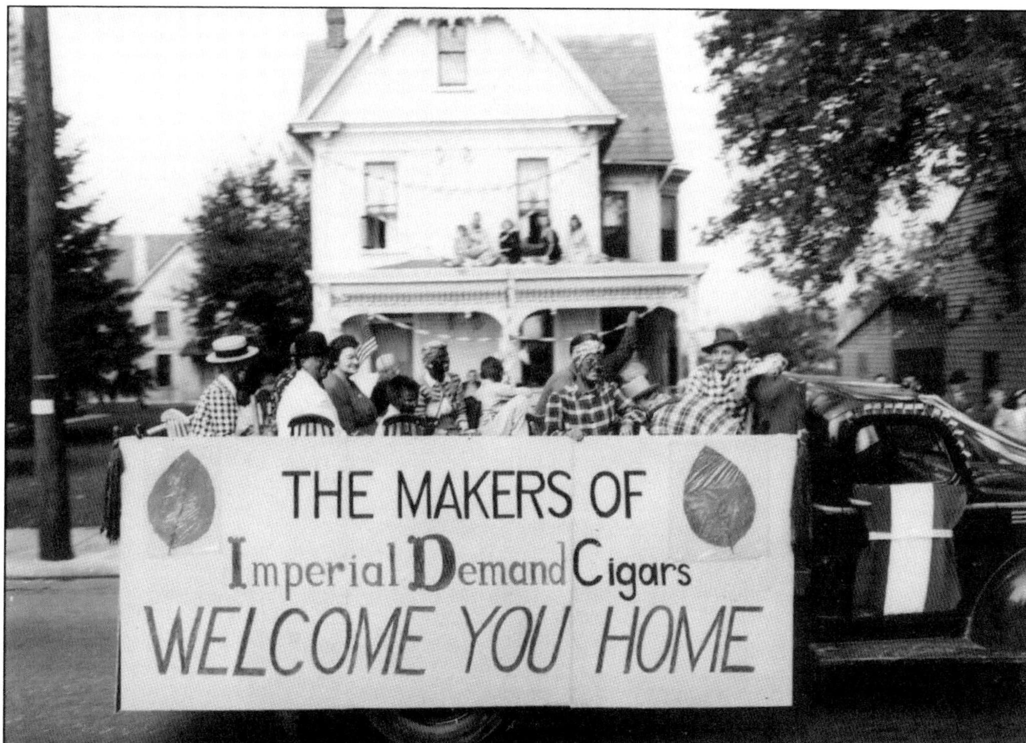

The Imperial Demand Cigar Company float is depicted in this photograph from the 1946 World War II homecoming parade. Taken by Richard E. Gemmill, this image shows West Main Street in Dallastown. Note the people sitting on the roof of the house across the street from the float.

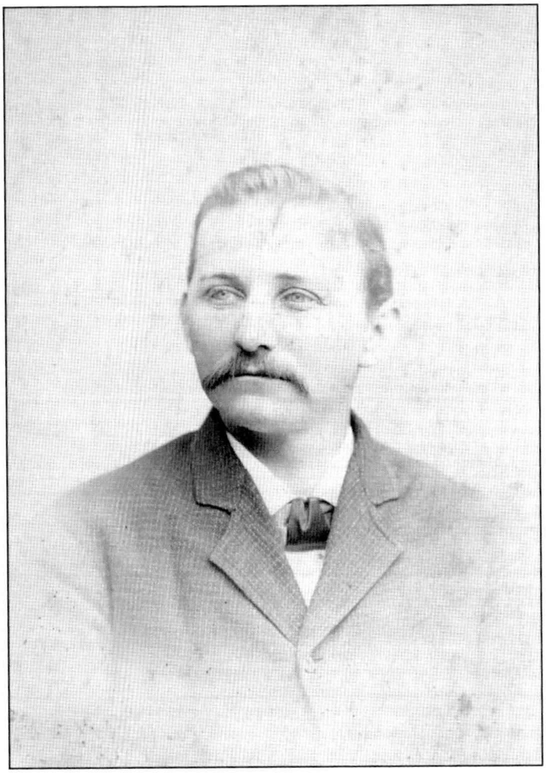

Adam Kohler was born in York Township in 1842. He married Alice Geesey in 1870. In the 1880 federal census, he is described as a dealer in buggies. Later, he operated a general store in Dallastown. By 1888, however, he was solely engaged in the cigar manufacturing business. Kohler was the proprietor of the Empire Cigar Factory. His factory employed 20 men and 8 women by 1895. (Courtesy of Schmidt Library, York College of Pennsylvania.)

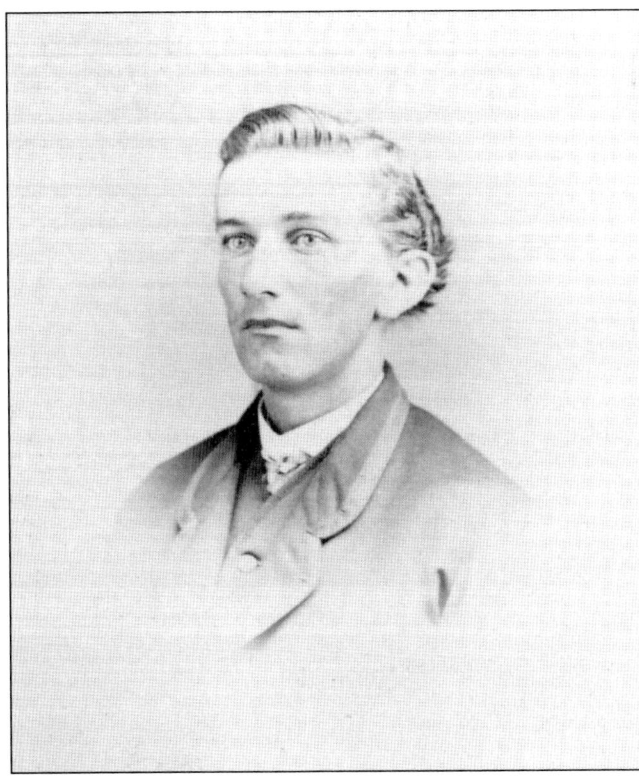

Charles Kohler was Adam Kohler's brother. Charles Kohler and Company was one of the largest cigar box manufacturers in Dallastown in the late 19th and early 20th centuries. In 1872, Kohler married Emaline Geesey. From 1873 to 1880, he sold carriages. In 1880, Kohler began to manufacture cigar boxes. By 1907, Kohler employed about 30 people and his factory was producing 3,000 boxes per day. (Courtesy of Schmidt Library, York College of Pennsylvania.)

Five

Transportation

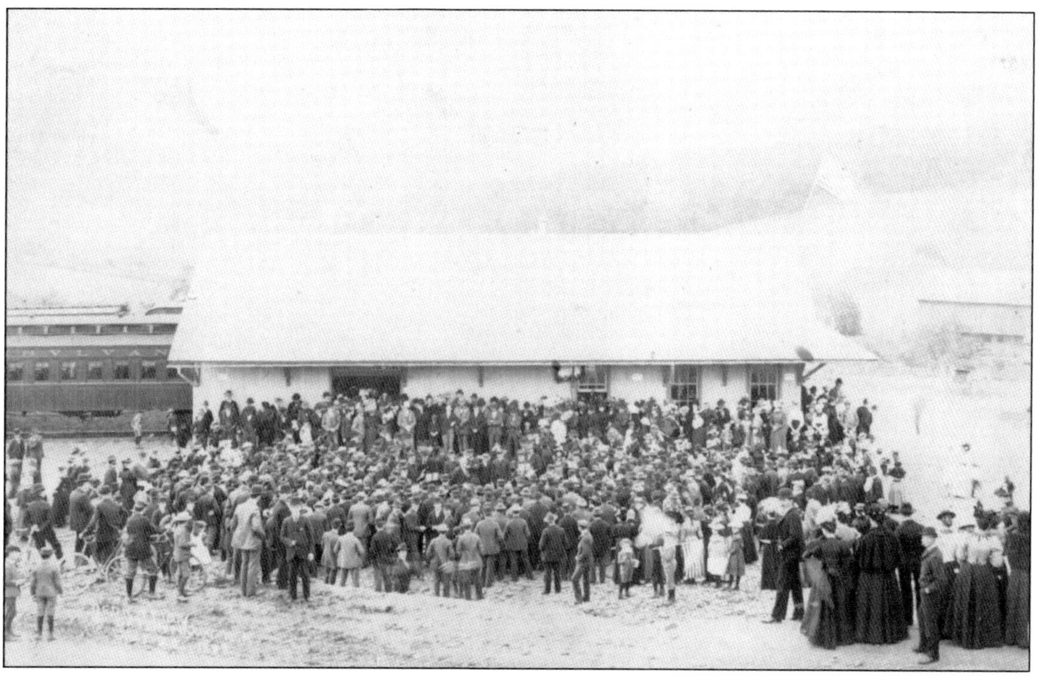

The dedication of the railroad station in Dallastown was a highly anticipated event. A large crowd is shown attending the dedication ceremonies at the station building on May 20, 1899. Members of a local band are in the center of the crowd holding their instruments. Behind the building and to the left is a Pennsylvania Railroad coach. The train station was located near the corner of East Maple and North Walnut Streets.

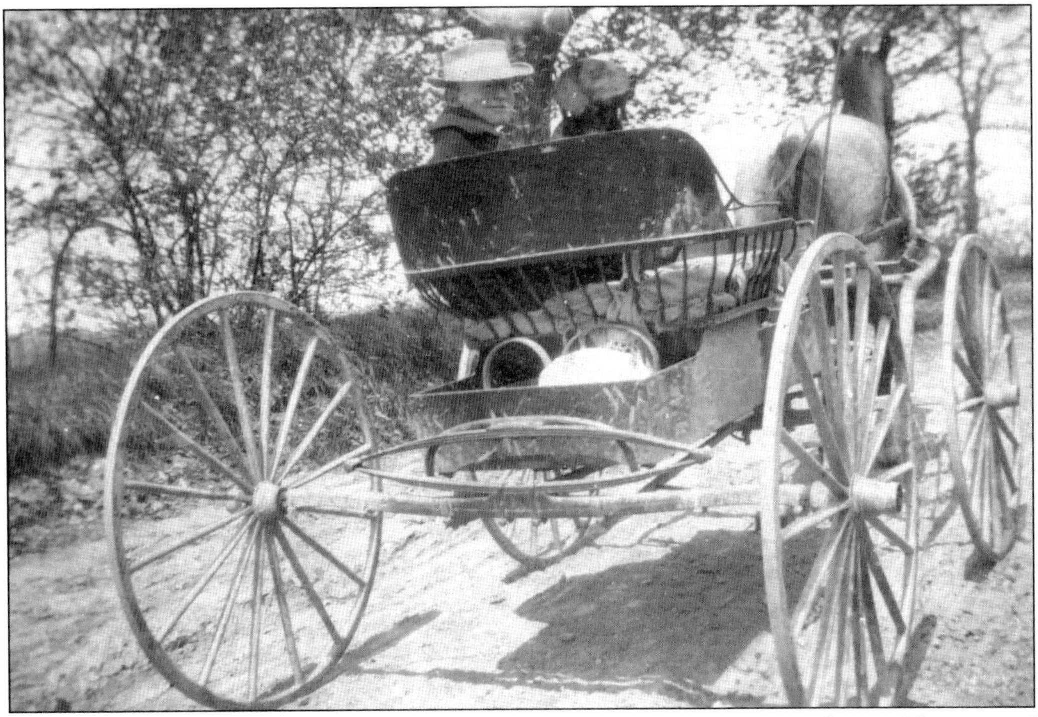

This one-horse buggy is being driven along a dirt road in Dallastown around 1900. This type of vehicle was the primary mode for short-distance transportation in the United States throughout most of the 1800s and into the beginning of the 1900s. A black dog rides on the passenger side of the seat, next to the driver. Two baskets are packed behind the seat of this open carriage.

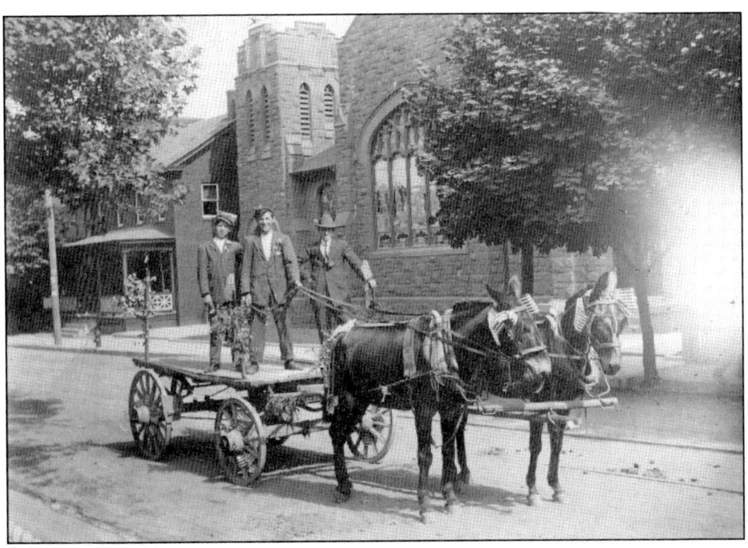

Taken on East Main Street in front of Bethlehem United Brethren Church in Dallastown, this postcard shows Frank Taylor driving his team of donkeys and a cart. This image was made between 1904 and 1918. Donkeys and horses were used for transportation and working fields throughout the Dallastown area during this era. (Courtesy of Lance Wolf.)

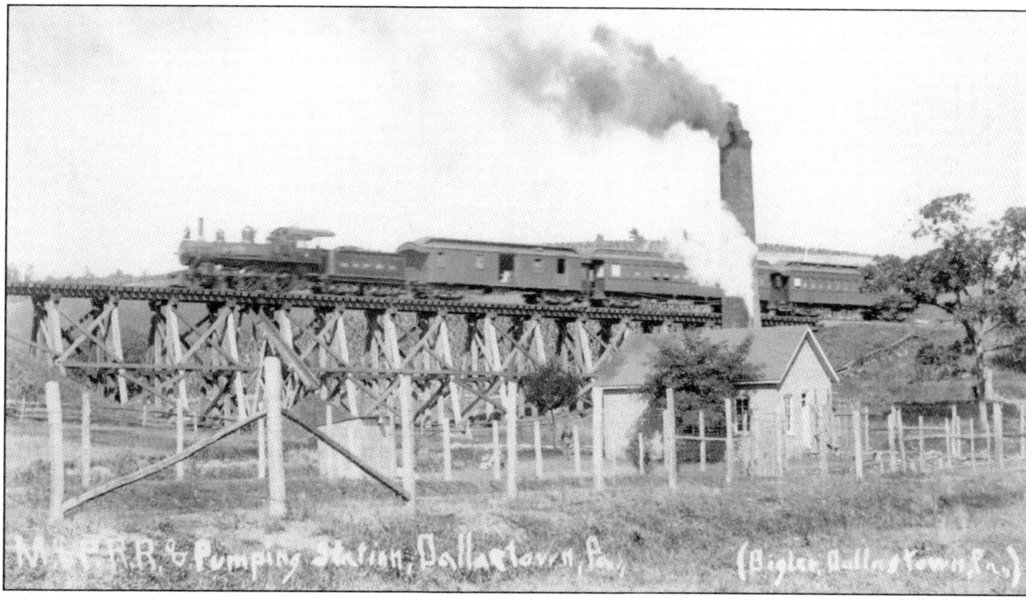

This postcard shows a Maryland & Pennsylvania Railroad passenger train crossing Kendig's trestle on the main line near Dallastown's water pumping station. The pumping station is in the foreground of the image, with steam and smoke billowing from its chimneys. This water pumping station was located between Springwood Road and East Locust Street. The image was taken by William M. Bigler between 1904 and 1918. (Courtesy of Tom Taylor.)

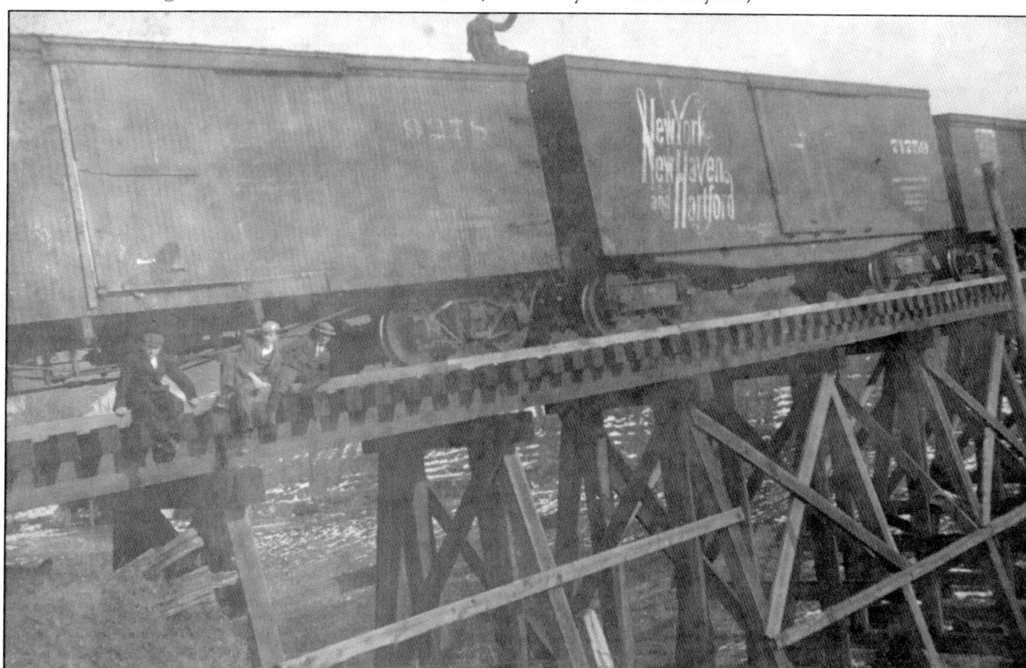

This image shows Kendig's trestle along the Maryland & Pennsylvania Railroad main line near Dallastown. The train has stopped, and three people pose on the bridge itself, next to the wheels of the train. Another man poses on top of one of the coaches. The Dallastown Branch was a 1.2-mile-long standard-gauge line, leaving the main line west of Red Lion at Dallastown Junction.

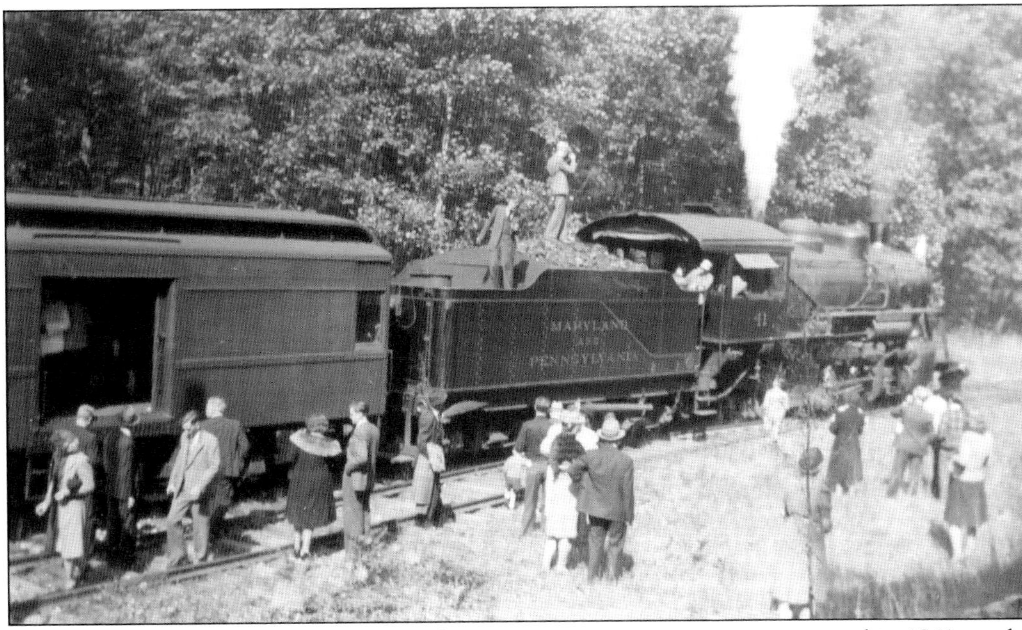

This Maryland & Pennsylvania Railroad Extra No. 41 train image was captured in 1941 on the Dallastown Branch. This steam locomotive, tinder, and coach are backing towards Dallastown Station, while train enthusiasts observe. Trains had to back into Dallastown due to the single track laid from Dallastown Junction. Passenger service ended in 1954. The station closed in 1957 and burned in 1959. The railroad abandoned the Dallastown tracks in 1983.

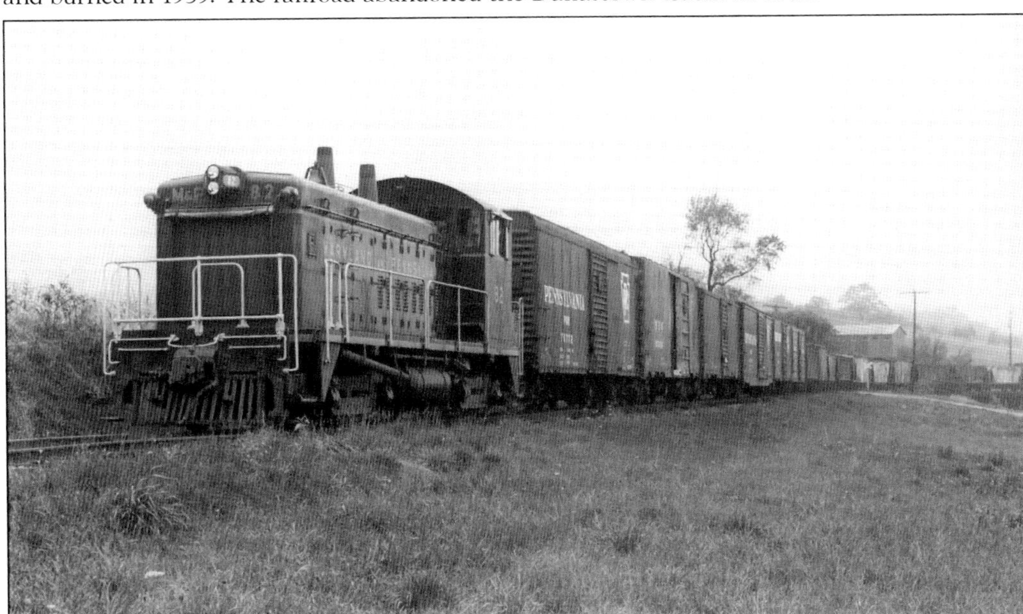

Freight service on the Dallastown Branch continued into the late 1970s. This photograph of the Maryland & Pennsylvania Railroad diesel-electric No. 82 heading south on the main line was taken near Dallastown Junction, at the crossing with East Locust Street, in the late 1960s by Jim Shaw. The back end of this train extends onto Kendig's trestle heading towards Yoe, on the far right edge of the picture. (Courtesy of Kurt Bell.)

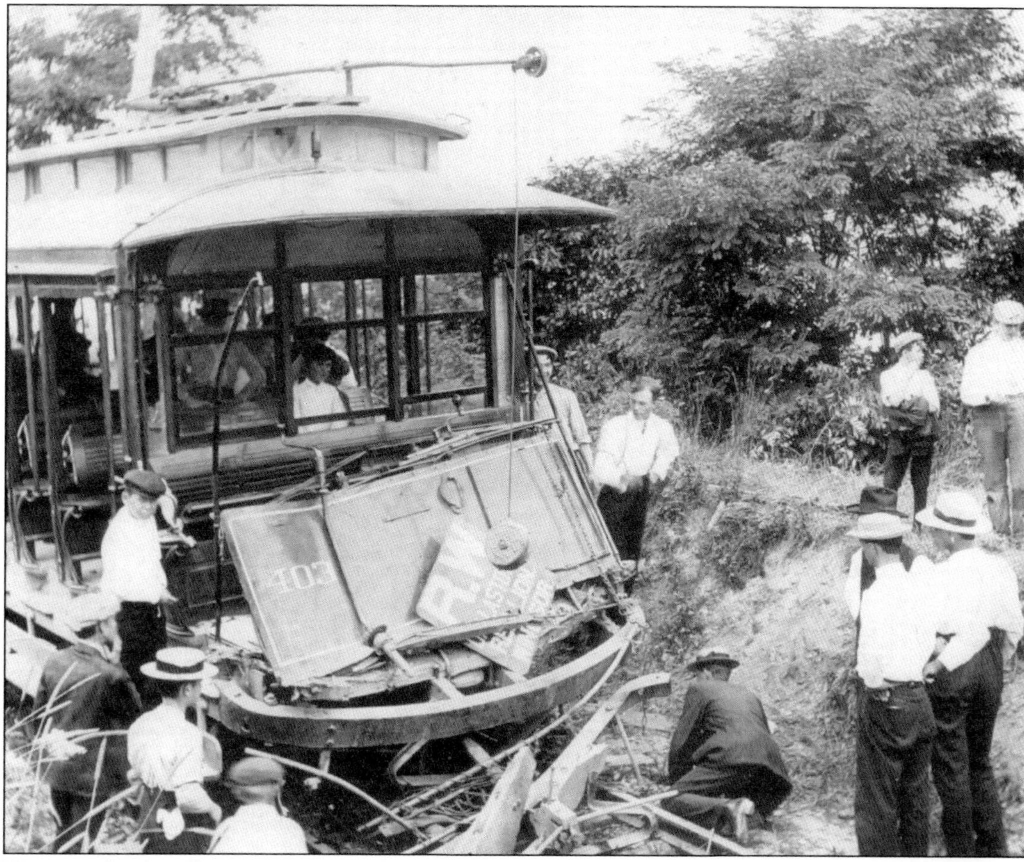

The wreck of trolley car No. 403 of the electric railway on the Dallastown line occurred on October 11, 1902, when the overcrowded trolley car bound for the York Agricultural Fair passed cars standing at the switch at the western edge of Dallastown. As the traveler-laden car passed the cars standing at the switch, numerous passengers hanging on the side of the York-bound car were almost crushed to death.

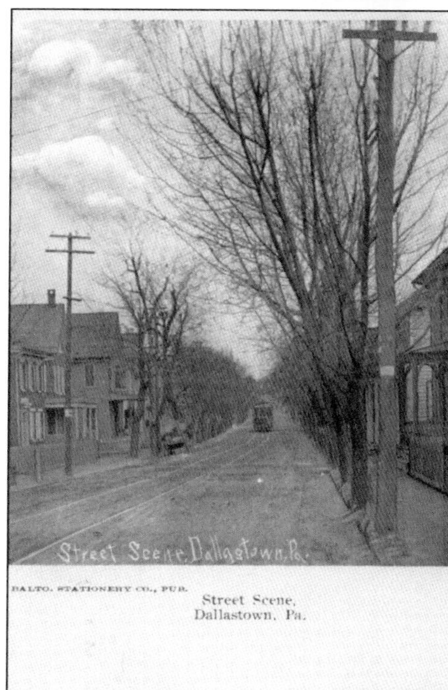

This c. 1901 postcard depicts the electric trolley tracks and car on West Main Street. The area in the foreground was once known as Drunkard's Flat. The York and Dallastown Electric Railway Company formed in 1889. In 1901, the extension of tracks from Dallastown to Red Lion, Windsor, and Bittersville was completed. The company merged with other trolley companies to form the York Railways Company in 1907.

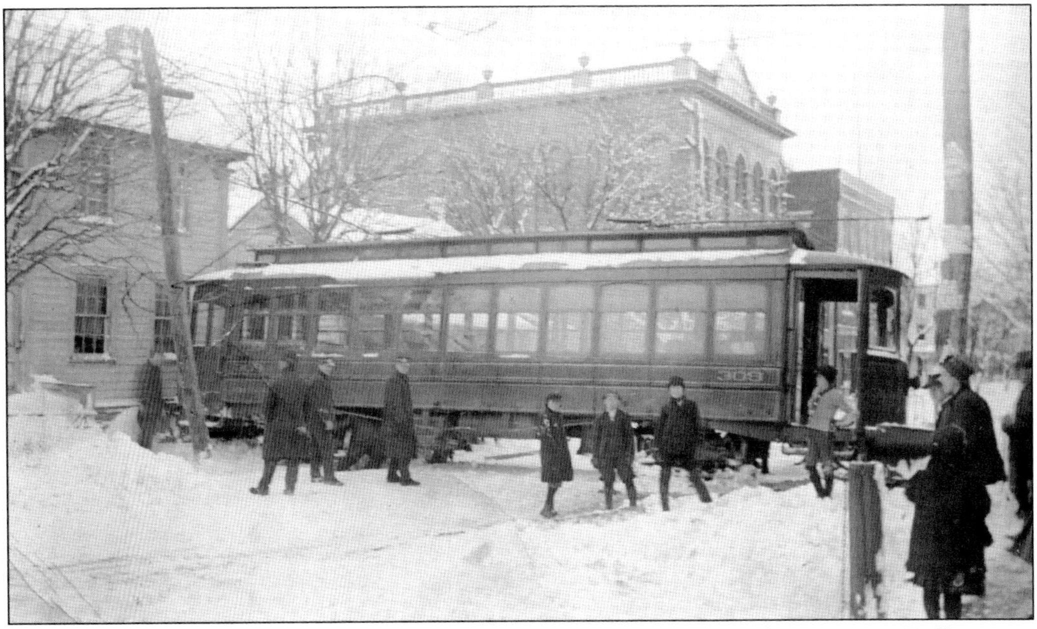

Trolley car No. 309 is shown off the tracks on East Main Street near the square in Dallastown, shortly after a snowstorm around 1911. Townspeople regularly complained that the trolleys often exceeded the seven-miles-per-hour speed limit through the borough. The largest structure, at the center top of the photograph, is the Hose Building, located at the southwest corner of Main and Walnut Streets.

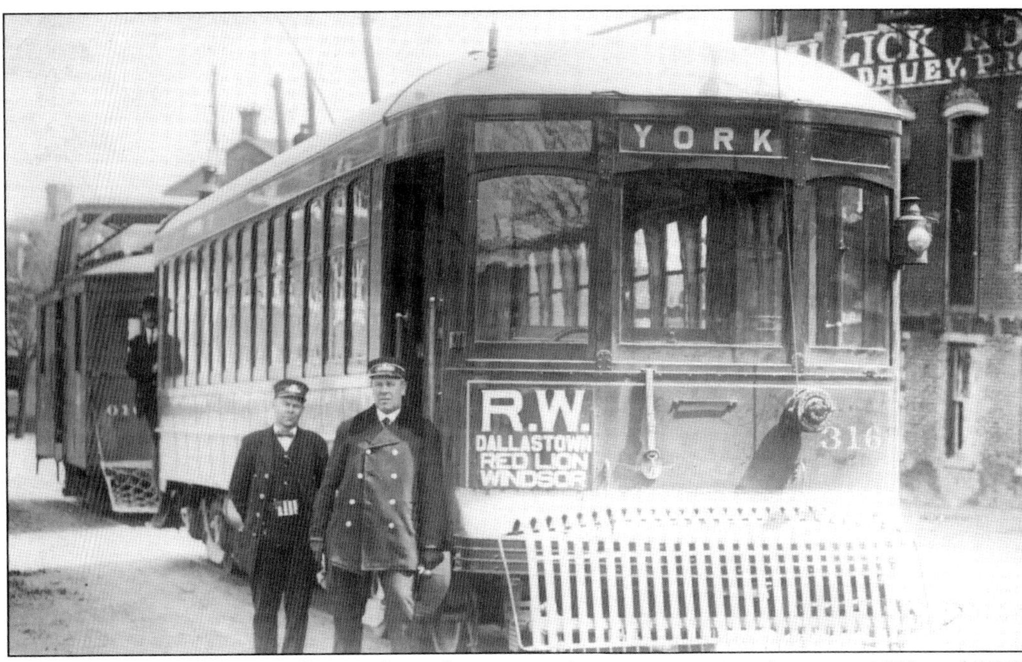

York trolley car No. 316 is depicted on this postcard image sometime between 1913 and 1918. This car made multiple runs daily to Dallastown, Red Lion, and Windsor from 1913 to 1939. At its zenith, the York Railways Company ran 68 streetcars over 85 route miles of standard-gauge track throughout York County. (Courtesy of Tom Taylor.)

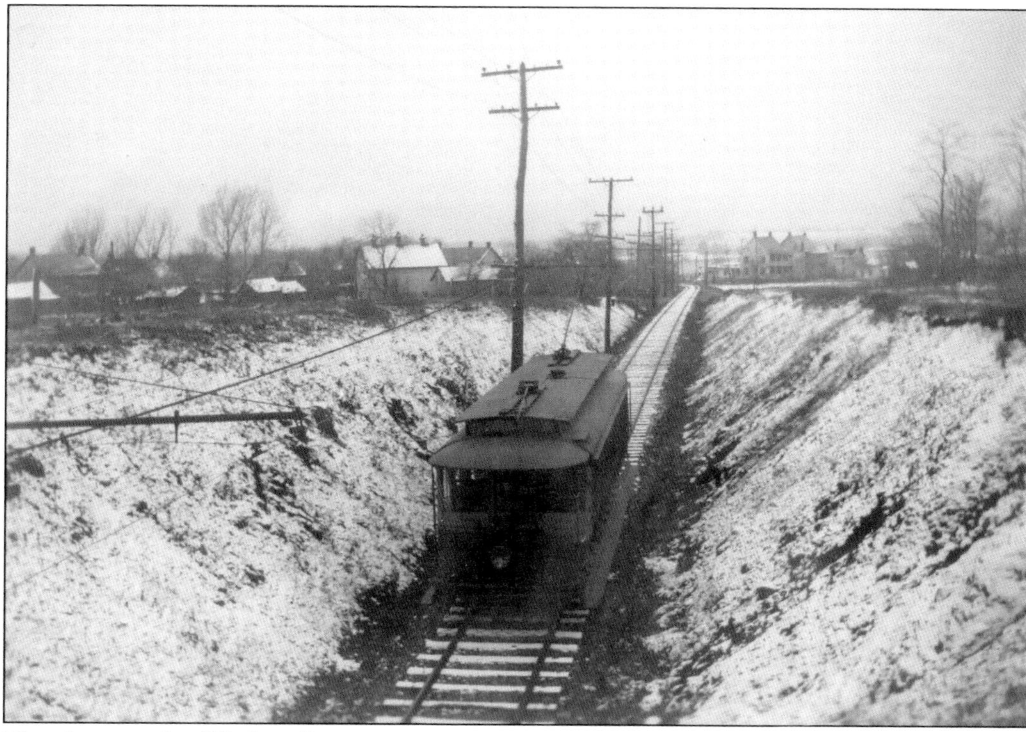

The photograph of York trolley car No. 402 was taken in February 1935 by Richard H. Steinmetz at a cut just west of Dallastown on a National Railway Historical Society excursion. This car was made by Brill and was retired in 1939. Cuts like this one were made when tracks were being laid from York to Dallastown in 1901. (Courtesy of Cathy Bankoske.)

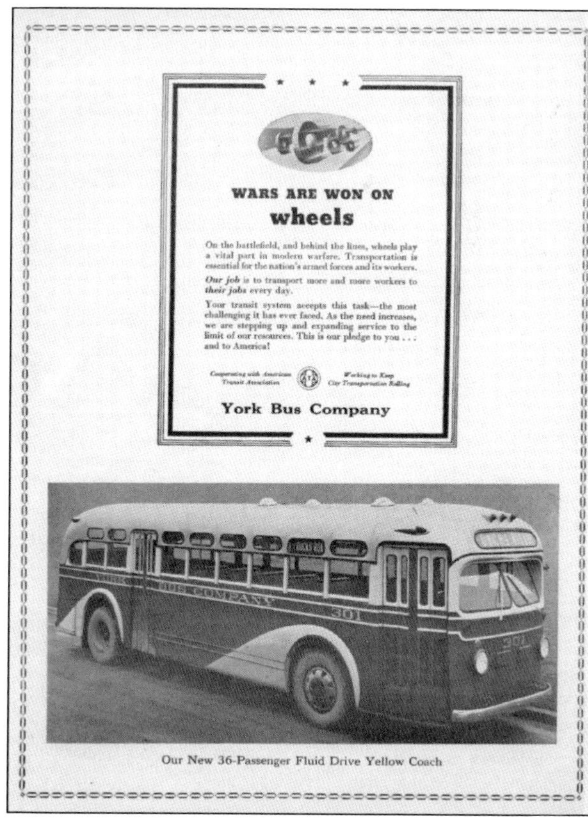

After the trolley cars stopped running to Dallastown in 1939, bus service took over the former route. This advertisement for the York Bus Company shows the second-generation style of buses that operated along the route to Dallastown during the war years 1941–1945. Public transportation through bus service had increased importance during World War II due to gasoline rationing. (Courtesy of Barry Arnold.)

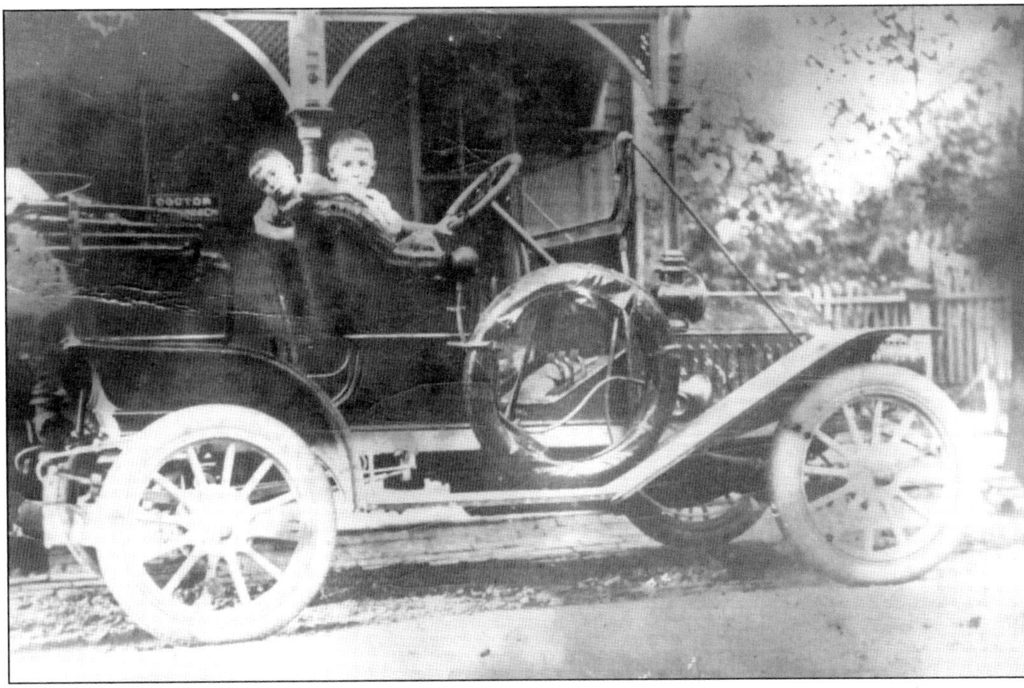

The two boys in this automobile are Dr. William Henry Minnich's sons John (at the steering wheel) and William Jr. The car is parked in front of Dr. Minnich's office on East Main Street around 1913. Minnich used this car to go on house calls around the Dallastown area. In April 1915, Dallastown's burgess F.A. Zeigler proclaimed a speed limit of 15 miles per hour for automobiles and motorcycles. (Courtesy of Roger Fuller.)

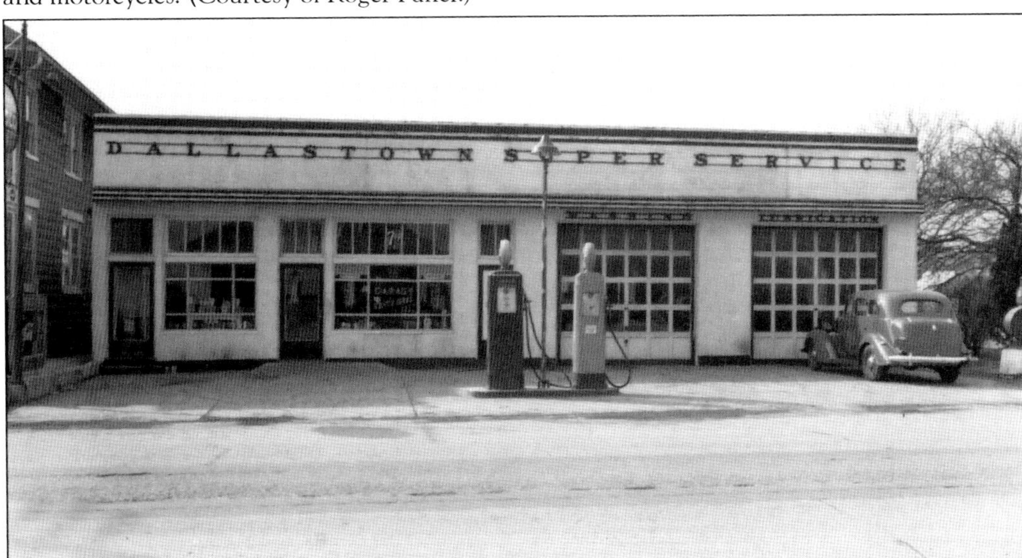

Dallastown had many service stations in the 20th century. One of them was the Dallastown Super Service, which was located at 466 East Main Street, according to a 1935 city directory. James V. Waltemyer was the owner of this service station and its accompanying lunch counter in the 1930s and 1940s. This photograph was taken in 1948 by Richard E. Gemmill. The building, for many decades now, has housed Red's Auto Body.

Six

Military Service and Fire Rescue

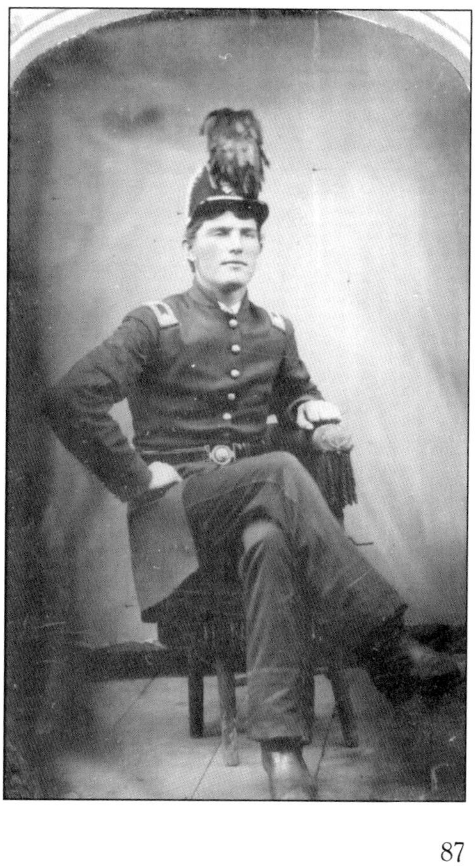

Adam Kohler was a Civil War veteran from Dallastown who served honorably from April 12, 1865, to June 25, 1865, in Company G of the 103 Pennsylvania Volunteer Infantry Regiment. He was also a skilled musician. During his service, Kohler was one of eight United States Army trumpeters who performed at Lincoln's funeral in Springfield, Illinois, in 1865. This tintype image of Kohler in uniform was made sometime between 1860 and 1865. (Courtesy of Schmidt Library, York College of Pennsylvania.)

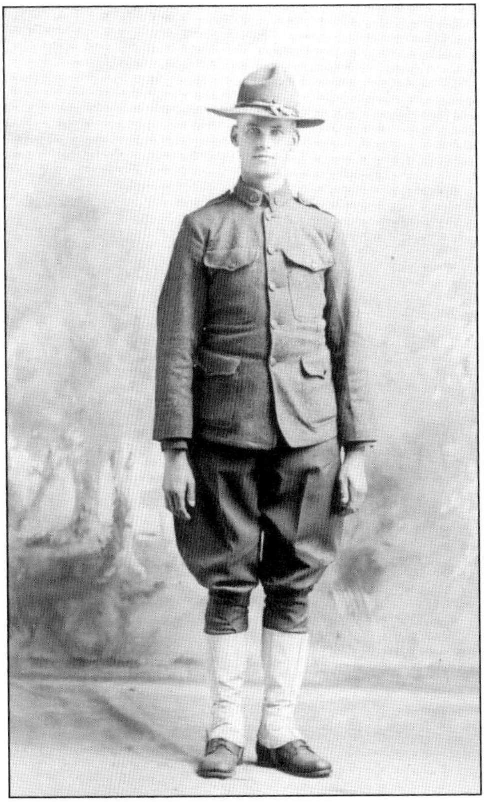

This c. 1918 photograph is of World War I doughboy Samuel G. Ferree from Dallastown. Ferree was born on January 29, 1888. He served in the United States Army from February 24, 1918, to February 19, 1919. Ferree lived on East Broad Street near Lombard Street. After the war, he returned to Dallastown and worked as a mason. He died on February 17, 1956.

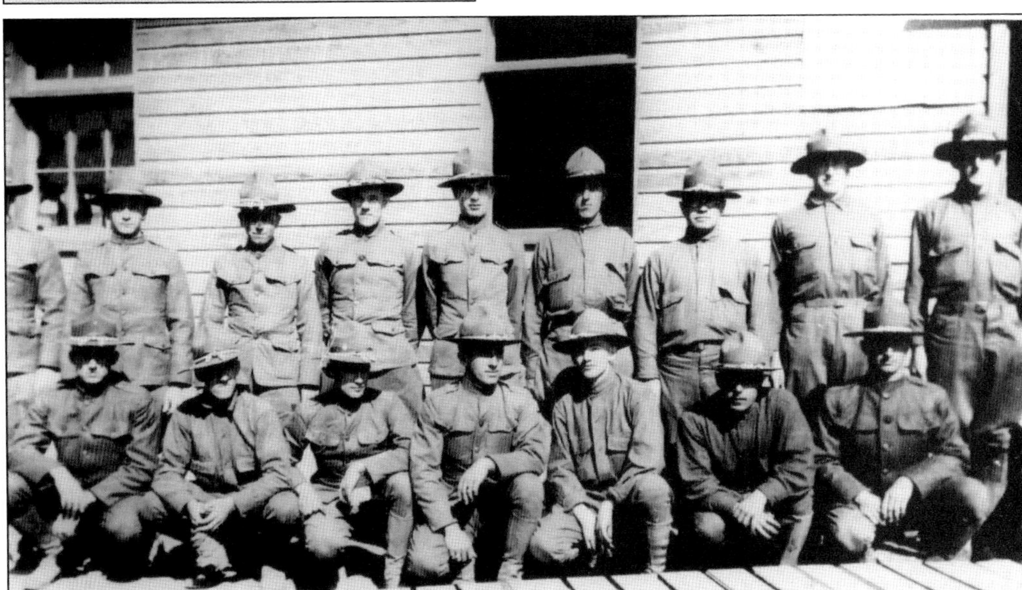

US soldiers from World War I pose in front of barracks in this photograph around 1918. A number of Dallastownians are in this image. From left to right are (first row) Bill Sechrist, Bill Geesey, unidentified, John Heisler, George Dellinger, Tibertus Grim, and unidentified; (second row) Clem Keller, Gehra Shaffer, Harry Bailey, Wilbur Daugherty, Moise Hartman, Albert Benedict, Sam Hess, and unidentified. (Courtesy of Roger Fuller.)

The photograph shows the front entrance of St. Joseph Catholic Church in Dallastown around 1940. A priest stands next to Thomas Aloysius Eck (right). Eck enlisted in the Army on December 7, 1941. He saw combat action during the invasion of Italy as a tank commander, where he earned both Silver and Bronze Stars. He was the son of Thomas J. and Bernardine E. Eck, longtime parishioners of St. Joseph Catholic Church. (Courtesy of Jeanne M. Saylor.)

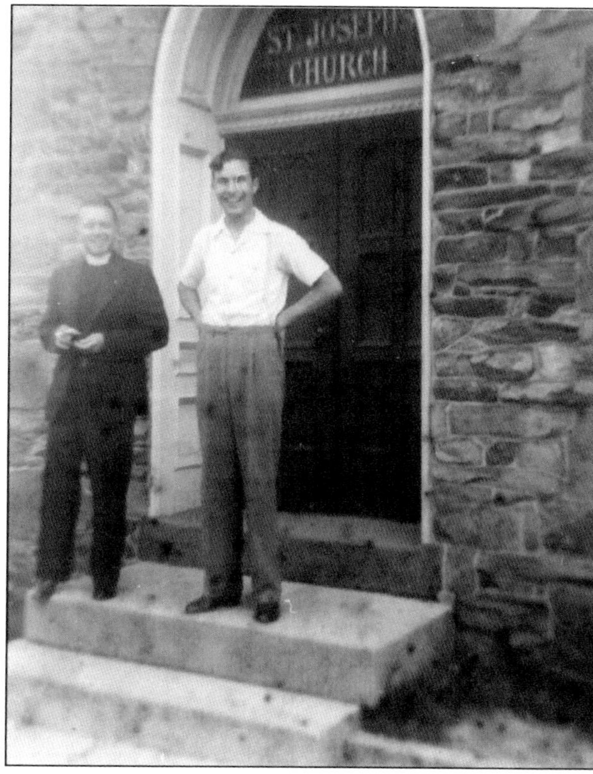

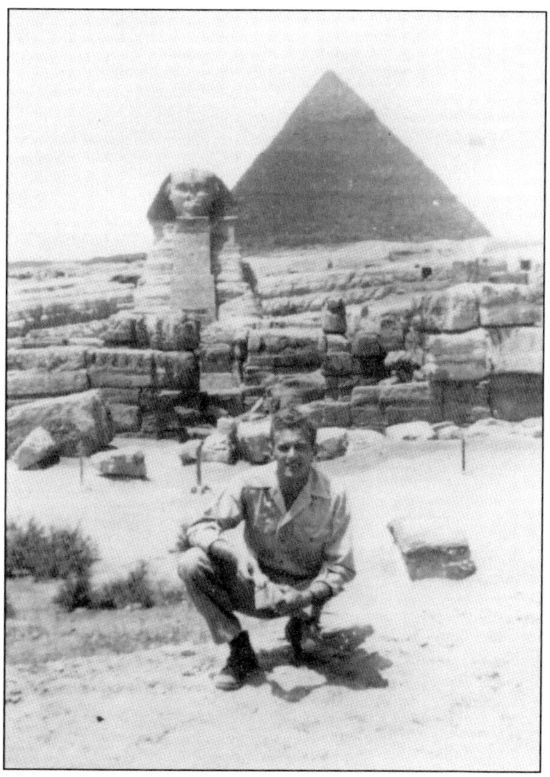

This image shows Dallastown native Palmer Sechrist (1922–1946) posing in Egypt in front of the Sphinx and the Great Pyramid of Giza. Sechrist served in the United States armed forces during World War II. This image was taken around 1944. Tragically, Sechrist and his cousin Kenneth Sechrist both drowned in a canoe accident in the Susquehanna River in 1946.

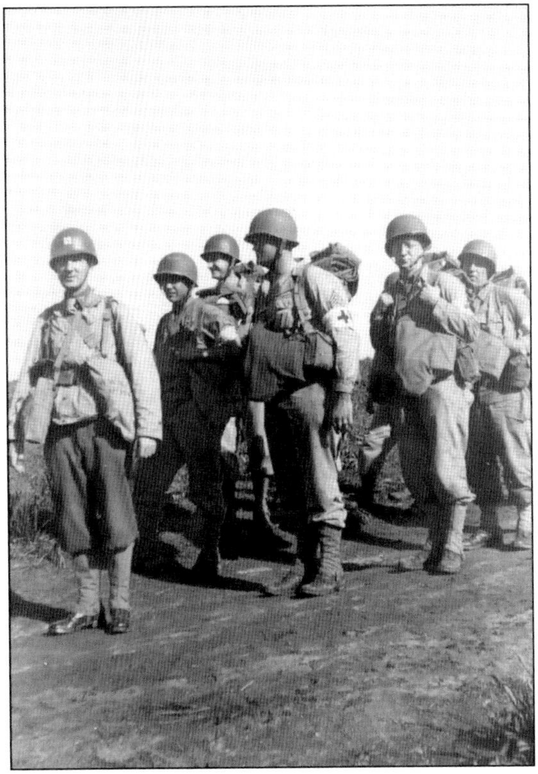

This photograph is of William H. Minnich of Dallastown and a group of United States Army medical personnel during World War II. From left to right are William H. Minnich, ? Auguston, ? Shaggenhein, Ed Wraney, ? Blackeby, and Gregory Dowgun. Most of the men in the image have a Red Cross armband on their left arms. (Courtesy of Roger Fuller.)

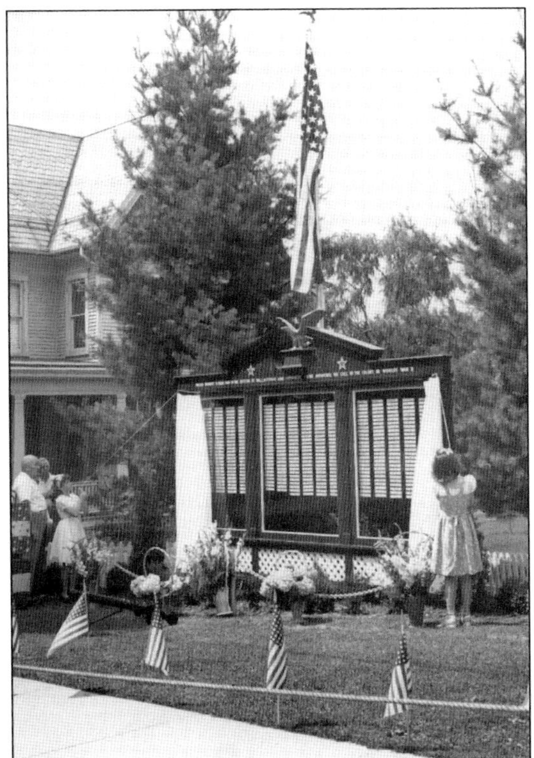

Erected in Dallastown at Zarfoss Hardware on West Main Street, this war memorial and honor roll is inscribed "Proud Tribute Is Here Paid To The Citizens of Dallastown And Community Who Answered The Call To The Colors In World War II." A total of 354 sons and daughters of the borough served in United States armed forces during World War II. This image was taken when the honor roll was dedicated in 1946.

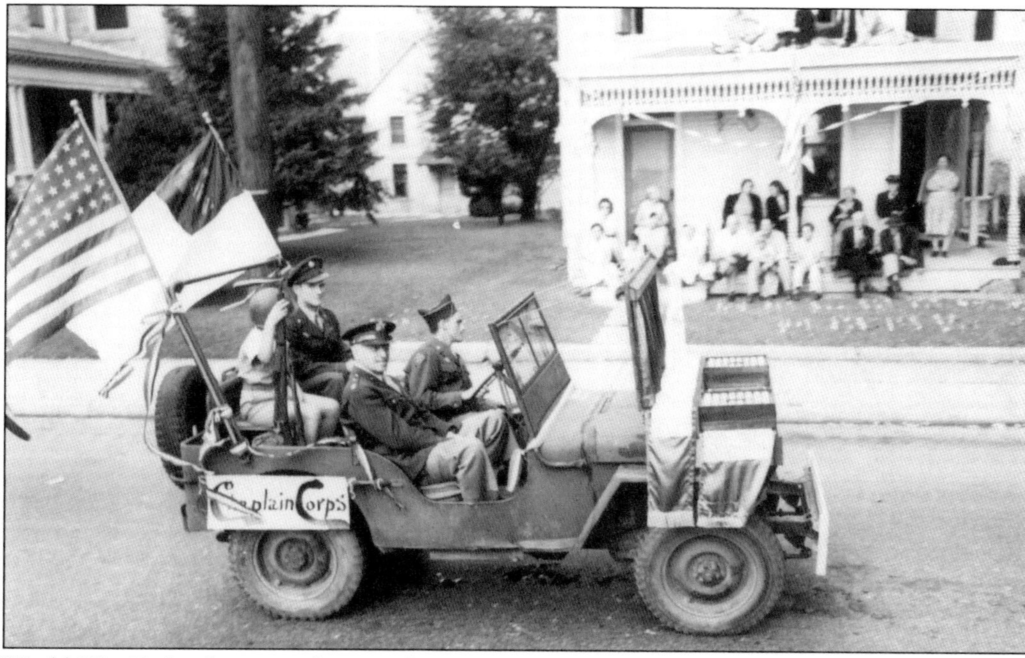

World War II chaplains are shown riding in a jeep in Dallastown's 1946 welcome home parade; it included Dallastown's Reverend Stiles, who was one of the Army chaplains. The house across the street from the jeep has the words "Welcome Home" spelled out on its front yard in rocks. The photograph was taken by Richard E. Gemmill.

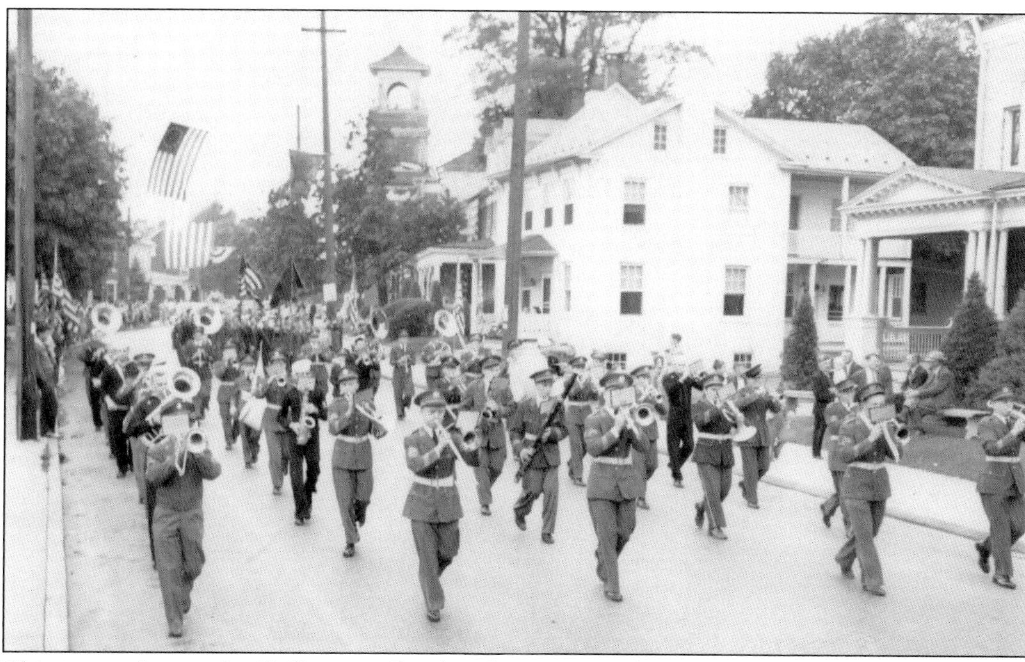

This image depicts the Dallastown Band and musicians who served in various branches of the armed services during the Second World War, playing their respective instruments while parading together through town. The photograph, with a view looking west, was taken by Richard E. Gemmill during the 1946 Dallastown welcome home parade on West Main Street.

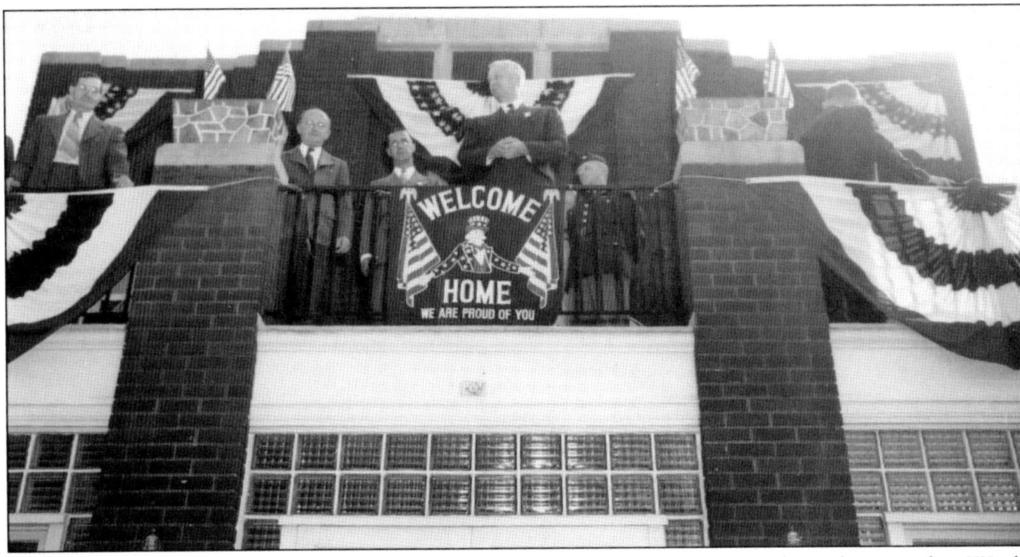

Gov. Edward Martin prepares to watch Dallastown's welcome home parade, in honor of its World War II veterans, from the balcony of Austin Eberly's Funeral Home on West Main Street. To the left of Martin is Dallastown mayor Charles B. Koontz. The other people at the rear of the balcony are unidentified parade judges. Richard E. Gemmill took this photograph in 1946.

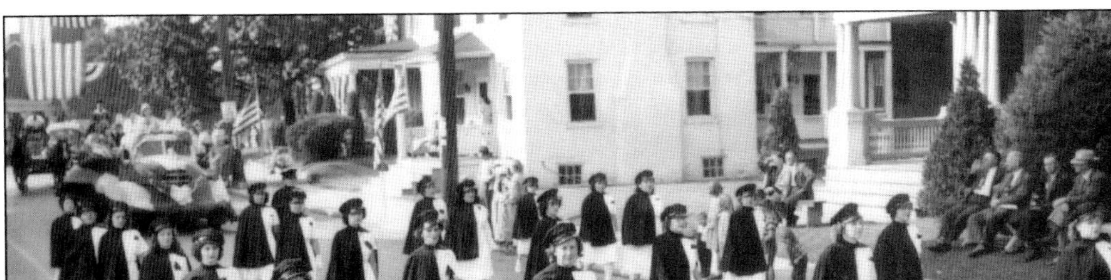

This image depicts Dallastown Fire Company's Ladies Auxiliary marching in the welcome home parade in 1946. Among its various duties, the Ladies Auxiliary helped to raise funds to support the volunteer fire company. The view in this image, taken in 1946 by Richard E. Gemmill, is looking west on West Main Street.

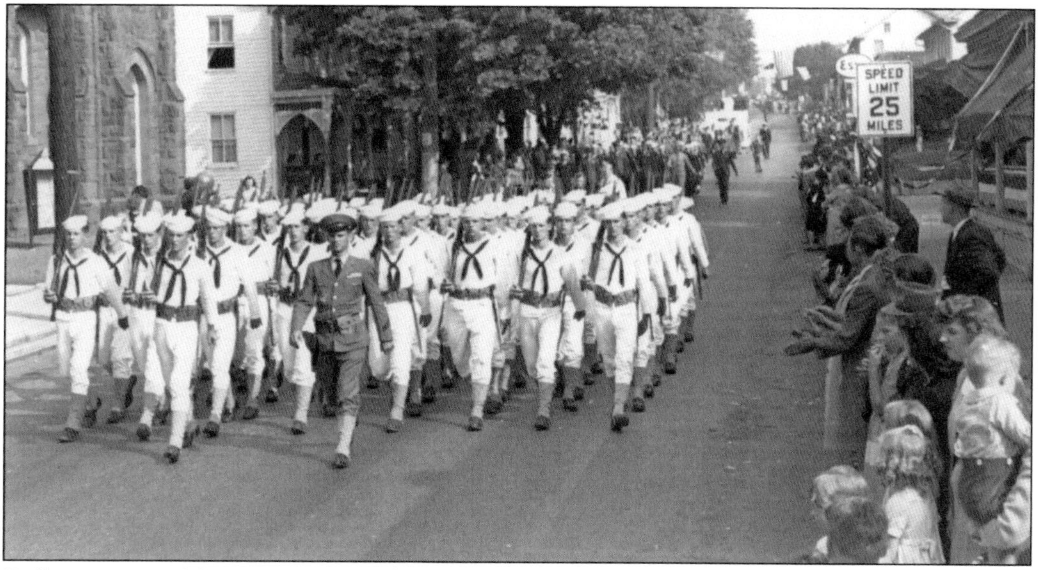

Dallastown-area Navy veterans are shown participating in a homecoming parade in the borough in 1946. The sailors are marching west on East Main Street, next to Bethlehem United Methodist Church. Townspeople line the street cheering for the veterans. The Esso service station sign, at 150 East Main Street, is visible on the south side of the street. Richard E. Gemmill took this photograph in 1946.

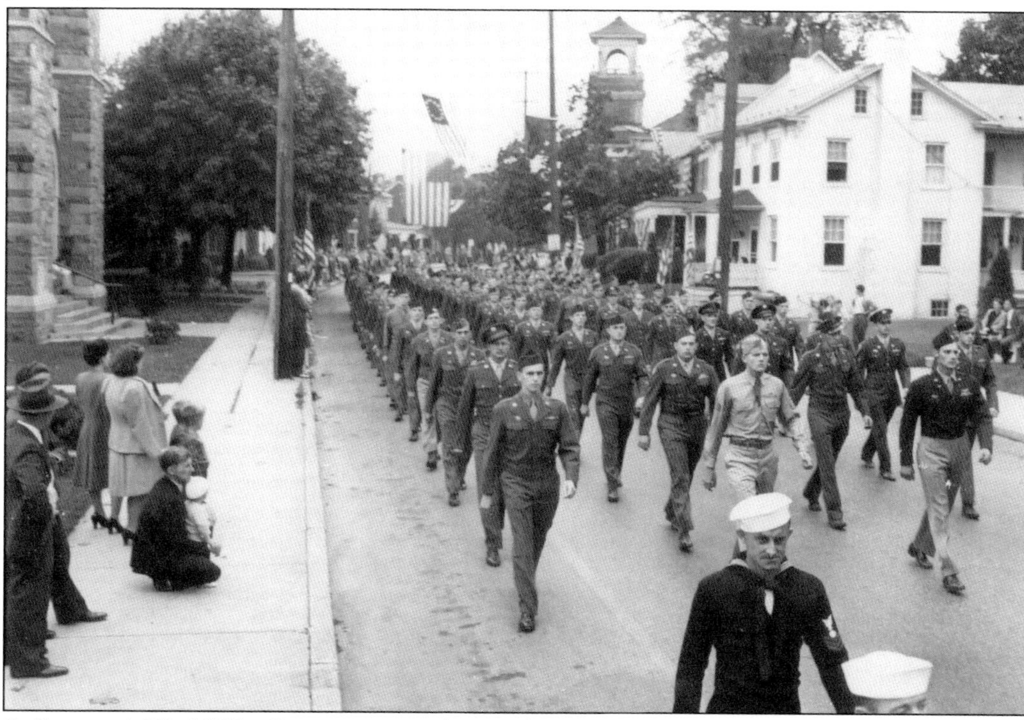

Dallastown's World War II veterans march east along Main Street during the borough's welcome home parade in 1946. Photographer Richard E. Gemmill took this image near Christ Evangelical Lutheran Church at 126 West Main Street. Dallastown's public elementary school's bell tower is visible near the top center of the image.

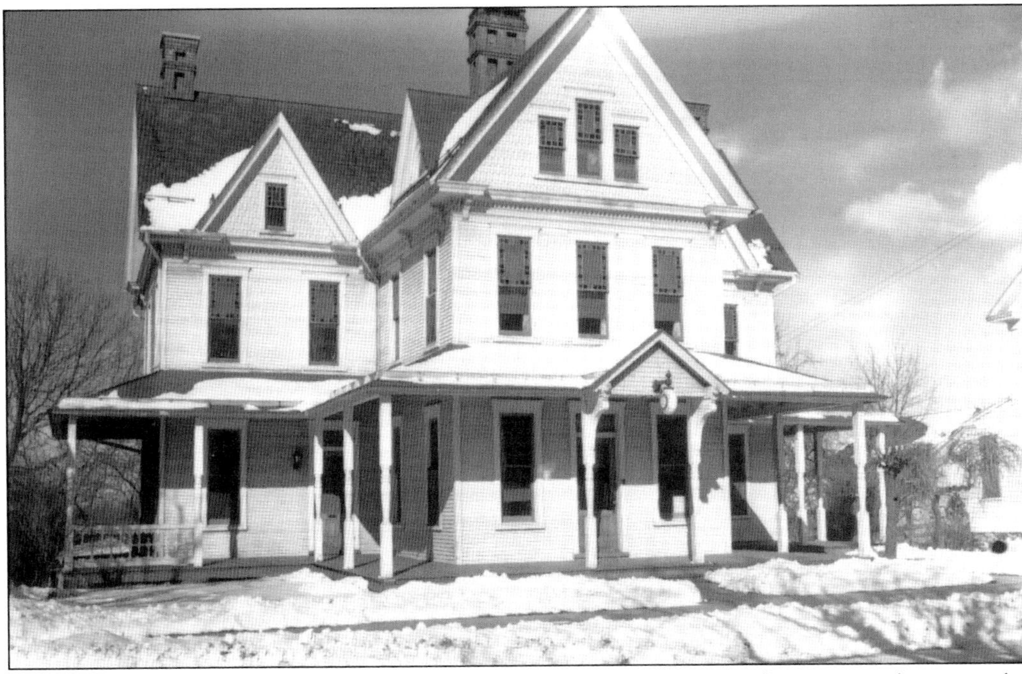

The American Legion building, located at 57 West Main Street in Dallastown, is shown in this Richard E. Gemmill image from 1946. Prior to the American Legion purchasing it, this structure was used by Ambrose Helder as a furniture and undertaking business. At one point, it was also home to Dr. Edward Fisher and his medical practice. The building was remodeled by the Legion in 1934.

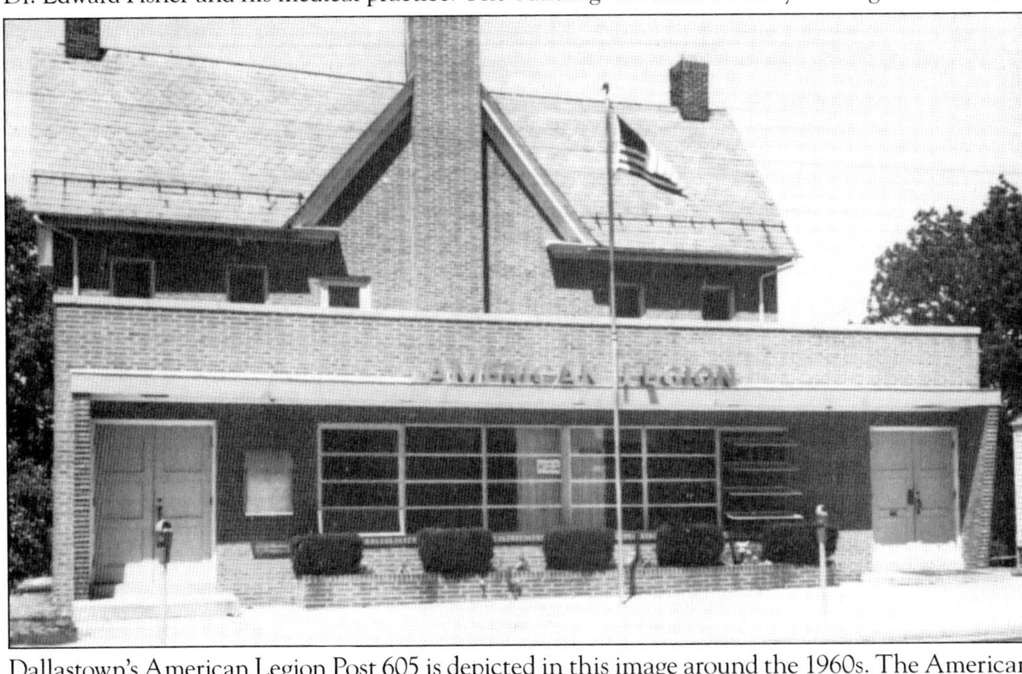

Dallastown's American Legion Post 605 is depicted in this image around the 1960s. The American Legion was founded in 1919, following the First World War. This American Legion building was originally a normal three-story structure. By this time, the Legionnaires had constructed a brick addition onto the front of the building to create more space.

This photograph was taken in December 1951 in Dallastown while Korean War soldier Richard E. Saylor was home on leave. Saylor was drafted into service in January 1951. Stationed at Camp Polk, Louisiana, he was promoted to corporal in 1952 in Headquarters Battery, 560th Field Artillery Battalion, US Army. Honorably discharged in January 1953, Saylor lived with his family at 56 East Frederick Street in Dallastown for over 40 years. (Courtesy of Jeanne M. Saylor.)

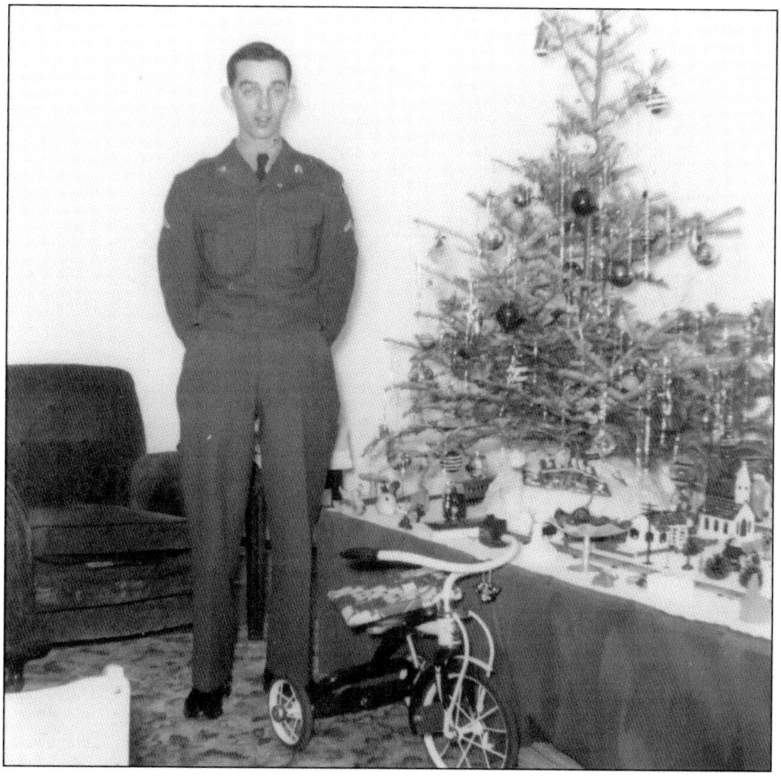

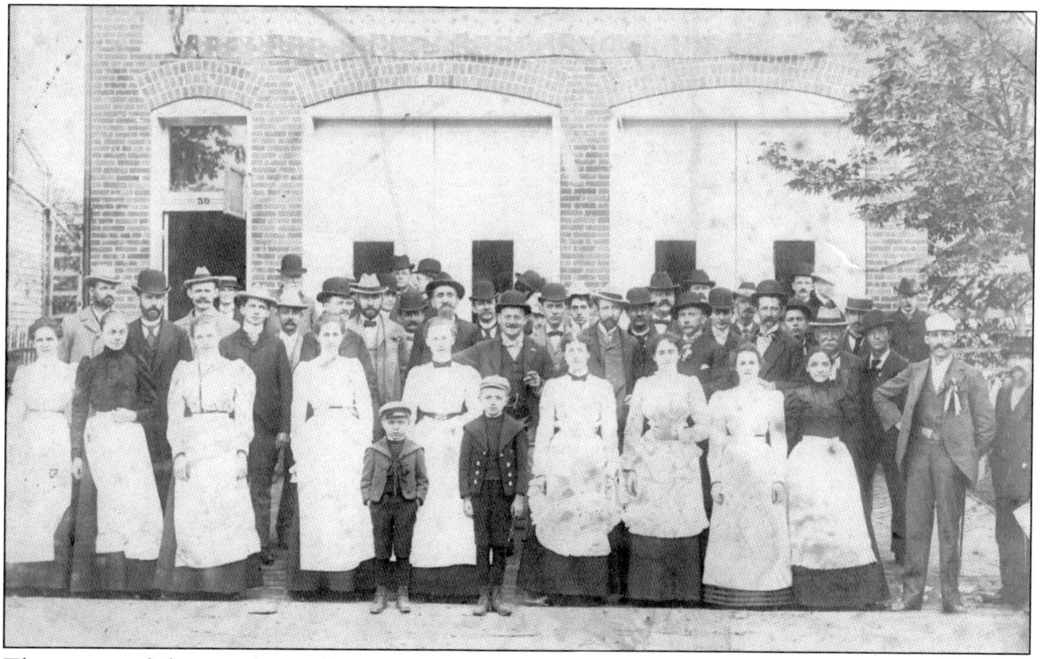

This postcard depicts the Dallastown Firemen's Convention around 1900. The conventioneers are posing in front of Dallastown's first fire engine house. The building was completed in 1899 and was located at 50 East Main Street. It would be replaced in 1913 when a new firehouse was built at 118 East Main Street.

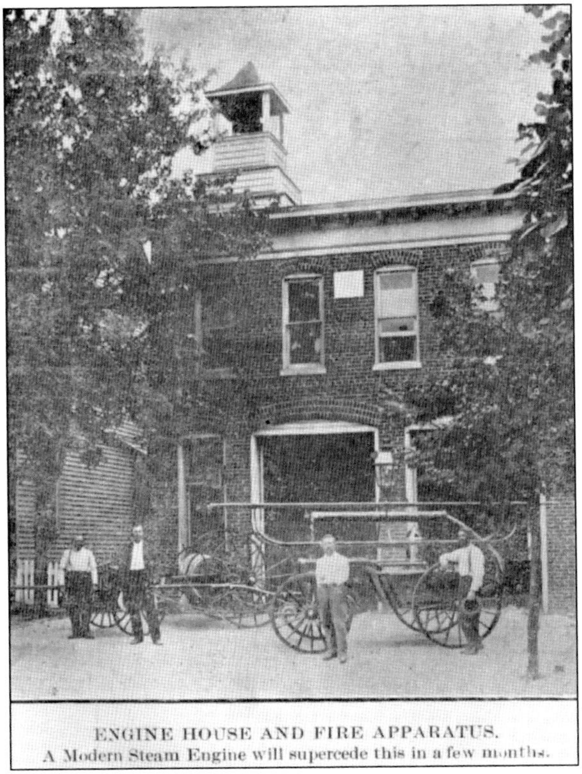

Dallastown's first fire engine house is depicted in this image, along with the fire company's hose and ladder cart and its 1892 Rumsey black and burgundy hand-drawn pumper. This building was completed in 1899 and was located on East Main Street. It was replaced when the second firehouse was dedicated in 1914 at 118 East Main Street. (Courtesy of Roger Fuller.)

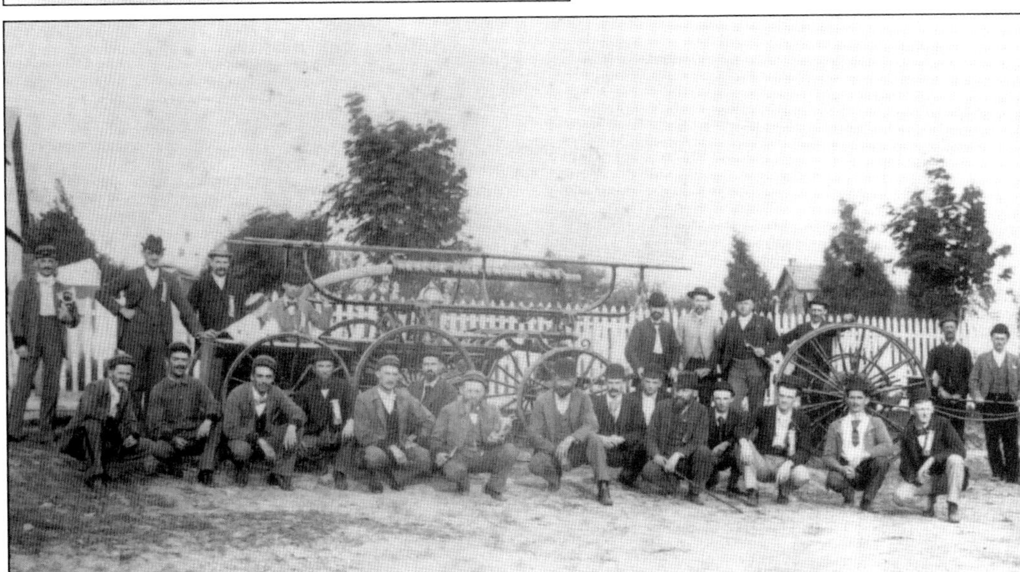

This photograph shows Dallastown's first two fire apparatuses, a hand-pulled fire pump cart and a hose and ladder cart. Posing alongside the equipment are members of Dallastown's fire company. From left to right are (kneeling) unidentified, George Heisler, Will Wallick, William Sechrist, Frank Spotz, John Heckert, ? Kohler, four unidentified, Charles Fix, two unidentified, and Sterling Raab; (standing) Dr. Charles Heisler, unidentified, Wilson Glatfelter, unidentified, Fred Heisler, unidentified, Henry Sechrist, and two unidentified. (Courtesy of Roger Fuller.)

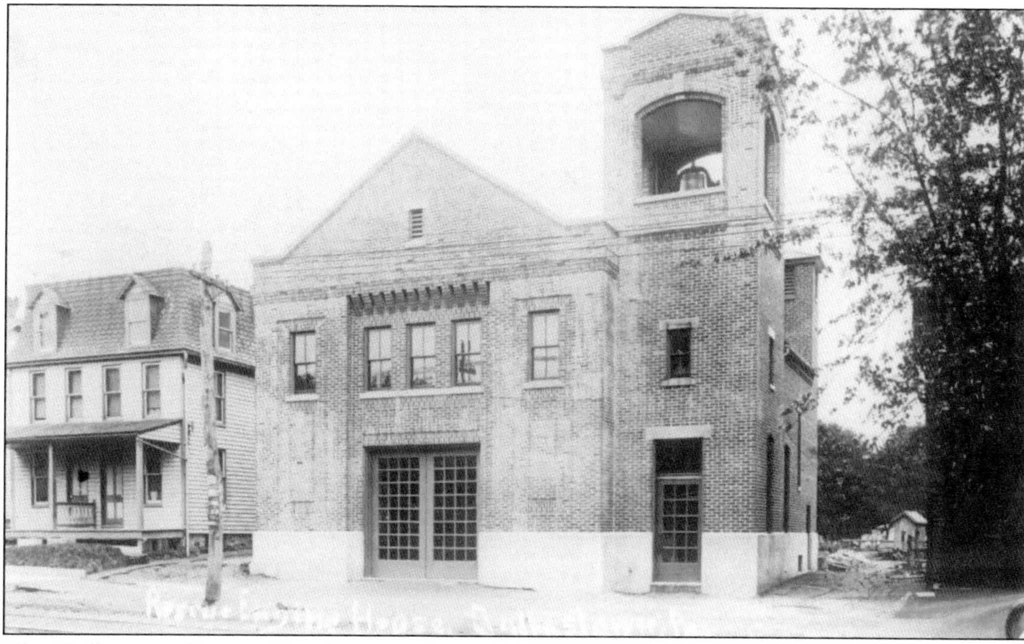

The Dallastown Rescue Fire Company's engine house was constructed in 1913 as a large two-story brick building that housed trucks and equipment on the first floor. Meeting rooms, a small recreation room, and the chief burgess's office were on the second floor. After the fire company built a new firehouse, this structure became home to the Dallastown borough offices and in 2000 to the Dallastown Area Historical Society.

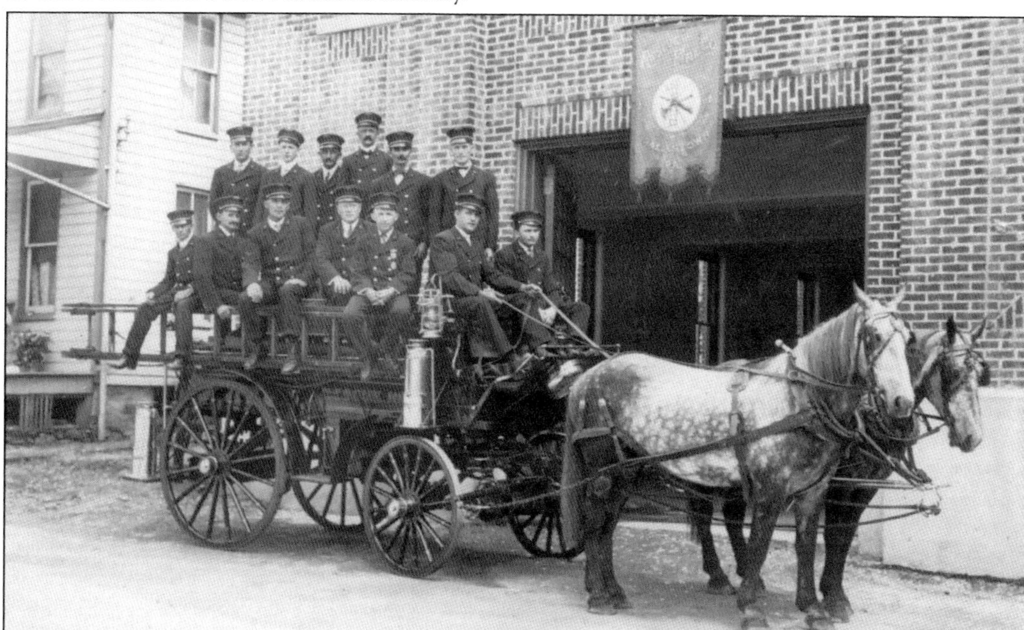

On this c. 1914 postcard, members of Dallastown's volunteer fire company are shown posing on their horse-drawn ladder cart in front of the firehouse. The vehicle had wooden wheels with metal rims. A banner attached to the engine house reads, "Rescue Fire Co. No. 1 Dallastown, PA." The doors of the engine house look like French doors, and a lantern hangs on a hook near the driver.

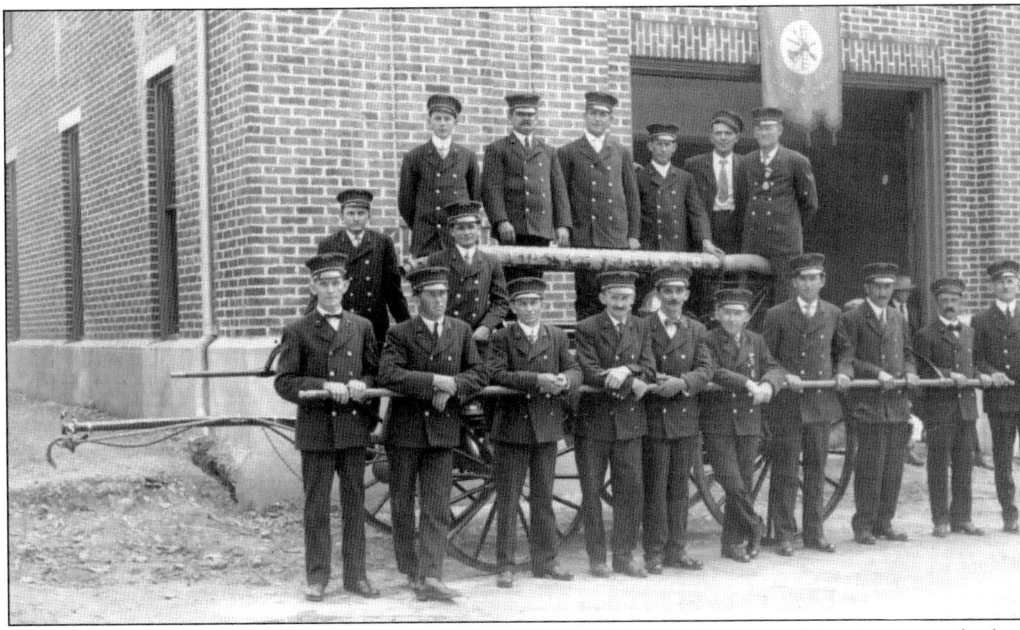

On this c. 1914 postcard, members of Dallastown's Rescue Fire Company No. 1 pose with their first hand-drawn fire pumper cart, an 1892 Rumsey Pumper, in front of the firehouse. Water from wells and bucket brigades were used to fill the pumper. The building's French doors are open wide behind the firemen, exposing the vehicle bay. The bay is where the fire company stored its firefighting apparatus.

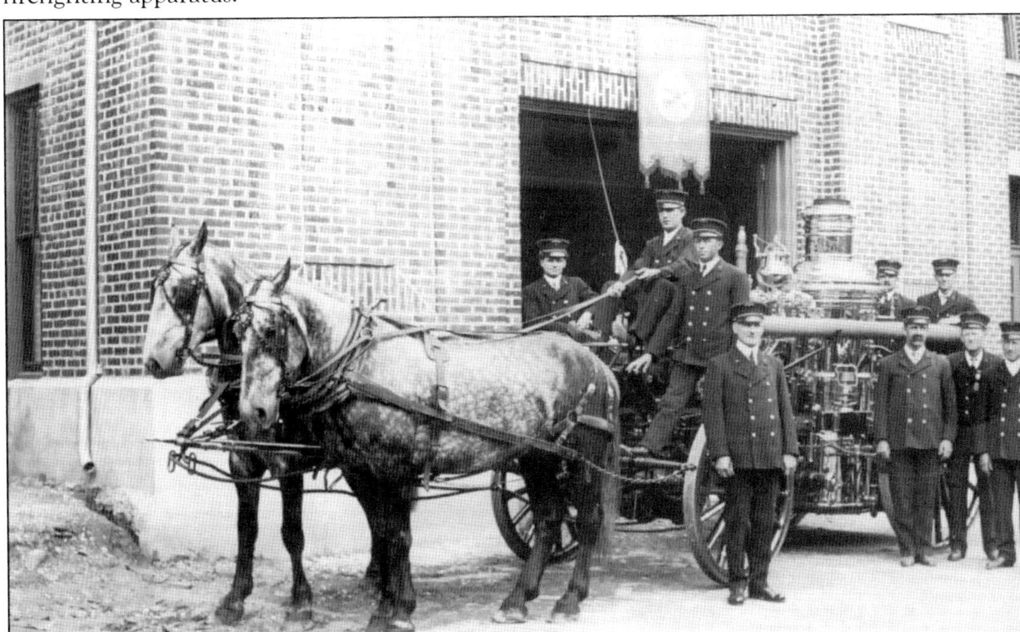

The postcard shows members of Dallastown's Rescue Fire Company No. 1 posing with their horse-drawn steam engine pumper in front of the firehouse around 1914. The bell located to the left of the driver was rung to alert people and other vehicles that a fire vehicle was approaching. The driver holds a horse whip that was used to encourage the horses to obey his commands.

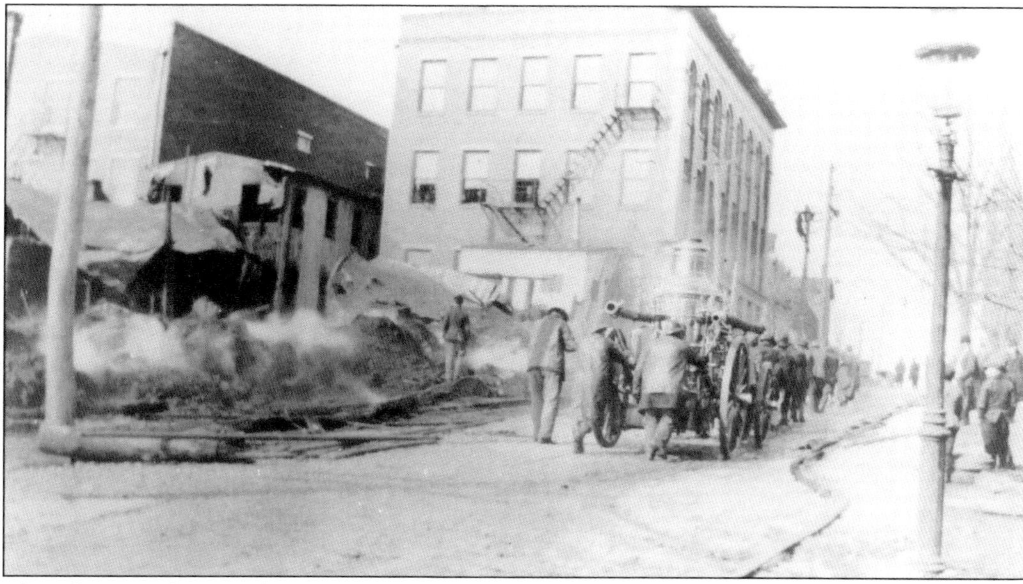

This photograph was taken on South Walnut Street, with a view looking toward the square in Dallastown in 1914. Dallastown Rescue Fire Company members are shown with their hand-pulled pumper moving north on South Walnut Street after battling a fire at the rear of the Hose Building. Smoke can still be seen rising from the rubble, while fire hoses lie on the east side of the street. Other buildings exhibit fire damage. (Courtesy of Roger Fuller.)

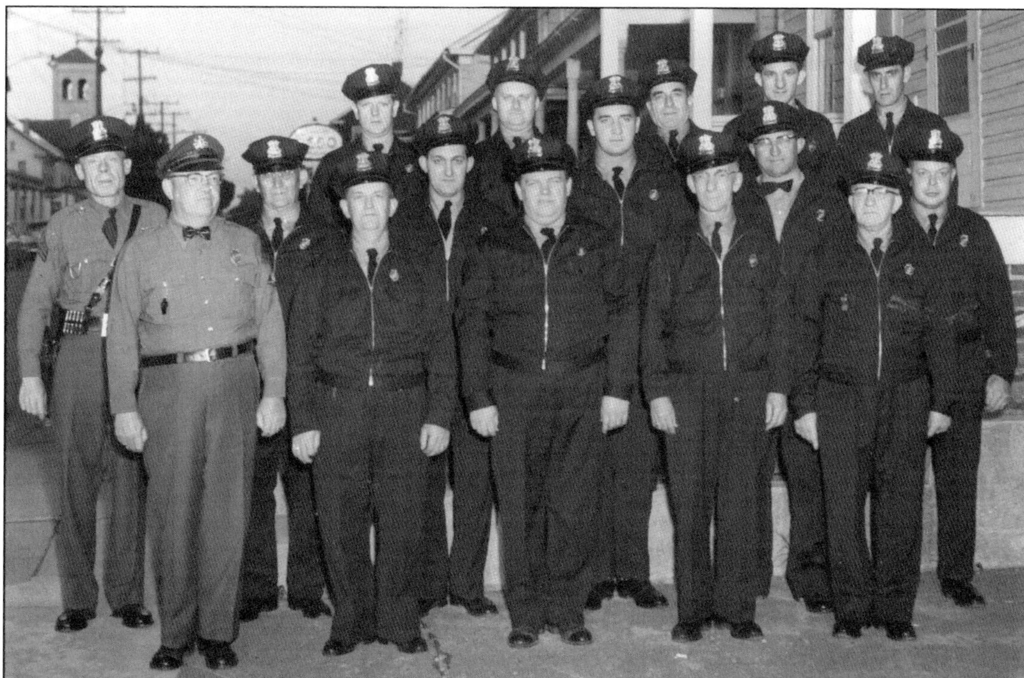

Posing to the east of the fire hall on East Main Street are the Dallastown Police force (left) and Dallastown Rescue Fire Company members (right). In the background on the south side of the street is the Esso service station. The bell tower of the original St. Joseph Catholic Church building is visible on the north side of the street.

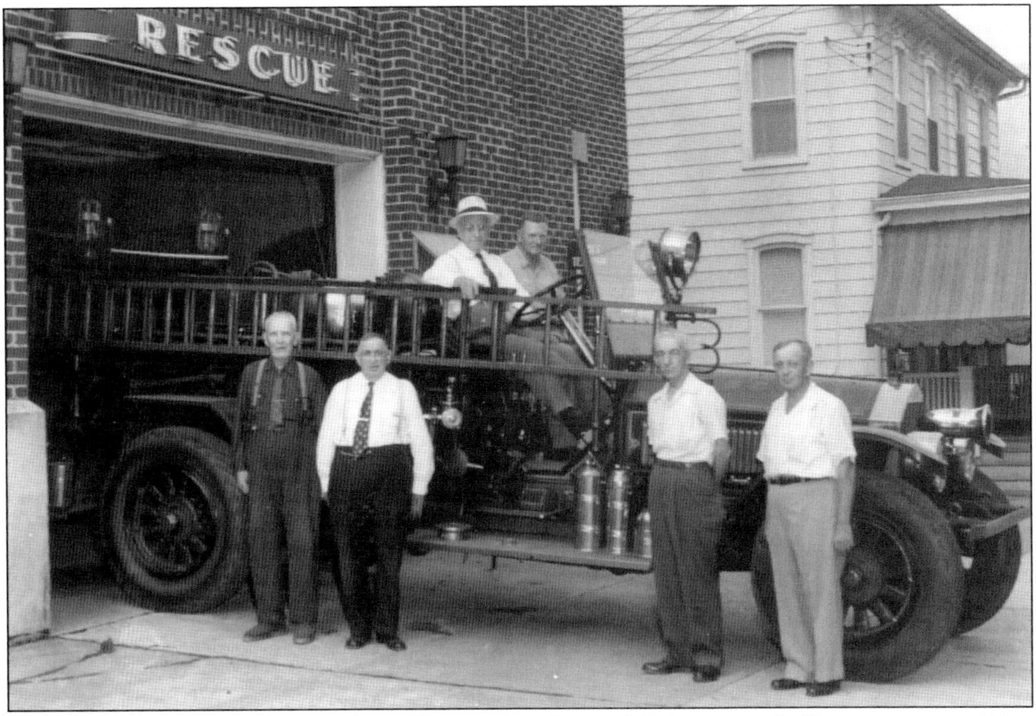

Fire company members pose with Dallastown's 1924 model American LaFrance pumper. This photograph was taken at the Rescue Fire Company No. 1 firehouse on East Main Street around 1957. A neon sign reads "Rescue" above the vehicle bay. Pictured are, from left to right, (standing) Henry W. Metz, Chester F. Heindel, Ivan G. Markle, and Vertus C. Keller; (seated) Leo Hollinger and William D. Raab.

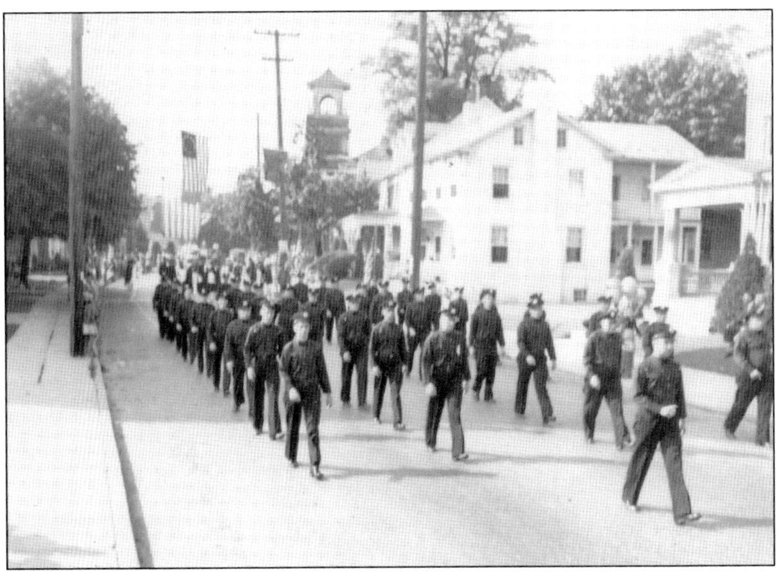

Dallastown firemen are pictured marching in the welcome home parade for veterans of World War II. The photograph, with a view looking west, was taken in 1946 by Richard E. Gemmill on West Main Street. The bell tower of the public school building at the corner of School Place and West Main Street is visible in the background.

Seven

Sports and Special Events

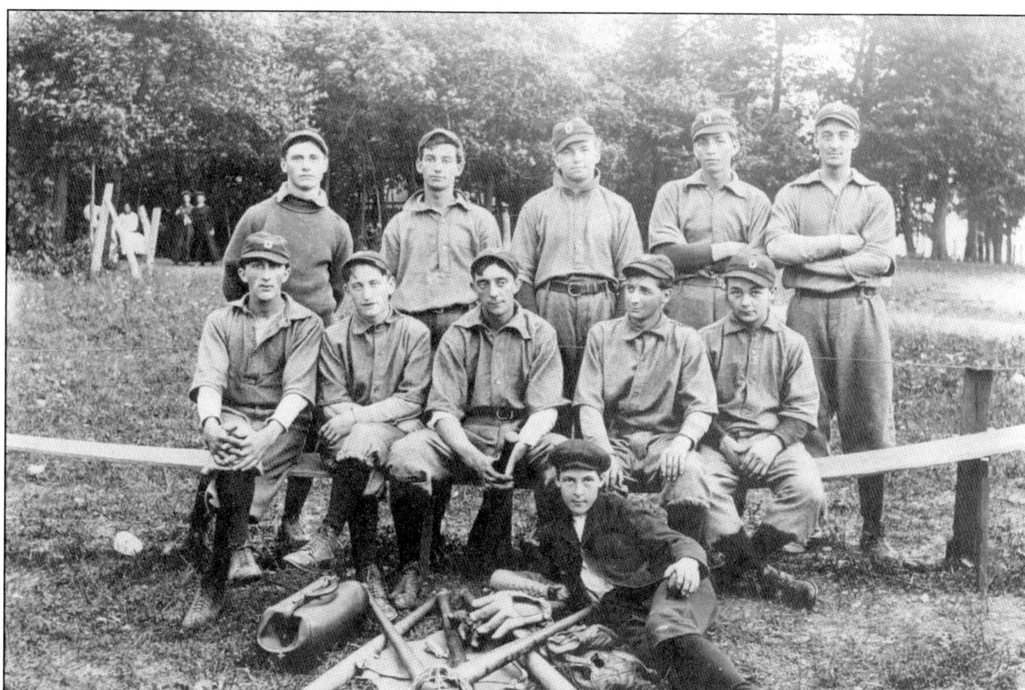

The 1904 Dallastown baseball team is depicted in this photograph. From left to right are (first row) batboy Jake Shenberger; (second row) Curvin Knaub, Martin Riedel, Eddie Hilbert, Harry Smith, and John Sheetz; (third row) Chauncey Orwig, Phil Riedel, Martin Lau, Ed Smith, and Curvin Dietz.

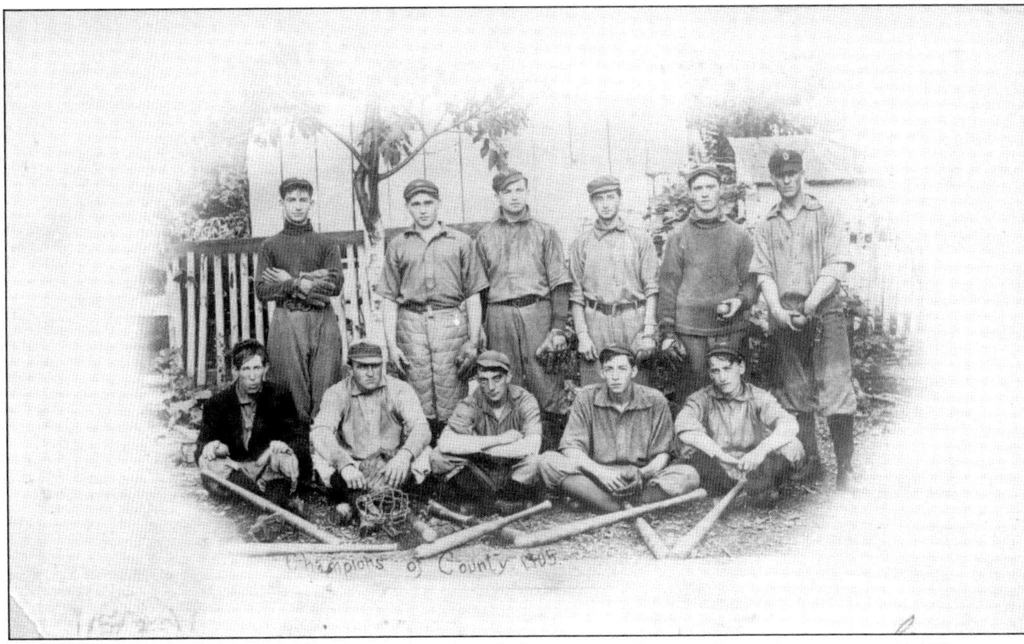

Dallastown's 1905 county championship baseball team is depicted on this postcard. This team played its home games at the Dallastown Athletic Grounds towards the west end of the borough. This was an era when almost every small town in York County had its own men's baseball team and town residents flocked to the games as a source of community pride. (Courtesy of Tom Taylor.)

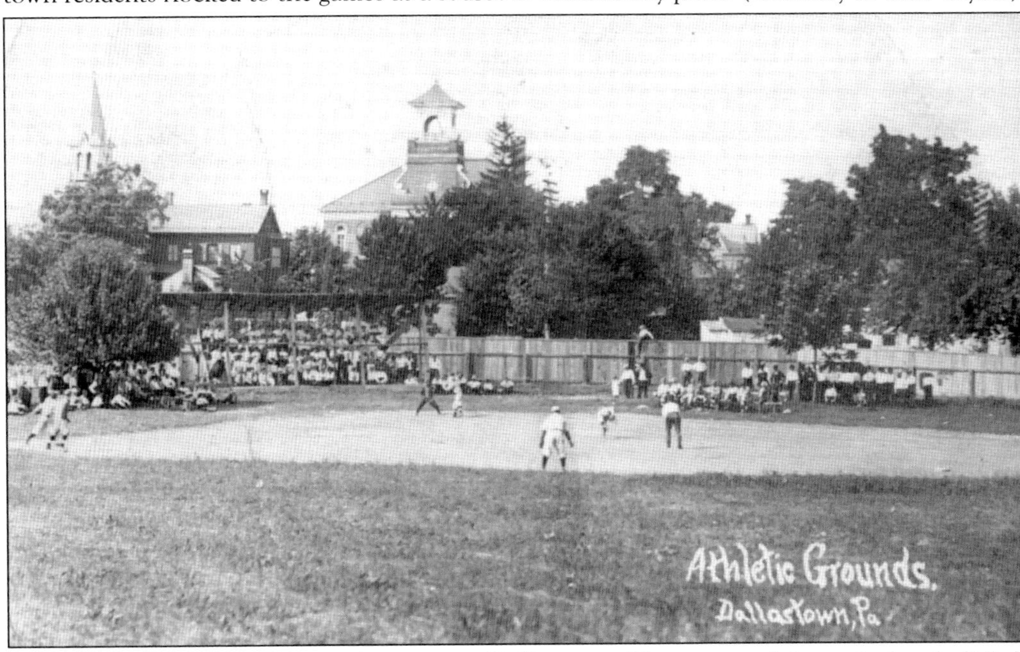

Baseball has always been a popular sport in Dallastown. This postcard shows its baseball field on the borough's athletic grounds at the town's west end. The grounds were located near where Rescue Fire Company No. 1 has its current firehouse. The public school building at the corner of School Place and West Main Street can be seen in the center rear of the image. This ball game was photographed around 1907. (Courtesy of Tom Taylor.)

Hunting has also always been a popular sport among the residents of Dallastown. This postcard shows a whitetail buck hanging from the sign at Meyers's pharmacy at 17 East Main Street. Druggist George A. Meyers (left) and Dr. Enos S. Mann admire the deer in the early 1900s. Interestingly, in the 1900s, Dallastown even had a foxhunting club. (Courtesy of Lance Wolf.)

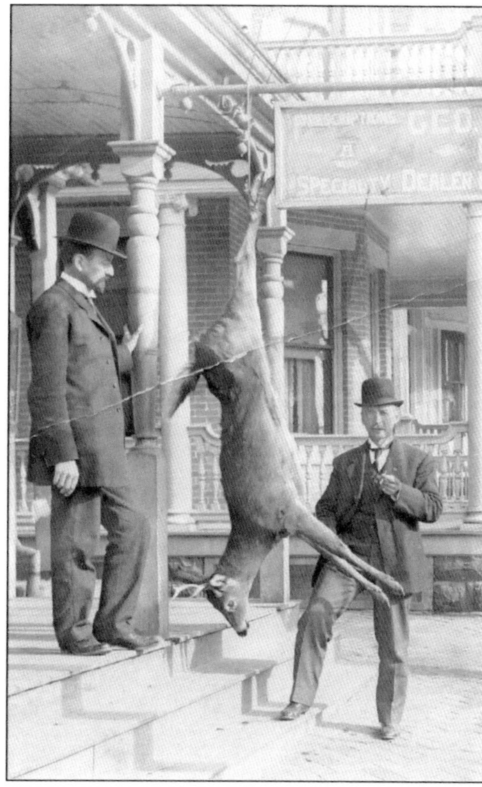

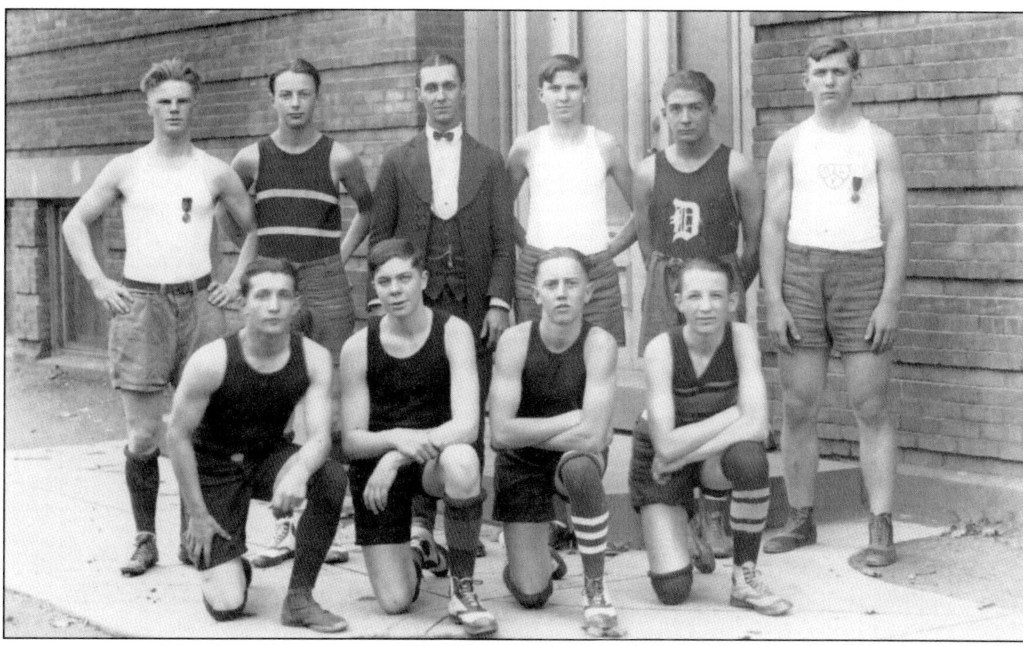

This postcard depicts Dallastown's high school track-and-field team around 1925. Pictured are, from left to right, (first row) "Cracker" Snyder, Donald Shenberger, Donald Eberly, and John Rojahn; (second row) Ernest Orwig, Donald Daugherty, Charles Koontz (coach), Palmer Poff, John Minnich, and Jake Flinchbaugh.

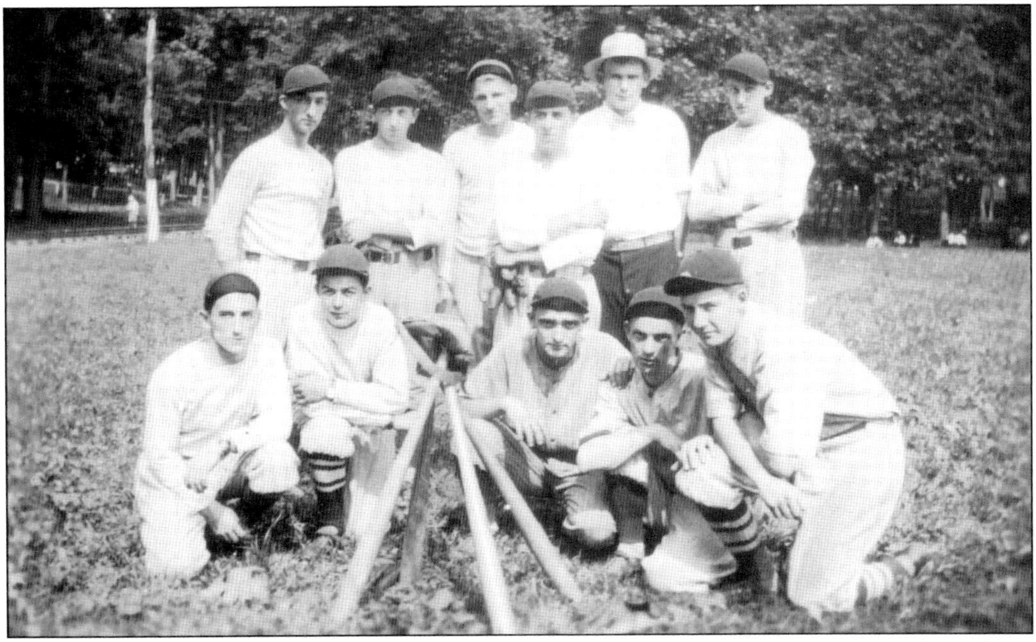

Dallastown's 1927 pennant-winning community-league (comprised of teams from towns throughout York County) baseball team is shown in this photograph. Team members are, from left to right, (first row) Harrold Reidel, Bob Thompson, Ervin Markey, Homer Dodson, and Phillip Rojahn; (second row) two unidentified, Elwood Smith, Leo Hartman, Ervin Smith, and Erdman Hartman.

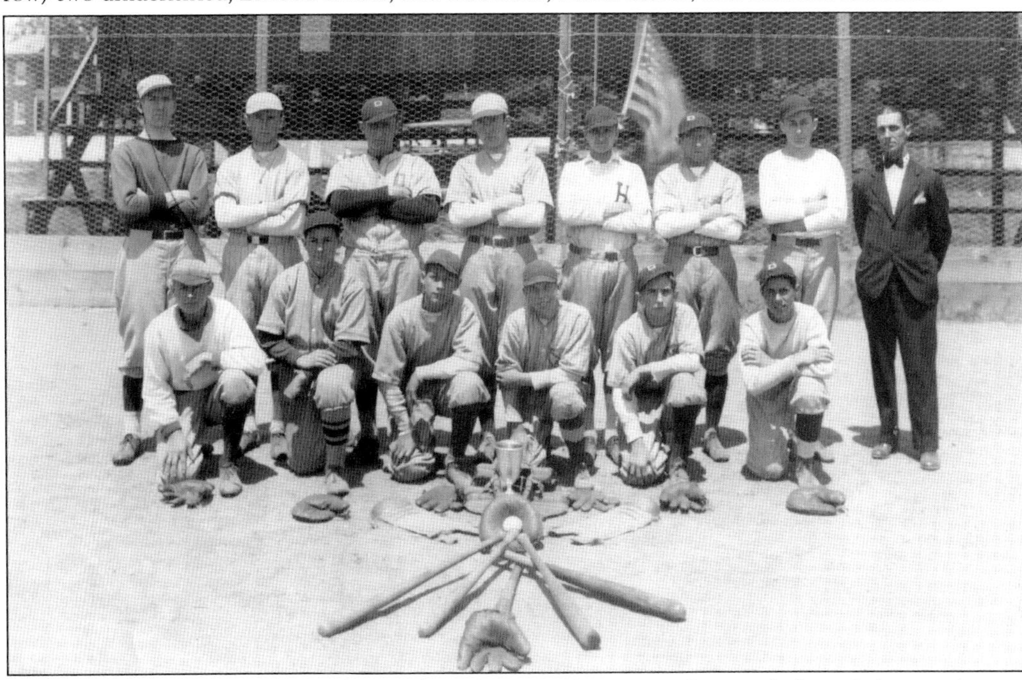

Dallastown's baseball team is depicted in this c. 1929 image. Pictured, from left to right, are (first row) Henry Raab, Jesse Hartman, Park Esbach, Robert Jackson, James Riedel, and Harris Holtzapple; (second row) Robert Flinchbaugh, Fred Barshinger, James Raab, Phil Rojahn, Sam Showalter, Woodrow Flinchbaugh, Robert Sechrist, and Charles Koontz (coach).

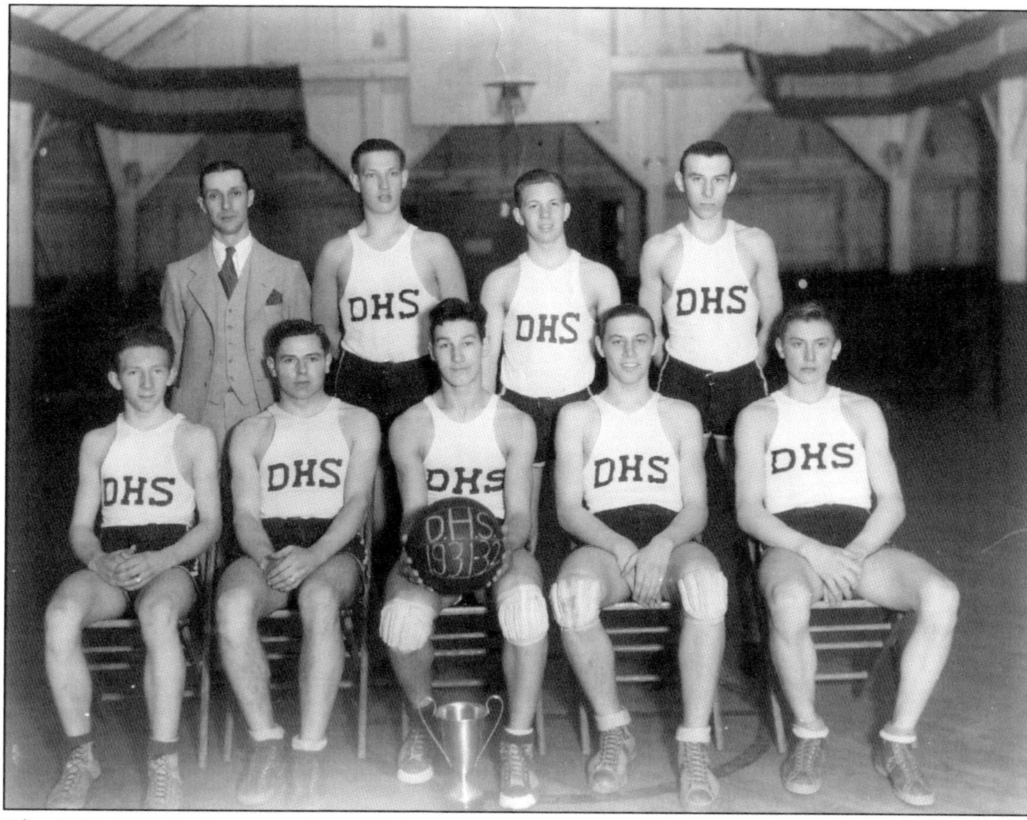

The 1931–1932 Dallastown Area High School boys' basketball team is pictured here. This team photograph was taken inside the school's original gymnasium on South Charles Street, which had once served as the borough's market house. From left to right are (first row) Phil Heisler, ? Waltemeyer, Park Eshbach, Hartman Keener, and Henry Raab; (second row) coach Charles Koontz, Austin Eberly, unidentified, and Emerson Keener. (Courtesy of Gretchen Frederich.)

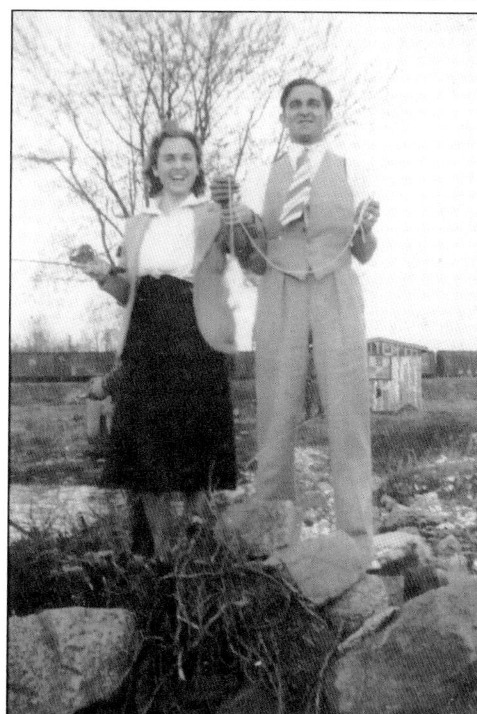

Cora Keller Deller and and her brother Pat Keller pose for a photograph while fishing in a Dallastown-area stream in the 1940s. The lack of leaves on the trees likely indicates that the picture was taken during spring trout season. Another fisherman stands behind the siblings fishing from the stream bank. Note the train in the background.

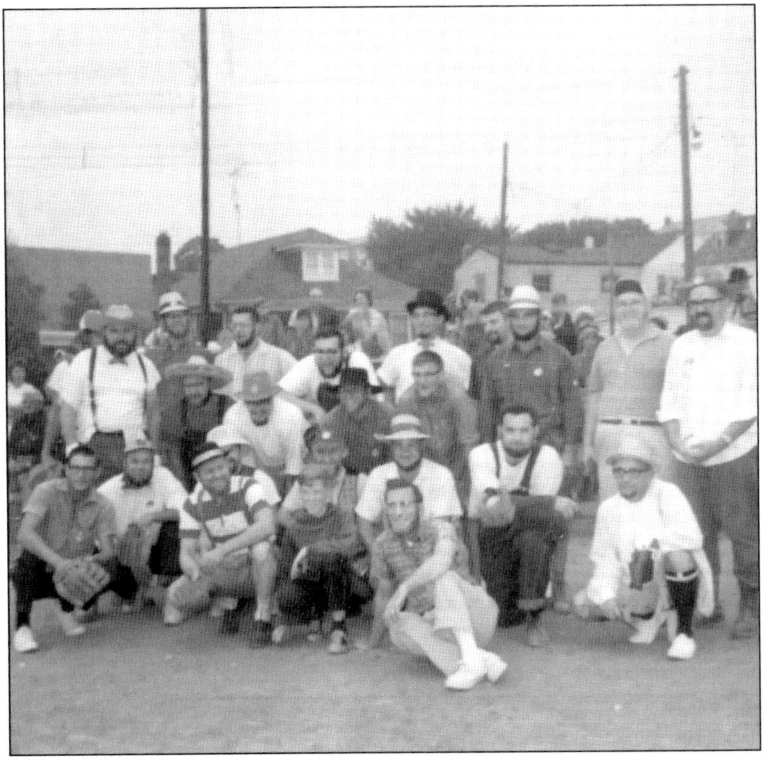

The Dallastown centennial baseball team is depicted at Cougar Field, located at the corner of East Queen Street and Franklin Avenue, on August 14, 1966. Organized as part of the town's centennial celebration, this team played a series of games against a team from Jefferson, Pennsylvania. Both municipalities celebrated their respective centennials in 1966. Most of the players have beards that they grew for the occasion.

This photograph is of a 1977 St. Joseph Catholic Church baseball team. The photograph was taken at Dallastown's Cougar Field. From left to right are (first row) Steve Snyder, two unidentified, and Damian Gallagher, (second row) two unidentified, Rich Saylor, and unidentified; (third row) Joel ? and two unidentified, (fourth row) assistant coach Richard "Dick" Saylor, Vincent Deller, and an unidentified head coach. (Courtesy of Richard C. Saylor.)

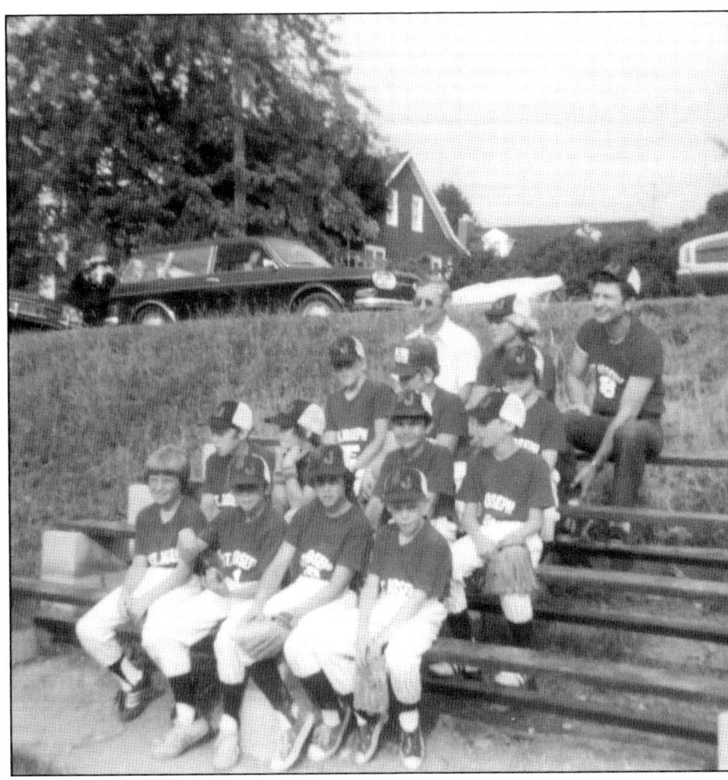

Michael Lee Sentz Jr. is depicted in this photograph taken in 1977. Sentz is shown wearing his Dallastown Cougars football uniform. As a nine-year-old, he played that year in the Rinks division. The uniform color was a maroon jersey with gold pants and helmet. This image was taken in the yard of 314 South Pleasant Avenue in Dallastown. (Courtesy of Michael L. Sentz Jr.)

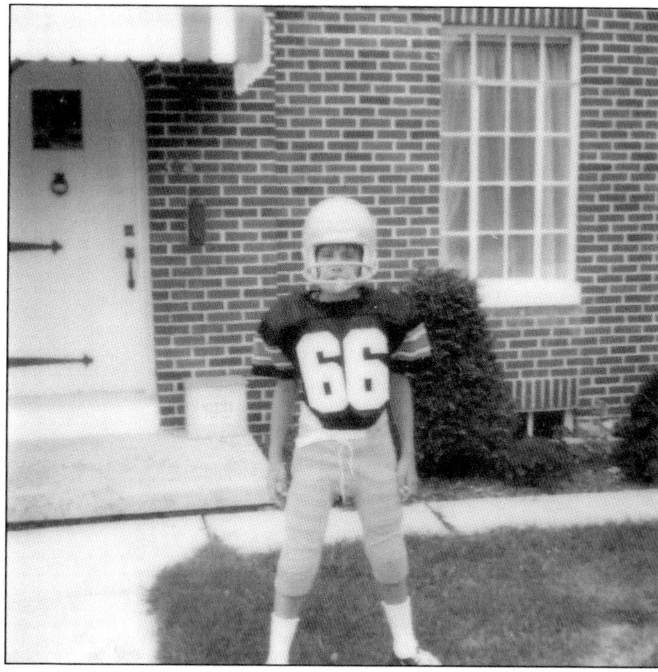

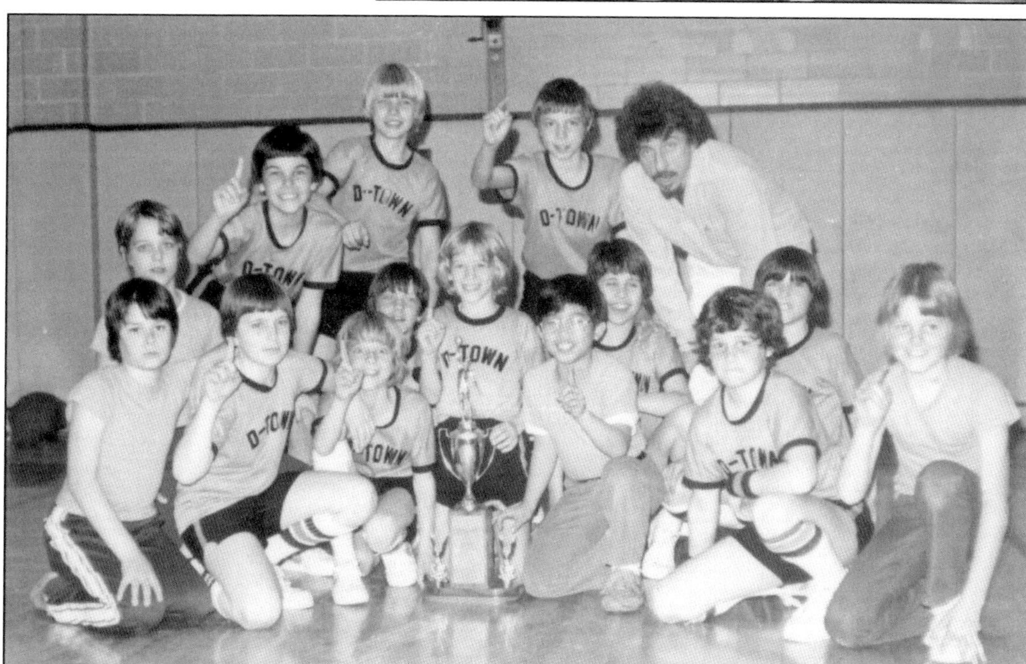

This Dallastown Elementary School Alleycats basketball team was undefeated in the preseason, regular season, and postseason tournament. The players are posing with the Dallastown Area School District's elementary tournament championship trophy, which they won during the 1978–1979 season. From left to right are (first row) Dwayne Combs, Steve Smith, T.J. Grove, Eric Heiser, Eugene Suk, Chris Clouser, and Rick Spyker; (second row) Tony Ryder, Mike Jones, Mike Sentz, and Mike Criswell; (third row) Rich Saylor, Daniel St. Clair, Steve Whitsel, and Barry Myers (head coach). (Courtesy of Richard C. Saylor.)

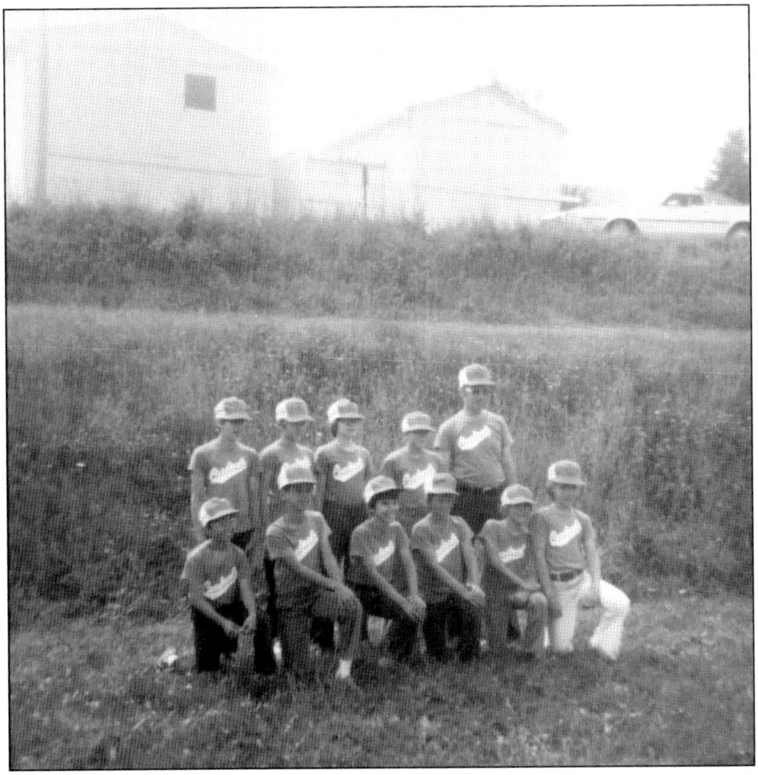

The 1979 Dallastown Cougars 10-to-12-year-old division's Cardinals baseball team is depicted in this image. The photograph was taken at Dallastown's Cougar Field. From left to right are (first row) Eugene Suk, Matthew Luchko, Rich Saylor, Patrick Strine, Chris Moore, and Daniel St. Clair; (second row) Michael Darr, Rick Marquette, Scott Bailey, Robert Amick, and coach Richard E. "Dick" Saylor. (Courtesy of Richard C. Saylor.)

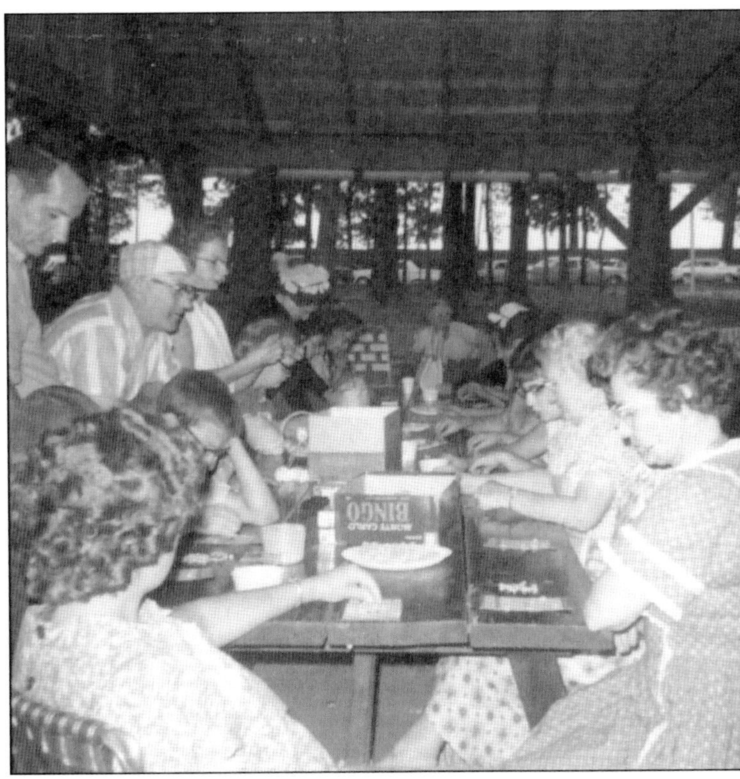

Picnickers at Dallastown's Lions Park are shown playing bingo. Many events were held throughout the summer of 1966 to celebrate the 100th anniversary of the incorporation of the borough of Dallastown. This park is located at 541 Lions Drive, not far from Dallastown Area High School. It has two baseball fields, picnic pavilions, a playground, and an outdoor amphitheater.

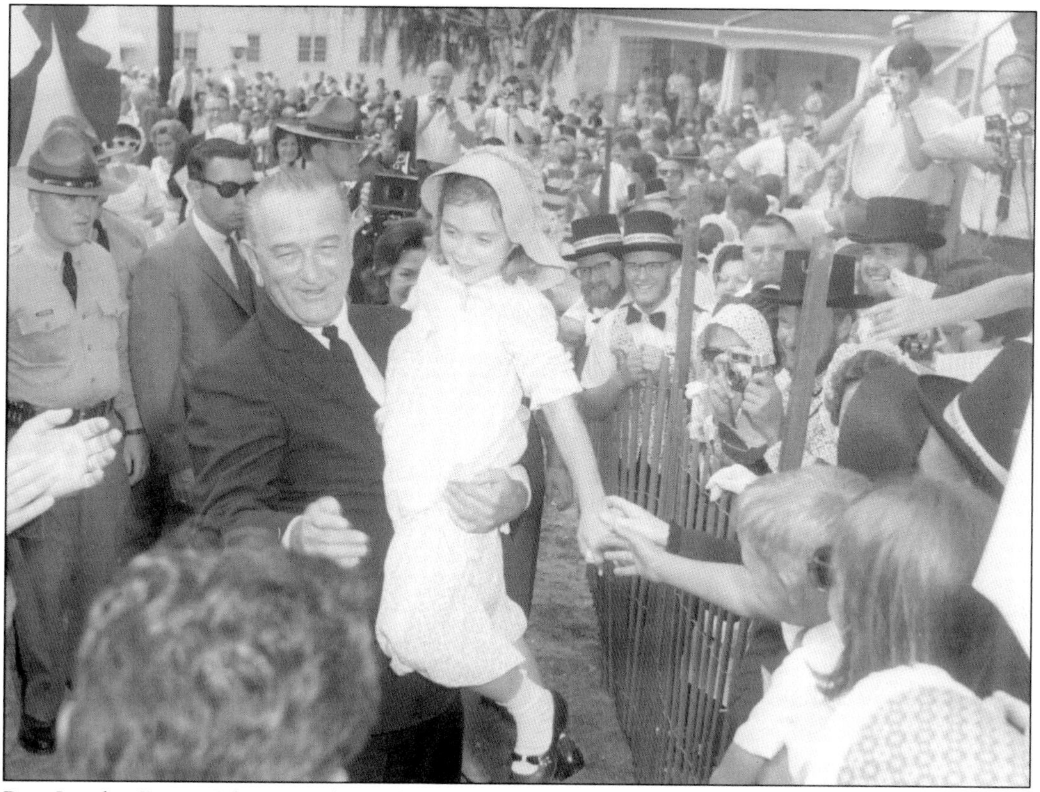

Pres. Lyndon Baines Johnson is shown holding Lesa Stultzfus during the borough's centennial in 1966. The president is surrounded by state police officers, Secret Service agents, and local townsfolk dressed in 1866 fashion. On September 3, 1966, President Johnson visited Dallastown, where he delivered a speech in which he stated that "Dallastown is one of the loveliest small towns in Pennsylvania." Photographer James Hayman Jr. took this image. (Courtesy of James M. Hayman III.)

A crowd estimated at around 30,000 people heard President Johnson deliver his speech in Dallastown. The town's normal population was 3,600. The grandstand where the president spoke is at right. This photograph was taken by James Hayman Jr. First Lady Claudia "Lady Bird" Johnson accompanied the president to Dallastown. Various politicians, including Pennsylvania governor William Scranton, were also guests of the borough that day. (Courtesy of James M. Hayman III.)

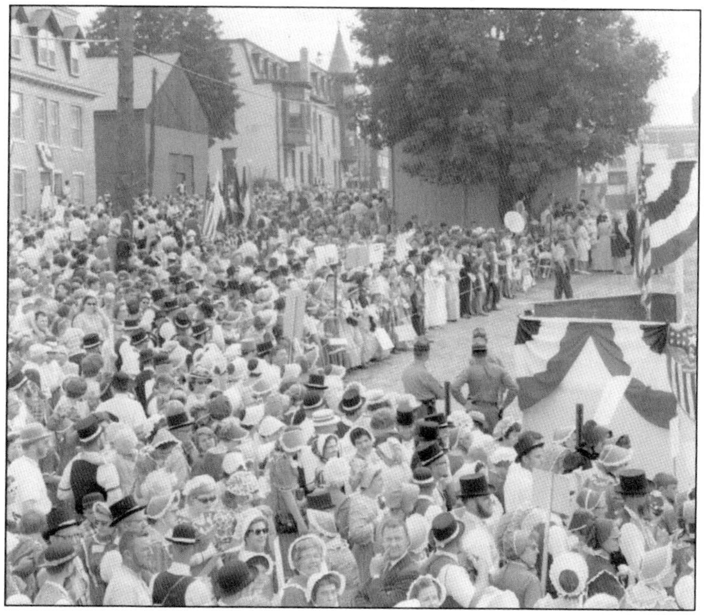

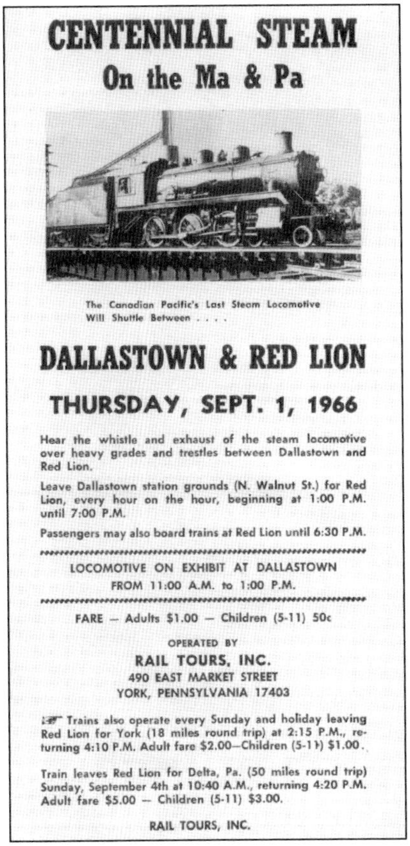

CENTENNIAL STEAM

On the Ma & Pa

The Canadian Pacific's Last Steam Locomotive Will Shuttle Between . . . .

DALLASTOWN & RED LION

THURSDAY, SEPT. 1, 1966

Hear the whistle and exhaust of the steam locomotive over heavy grades and trestles between Dallastown and Red Lion.

Leave Dallastown station grounds (N. Walnut St.) for Red Lion, every hour on the hour, beginning at 1:00 P.M. until 7:00 P.M.

Passengers may also board trains at Red Lion until 6:30 P.M.

LOCOMOTIVE ON EXHIBIT AT DALLASTOWN FROM 11:00 A.M. to 1:00 P.M.

FARE — Adults $1.00 — Children (5-11) 50c

OPERATED BY

RAIL TOURS, INC.

490 EAST MARKET STREET

YORK, PENNSYLVANIA 17403

☞ Trains also operate every Sunday and holiday leaving Red Lion for York (18 miles round trip) at 2:15 P.M., returning 4:10 P.M. Adult fare $2.00—Children (5-11) $1.00.

Train leaves Red Lion for Delta, Pa. (50 miles round trip) Sunday, September 4th at 10:40 A.M., returning 4:20 P.M. Adult fare $5.00 — Children (5-11) $3.00.

RAIL TOURS, INC.

During Dallastown's centennial in 1966, George M. Hart's Rail Tours Inc. ran Canadian Pacific steam locomotive No. 972 with passenger cars between Dallastown and Red Lion on the Maryland & Pennsylvania line. The special train ran on September 1, 1966, Founder's Day in Dallastown, every hour from 1:00 p.m. to 7:00 p.m. This original handbill from the event was used as advertising during the lead-up to the town's centennial celebrations. (Courtesy of Kurt Bell.)

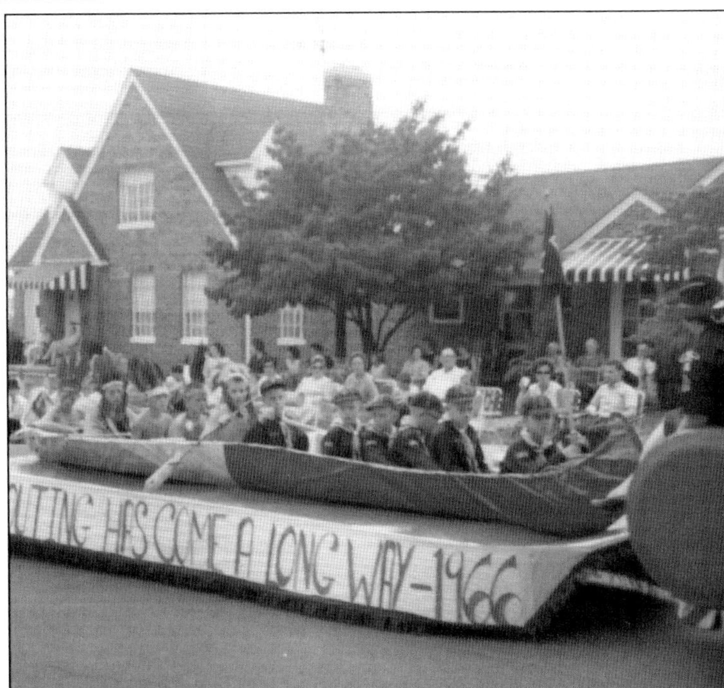

This is the centennial parade float for Scouting in Dallastown. The front of the canoe shows Cub Scouts in uniform, while the rear of the boat has Scouts dressed as American Indians. The slogan on the float states, "Scouting Has Come A Long Way—1966." Dallastown has a long tradition of having a number of Boy Scout and Girl Scout troops.

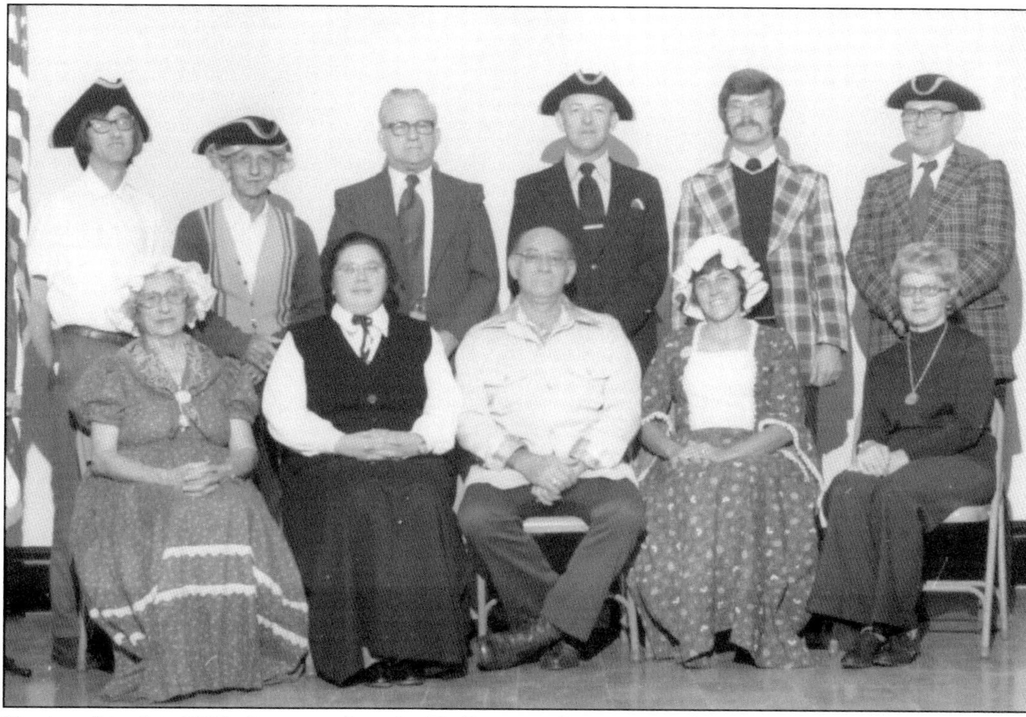

Depicted in this 1976 photograph is the Dallastown Bicentennial Commission. From left to right are (first row) Mamie McDowell (ladies division), Sister Dominica Lobiance (secretary), Gerald Flinchbaugh (general chairman), Lois Flegel (assistant ladies division), and Jean Capatch (window painting); (second row) Charles Snyder (public relations), John H. Kell (men's division), Harry Neuman (street decorations), O.V. Daugherty Jr. (vice chairman), Thomas Tome Jr. (treasurer), and Harold Good (parade marshal).

The Dallastown Carnival, or Fair, has been held in one form or the other for more than a century. For many decades, these festivals had livestock competitions for local farmers. This postcard image depicts the first-prize chicken from the 1908 Dallastown Fair. Interestingly, pigeon racing was also a popular contest at these events, as well as a hobby enjoyed by many Dallastown men through the 1970s. (Courtesy of Tom Taylor.)

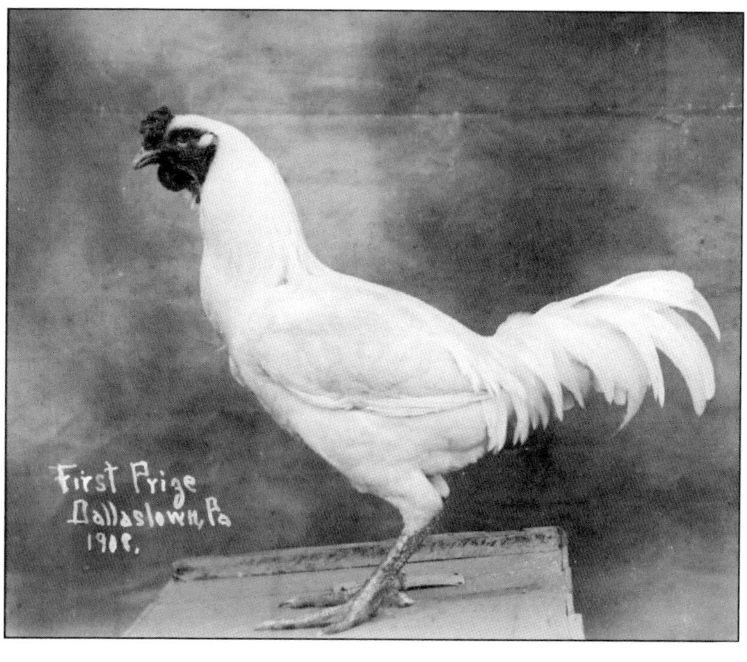

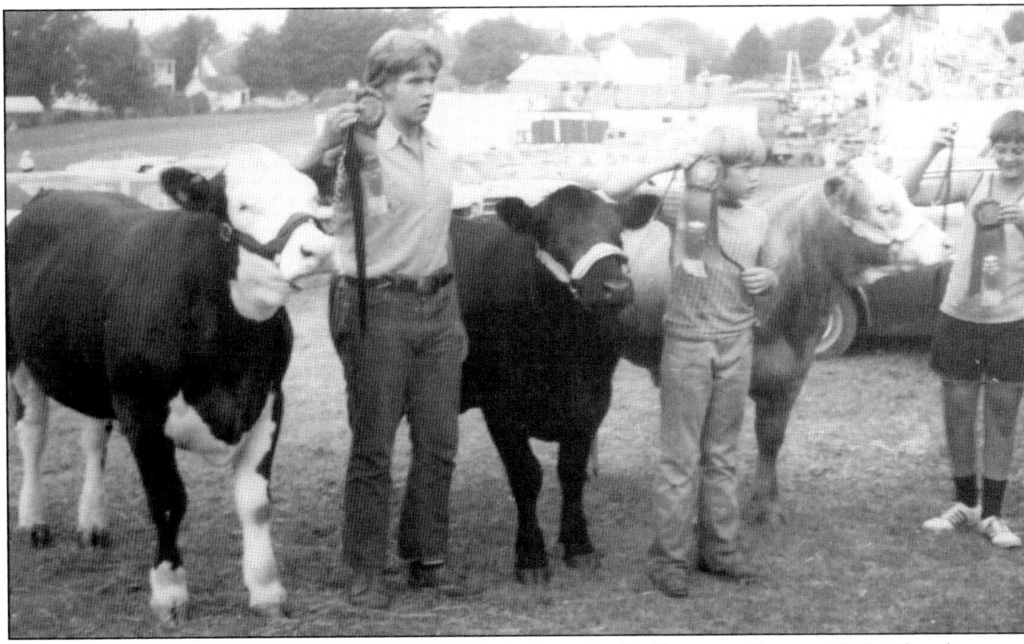

Prizewinning cows are displayed in this photograph at the Dallastown Fair in 1975. The three top prizewinners display their award ribbons alongside their respective animals. At that time, the fair still had a number of 4-H competitions that were a mainstay of the weeklong event's varied programs.

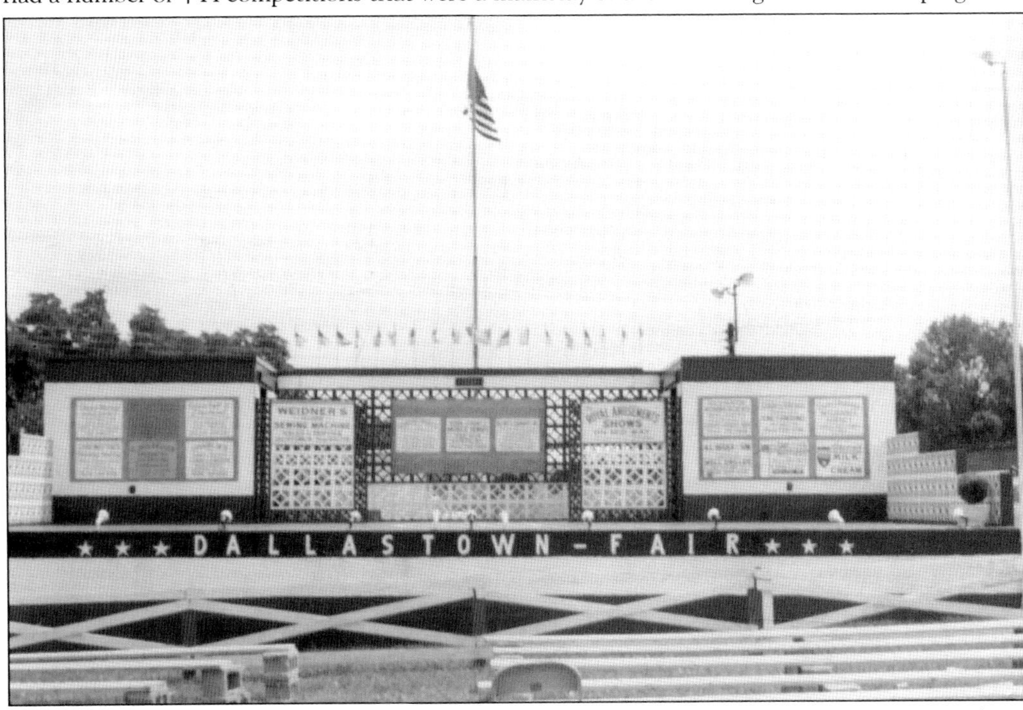

The main stage at the 1975 Dallastown Fair is depicted in this photograph. Numerous musical acts and other performers used this stage during the course of the fair. Various announcements were also made from this platform. Local businesses that supported the fair had their advertisements posted around the backdrop.

Eight

People

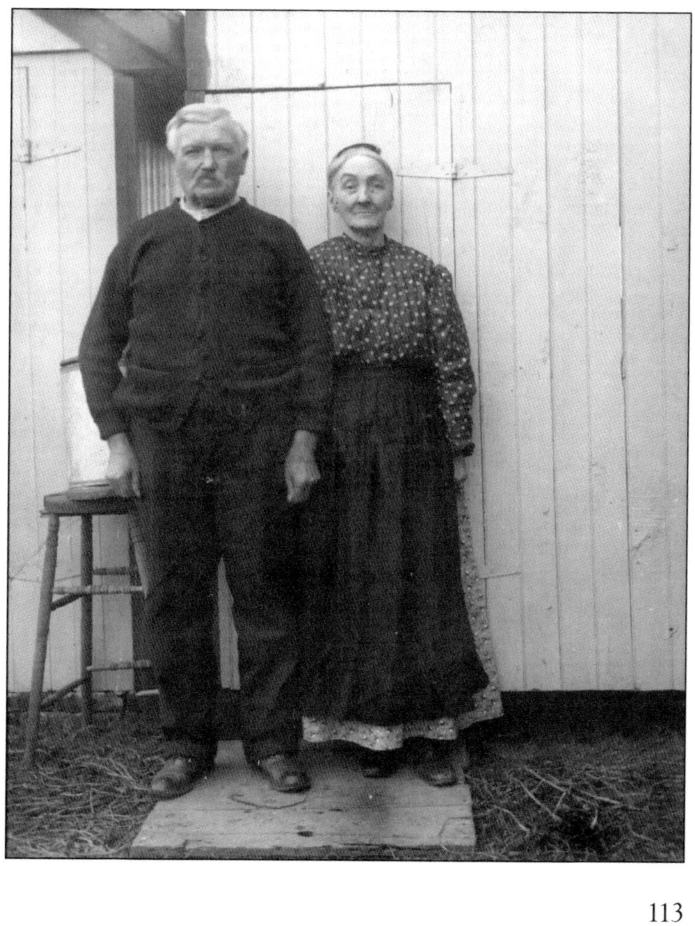

William Henry Raab and his wife, Mary Ann (Olp) Raab, are the subjects of this c. 1910 photograph. William was born on April 15, 1853. He was the founder and owner of W.H. Raab and Sons cigar manufacturers, which began business in Dallastown in 1874. At its peak, the company employed around 100 workers. (Courtesy of Tom Taylor.)

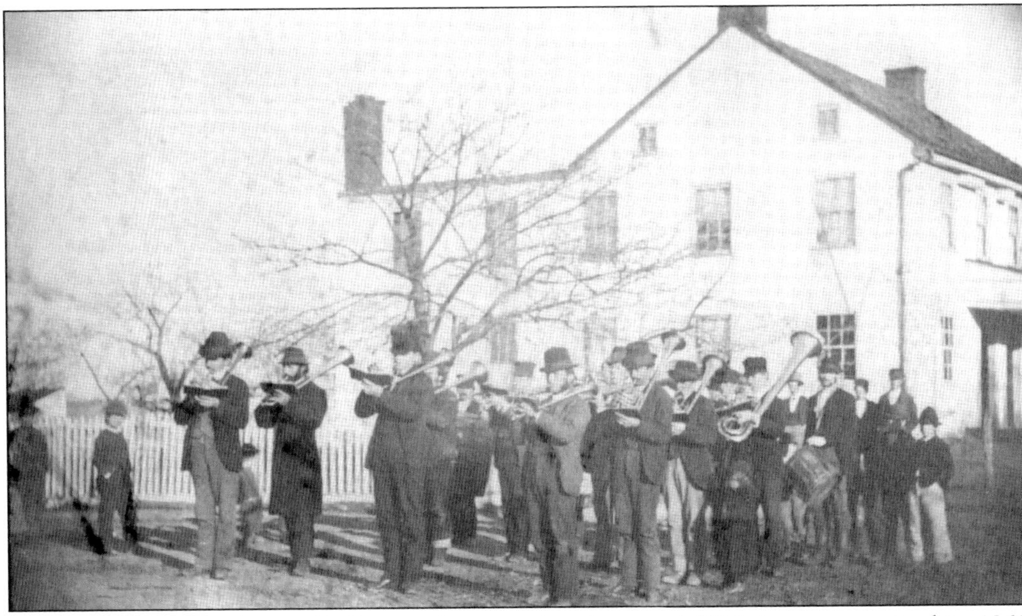

This carte de visite depicts Dallastown's cornet band around 1877; it was organized in 1861. The band was originally formed with the intention of becoming a regimental band for one of Pennsylvania's Volunteer Infantry regiments during the Civil War; however, the United States Army disbanded all regimental bands on July 17, 1862. Adam Kohler was the founder and musical director of this band, which transitioned into the Dallastown Band and eventually the Dallastown Band Association. (Courtesy of Schmidt Library, York College of Pennsylvania.)

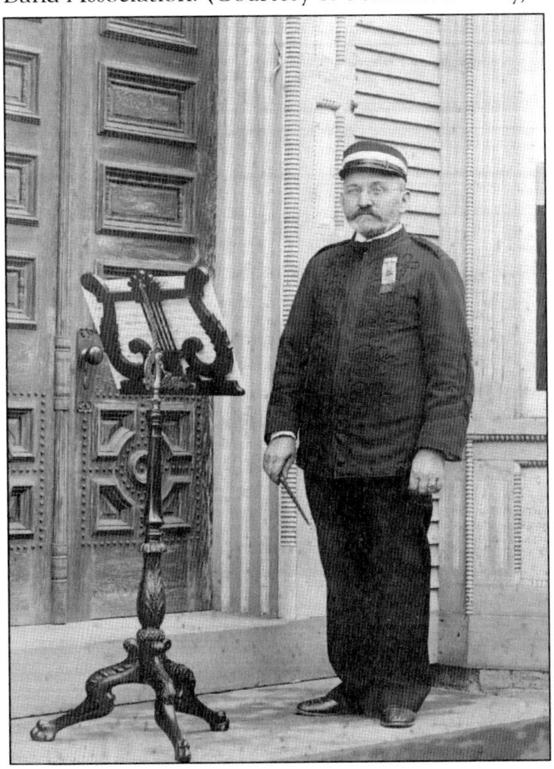

Adam Kohler is depicted in his role as leader of the Dallastown Band in this image captured by photographer William M. Bigler. Kohler was director of Dallastown's Band for 42 years, from 1861 to 1904. The wooden music stand in the photograph is now in the special collections of York College's library. In 1974, an annual music studies scholarship was created in Kohler's name at York College of Pennsylvania. (Courtesy of Schmidt Library, York College of Pennsylvania.)

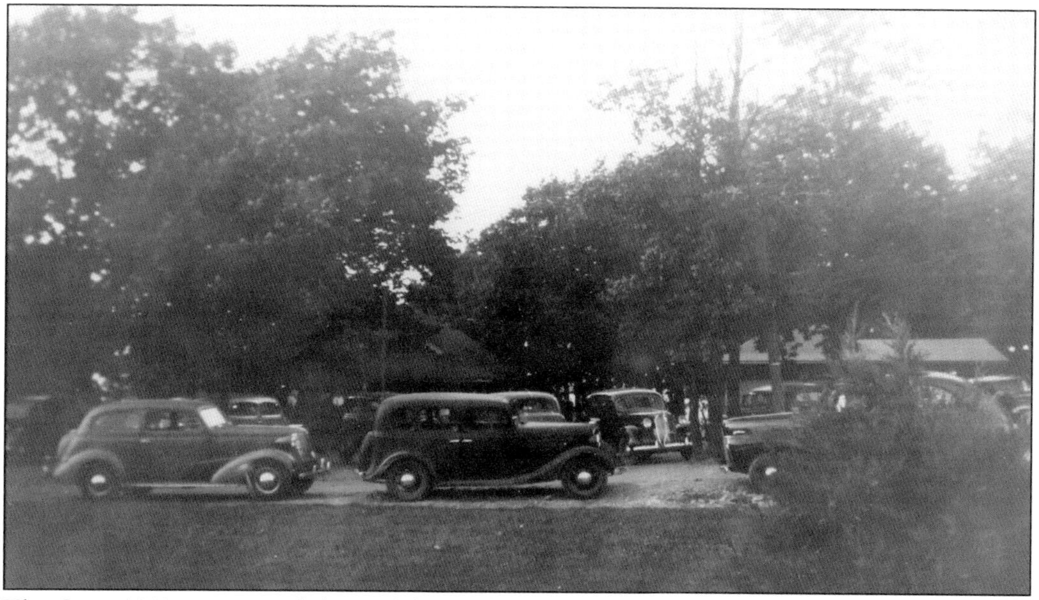

This June 1941 image is of the park located at the end of North Park Street in Dallastown. Originally named Simon Park for its first owner, Valentine Simon, it later became Boeckel Park from 1927 to 1945, when purchased by the Boeckel brothers of York. Finally, it became Harry Keller's Keller Park from 1946 into the 1950s. Saturday-night country-and-western dances were often held there. (Courtesy of Cathy Bankoske.)

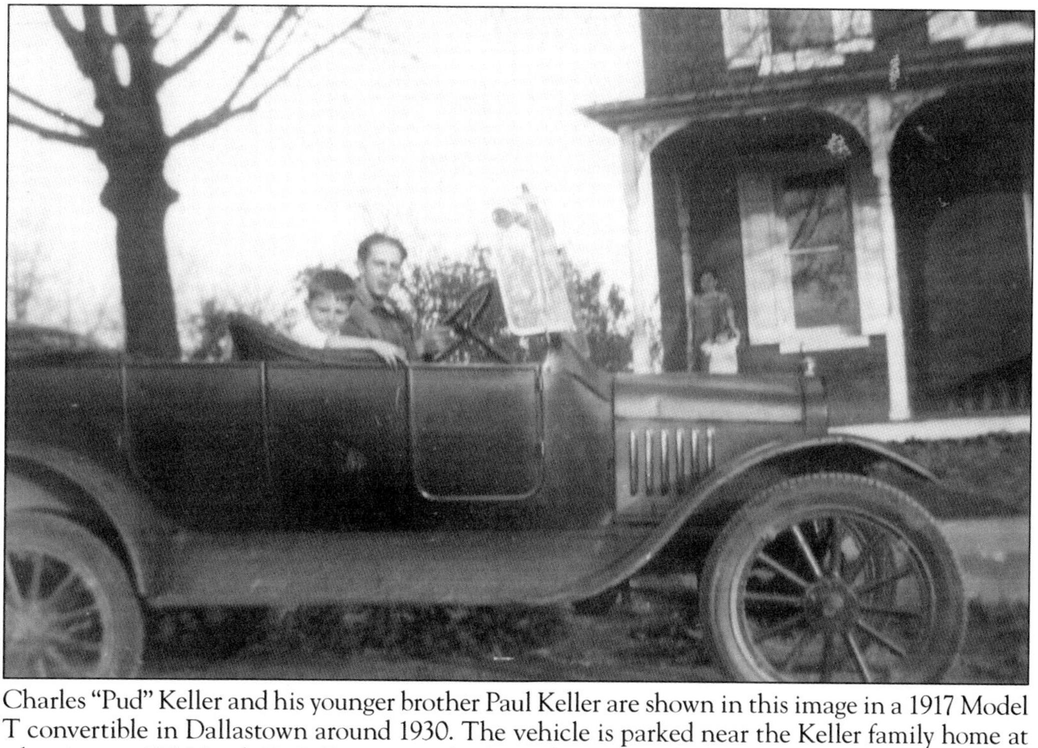

Charles "Pud" Keller and his younger brother Paul Keller are shown in this image in a 1917 Model T convertible in Dallastown around 1930. The vehicle is parked near the Keller family home at what is now 297 North Park Street, not far from the former site of Boeckel Park. (Courtesy of Cathy Bankoske.)

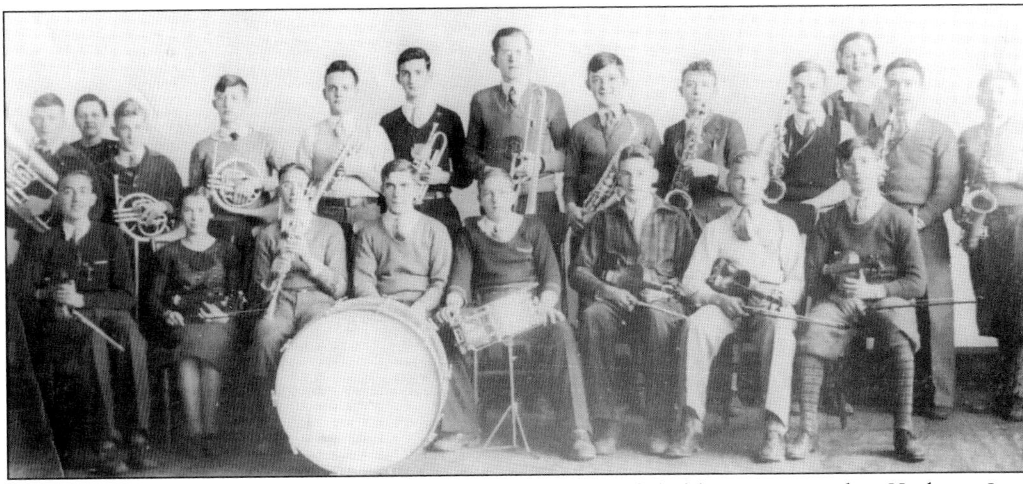

This photograph depicts the 1933 Dallastown school band, led by music teacher Kathryn Lutz Chance. Pictured are, from left to right, (first row) Earl Sechrist, Hazel Linburg Snyder, Vernon Straub, Willard Innerst, Charles Spotz, Preston Sechrist, Ammon Lentz, and John Stine; (second row) Ralph Strayer, Kathryn Lutz Chance (music teacher), Lewis Riedel, Vernon Shermyer, William McCormick, Dwight Daugherty, Bruce Rost, Richard Kauffman, Warren Sechrist, Robert Flinchbaugh, Marian Hench Hess, Robert Miller, and Richard Flinchbaugh.

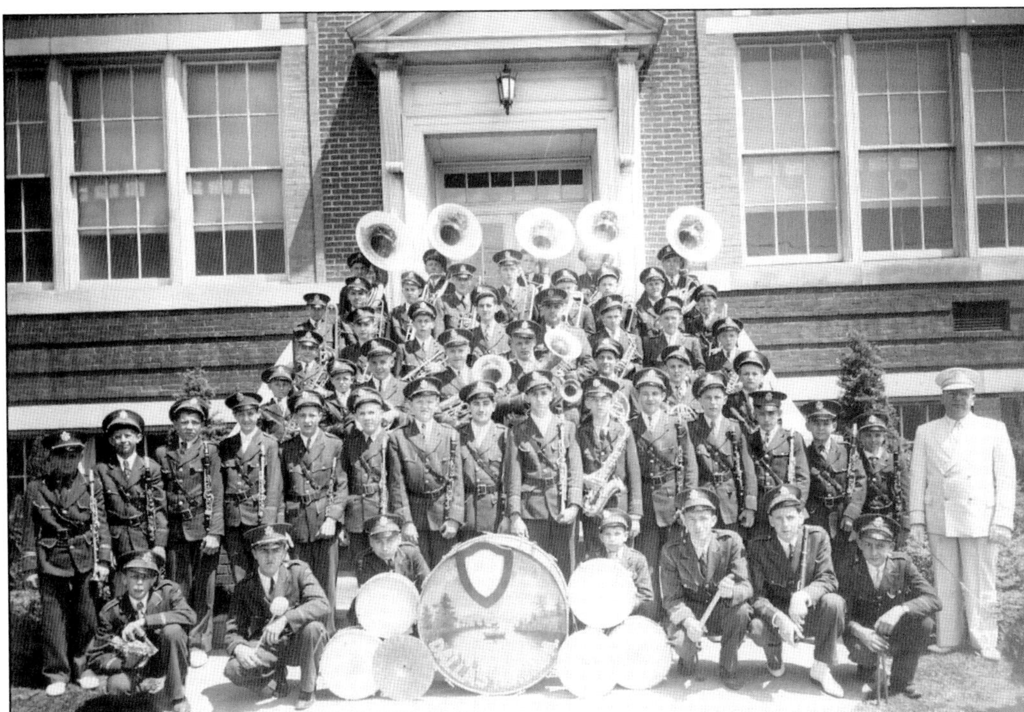

This photograph of the Dallastown Boys Band shows the band members posing with their instruments in front of the old high school in Dallastown. The Dallastown Boys Band was the junior group that fed into the Dallastown Band. This school, located on South Charles Street, is now the town's elementary school.

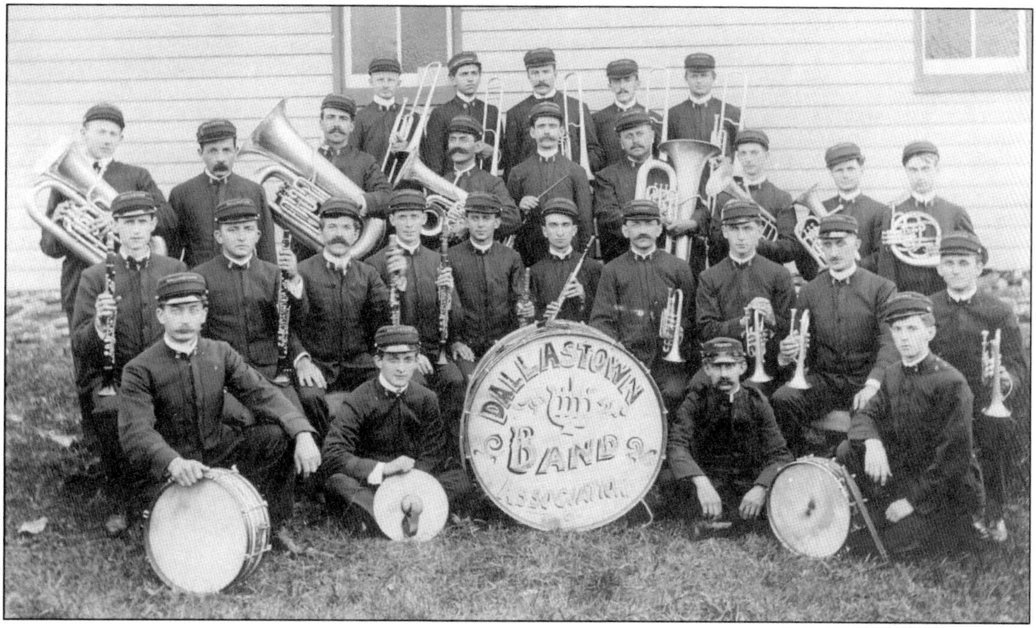

Dallastown Band Association members are posing with their musical instruments in this c. 1890s image. Most of the band members' caps have the name "Dallastown" on them. However, the band's "Porter," "Leader," and "Conductor" all have their position titles on their caps. The trombone player in the fourth row, second from left, has a cap with the initials "DBA" on it, for Dallastown Band Association.

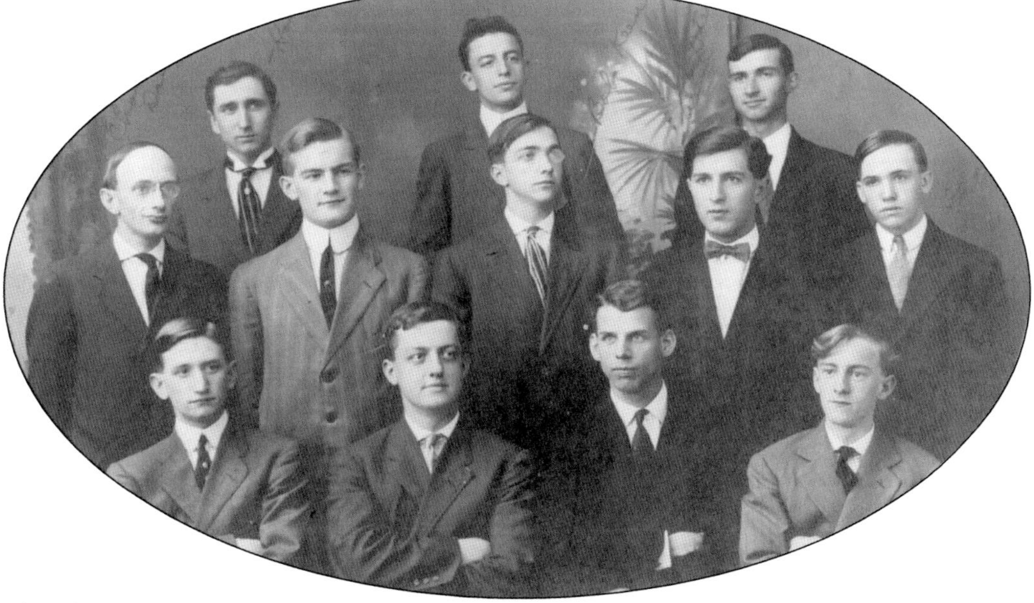

This photograph shows a men's choral group from Dallastown around 1910. Many of the men are wearing detachable shirt collars. From left to right are (first row) Norm Shenkmyer, unidentified, Hiram Peters, and Myles Riedel; (second row) Charles Daugherty (teacher), unidentified, Bob Keener, Art Stein, and ? Gates; (third row) Howard Perry and two unidentified. (Courtesy of Helen P. Stein.)

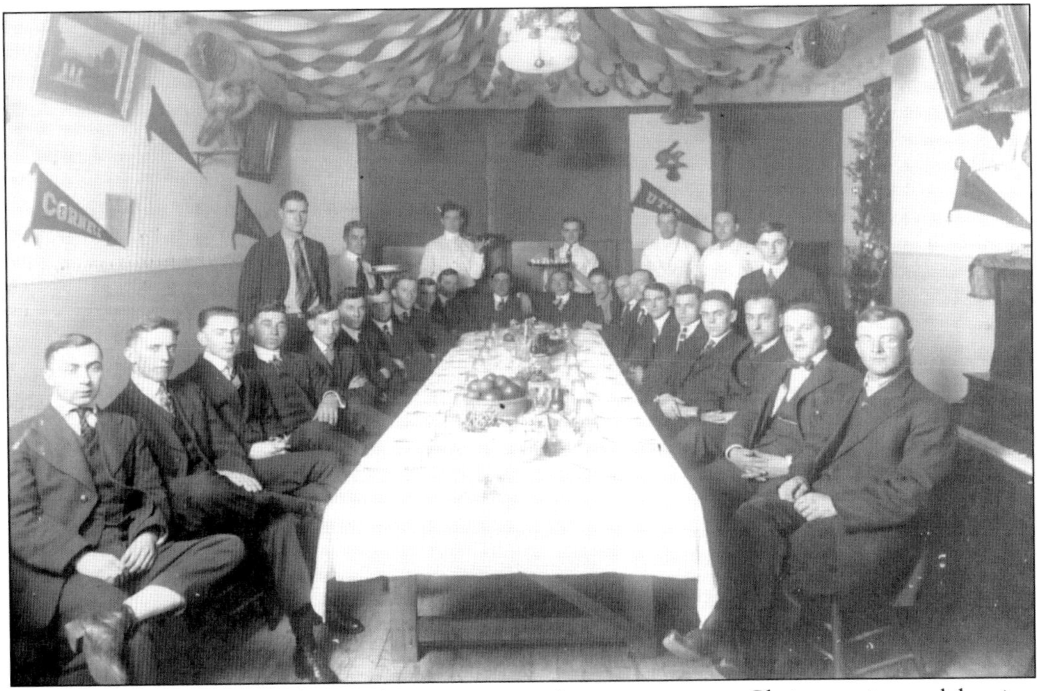

The photograph depicts a fraternal organization of young men at a Christmastime celebration in Dallastown. The members of the society sit around the table while waiters and cooks stand near the far wall. From left to right are (seated) Marvin Koontz, Raymond Peifer, Paul Dellinger, Peifer Steinfelt, Henry Deller, Harry Wagman, Lawrence Noll, Bill Deller, Clarence Flory, Tibertus Tuck Grim, Archibald Grim, Harry Bailey, Walter Deller, Jerome Keller, Austin Reidel, Henry Ryer, Jerome Ryer, Harry Reidel, William Douglass, and Peter Williams; (standing) Parsely Peters, Luther Reidel, Roland Grim, Charles Butcher, Oscar Deller, Allen Flinchbaugh, and Spurgeon Hildebrand.

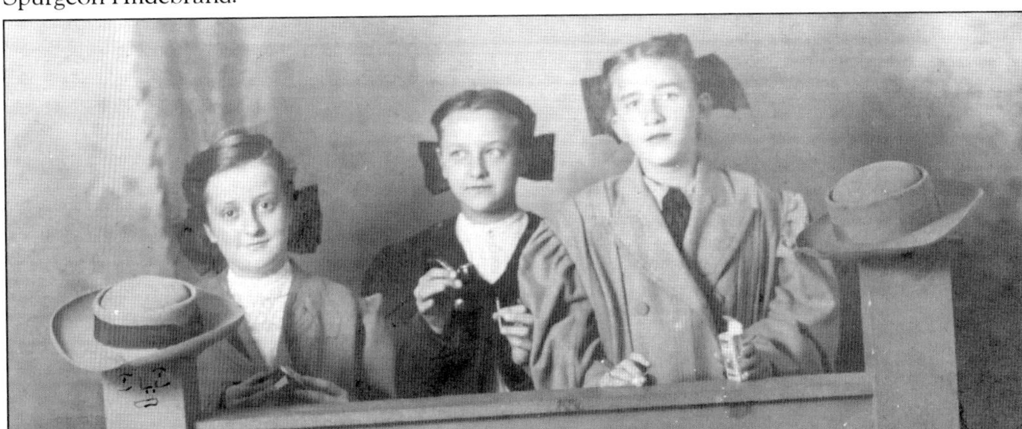

This studio portrait depicts a trio of friends. From left to right are Esther Stabley, Flora Horn, and Bell Kauffman. The photograph was taken around 1901. These Dallastown girls are posing with various smoking paraphernalia, including a pipe, matches, and a cigarette package. All three girls are wearing large bows in their hair, which was a popular fashion of that era.

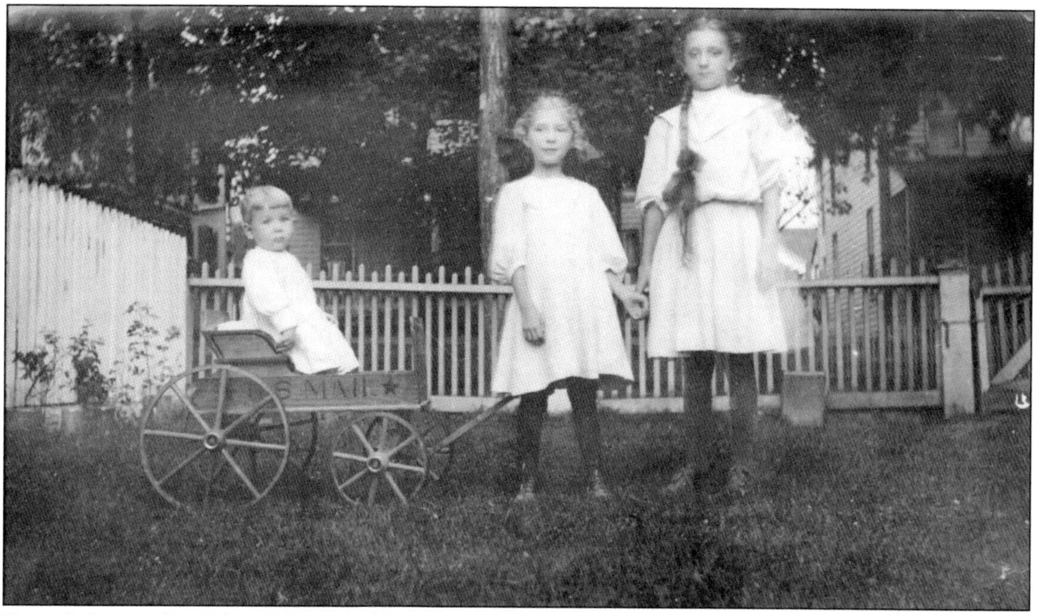

From left to right, John, Mary, and Janet Minnich are shown in this postcard image. They were children of Dr. William Henry Minnich and Elizabeth Crist Minnich of Dallastown. Note the wooden US Mail toy wagon with wooden wheels that John is sitting in. It was common for little boys like John to wear dresses up to the age of seven during this era. The postcard was made sometime between 1907 and 1912. (Courtesy of Roger Fuller.)

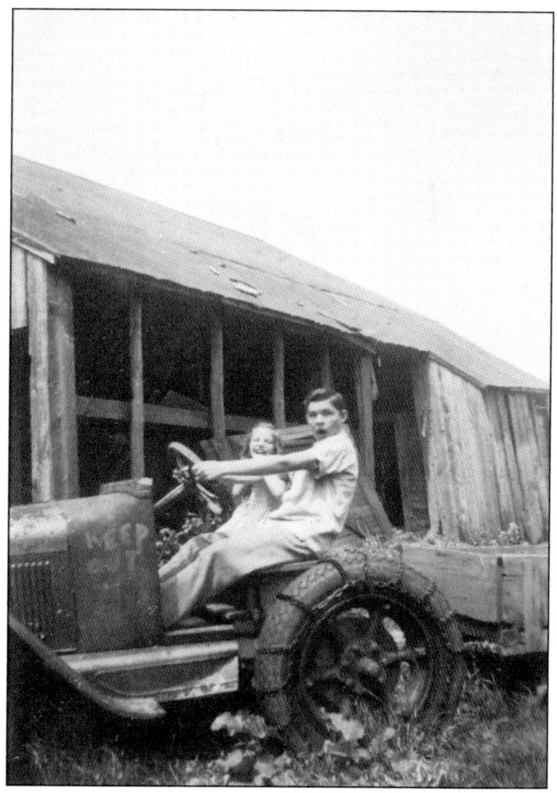

Emily B. Eck (left) and Gregory J. Eck pose on the family farm tractor in this c. 1940s photograph. This image was taken in front of the property's barn in RD No. 1 Dallastown. A lifelong resident of Dallastown, Gregory grew up to become a barbershop quartet singer whose group participated in international competitions. At one time, he also owned a gas station in Red Lion. (Courtesy of Jeanne M. Eck.)

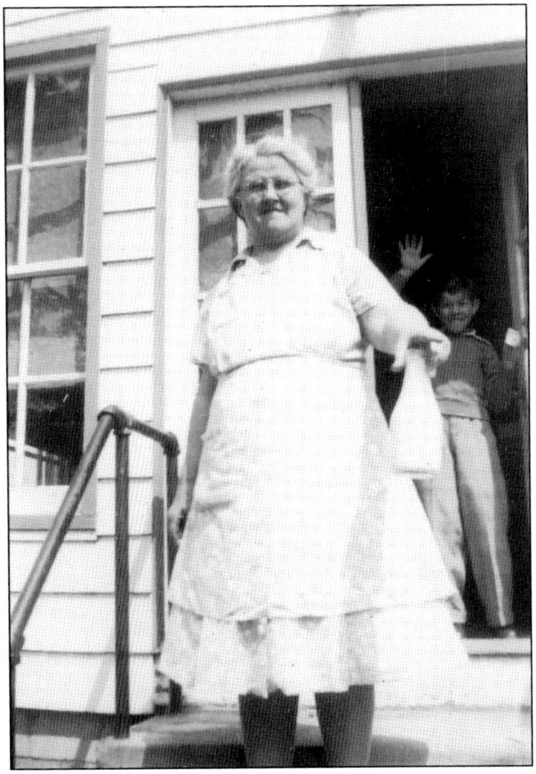

This photograph of Bernardine E. Eck was taken on the steps of her farmhouse porch in RD No. 1 Dallastown. Standing behind her is Richard, one of her 14 children. A housewife, Eck also stripped tobacco leaves at home for the local cigar trade. She was married to Thomas J. Eck. Their children were named Lawrence, Elizabeth, Rosemary, Thomas, Catherine, Pauline, John, Bernard, Jeanne, Gregory, Leo, Leona, Richard, and Emily. (Courtesy of Jeanne M. Eck.)

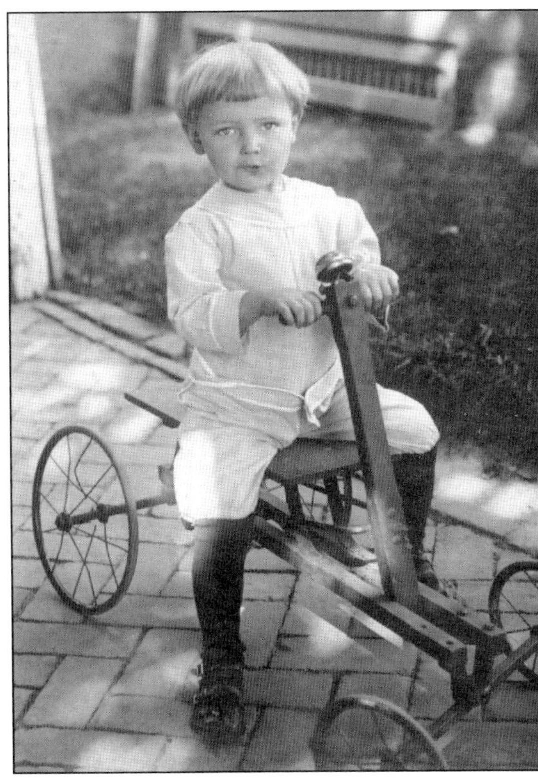

The image shows two-year-old Marlet W. Geesey in 1916 riding his toy cart. The photograph was taken at his parents' residence at 37 West Main Street in Dallastown, where Contino's Shoe Store and Repairs has been located since 1926. As an adult, Geesey became a hospital orderly in York, according to a 1935 city directory. In 1948, he built a new home at 201 West Broad Street. (Courtesy of Joan Klingenmaier.)

Cameron Mitchell (originally Mitzel) was born in Dallastown on November 4, 1918. His father, Rev. Charles Mitzel, was a minister. Cameron served as a bombardier in the United States Army Air Corps during World War II. After changing his last name to the less German-sounding Mitchell, he acted on stage, radio, motion pictures, and television. His best-known role in television was as Buck Cannon on the show *The High Chaparral*, which ran from 1967 to 1971. Mitchell passed away on July 6, 1994.

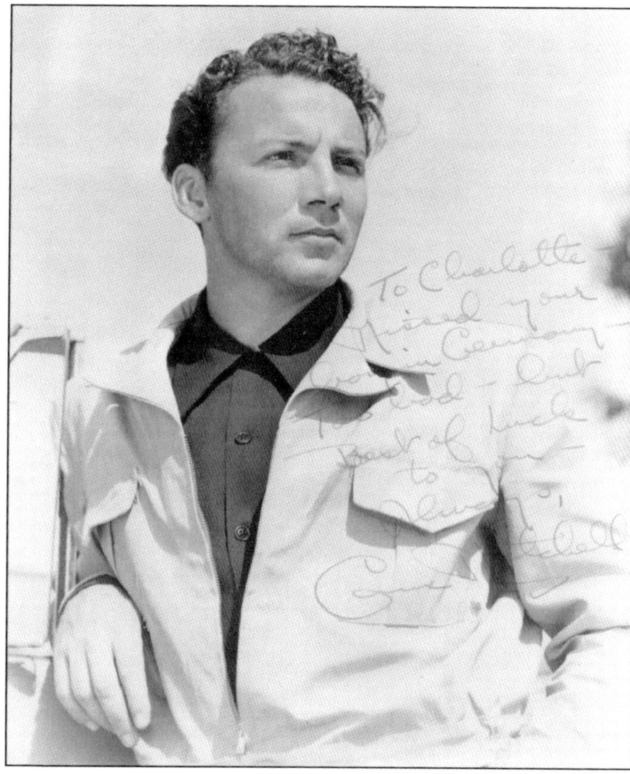

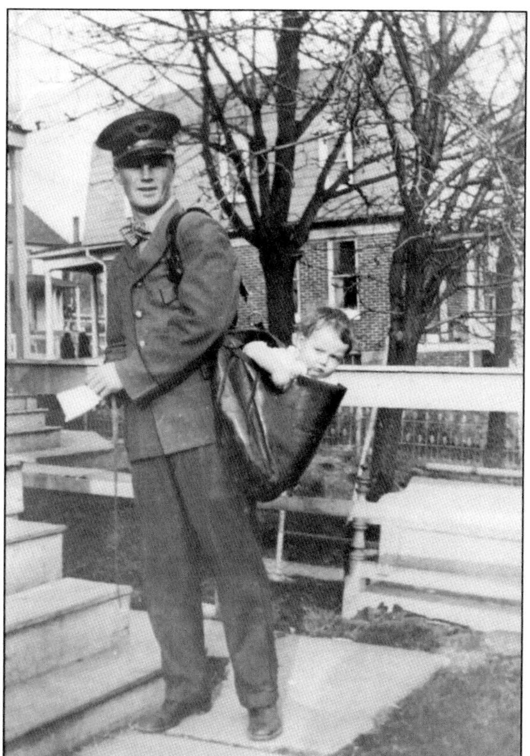

Mailman Ernest Orwig (left) and his son Ray Sherwood "John" Orwig (right) are shown delivering mail in Dallastown in the early 1930s. The photograph is titled "In the Bag." The town's post office was established on September 28, 1847, with James Edgar serving as the first postmaster. Ernest "Ernie" Orwig also enjoyed acting and singing in local plays. His son Ray followed in his footsteps and also became a mailman.

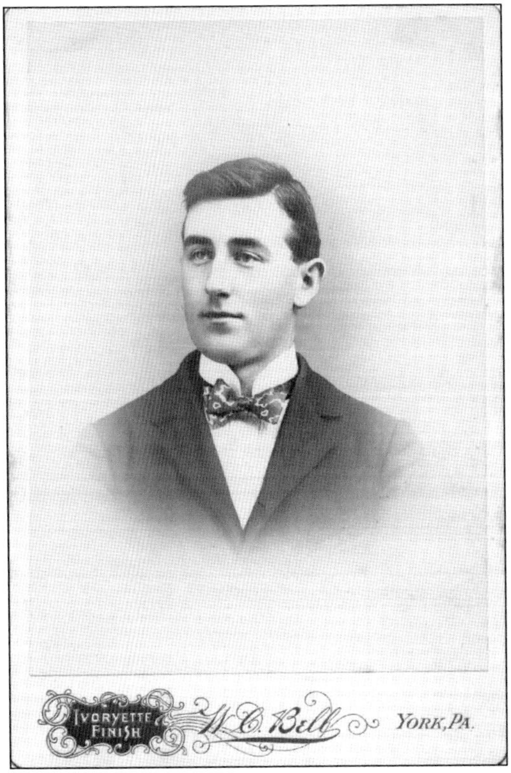

John D. Marshall was born on April 18, 1877, and worked for many years as a cabinetmaker at the Dallastown Furniture Company. This photograph was taken by W.C. Bell of York around 1900. A resident of Dallastown, Marshall voted in every US presidential election from 1900 through 1972. His first presidential vote helped reelect William McKinley to a second term in 1900. An avid fisherman, Marshall died in 1974. (Courtesy of Richard C. Saylor.)

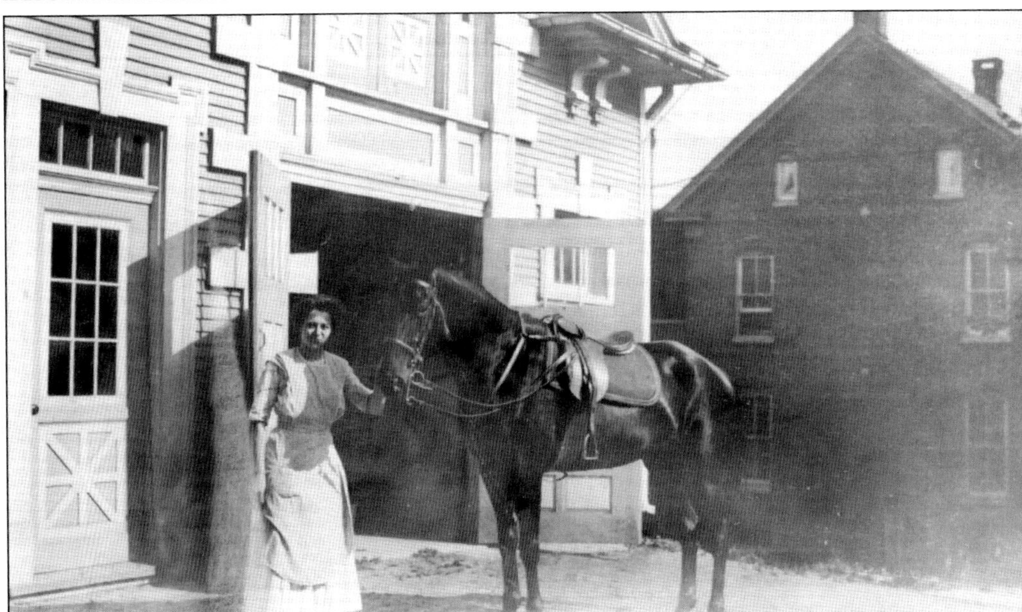

For thousands of years, man's chief form of transportation was the horse. Idabelle Day is shown in this 1912 image holding the bridle of the Minnich family's horse, Billy. They are standing in front of the carriage house along North Pleasant Avenue. Day was John W. Minnich's longtime housekeeper and the onetime fiancée of his son Chauncey. She was born on February 14, 1890, and died on February 6, 1972. (Courtesy of Lance Wolf.)

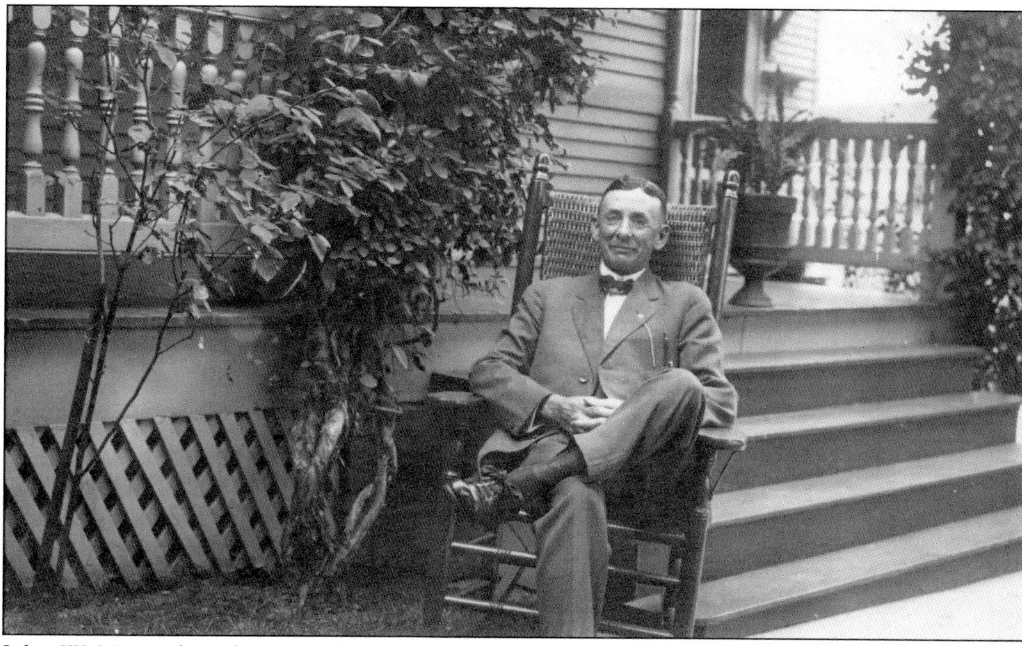

John W. Minnich is shown in this 1913 postcard sitting in a chair next to his house at 157 East Main Street. Born on January 21, 1860, Minnich died on May 10, 1940. He was the owner of J.W. Minnich Cigar Factory in Dallastown. He married Susan Geesey Minnich in 1882. Together, they had a son named Chauncey William Minnich. John's brother was Dr. William H. Minnich, also of Dallastown. (Courtesy of Lance Wolf.)

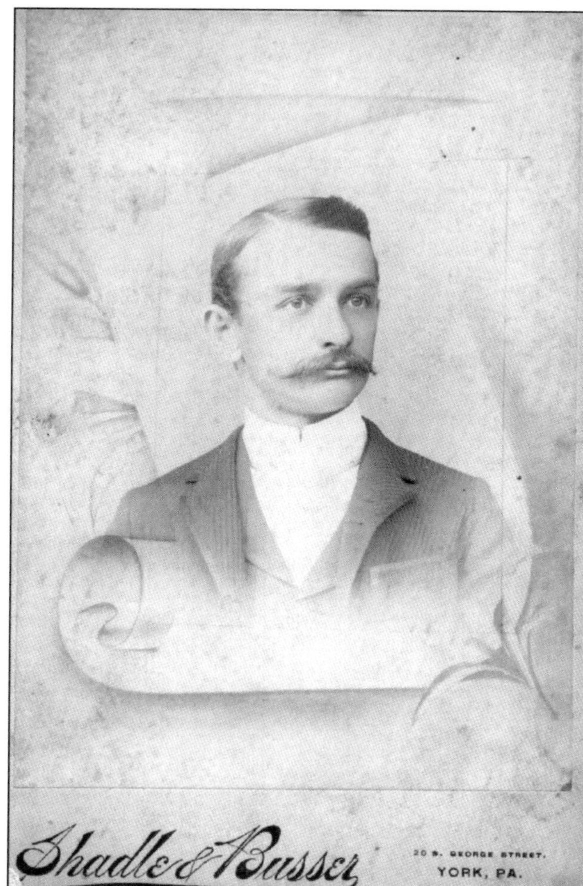

Dr. William Henry Minnich is depicted in this photograph made around 1890. Born on September 30, 1864, he studied medicine at the Baltimore Medical College and the College of Physicians and Surgeons. He was married to Elizabeth Crist Minnich in 1894. He practiced medicine in Dallastown, beginning in 1895, on East Main Street in a building that was located next to Bethlehem United Methodist Church. Dr. Minnich died on May 1, 1914. (Courtesy of Roger Fuller.)

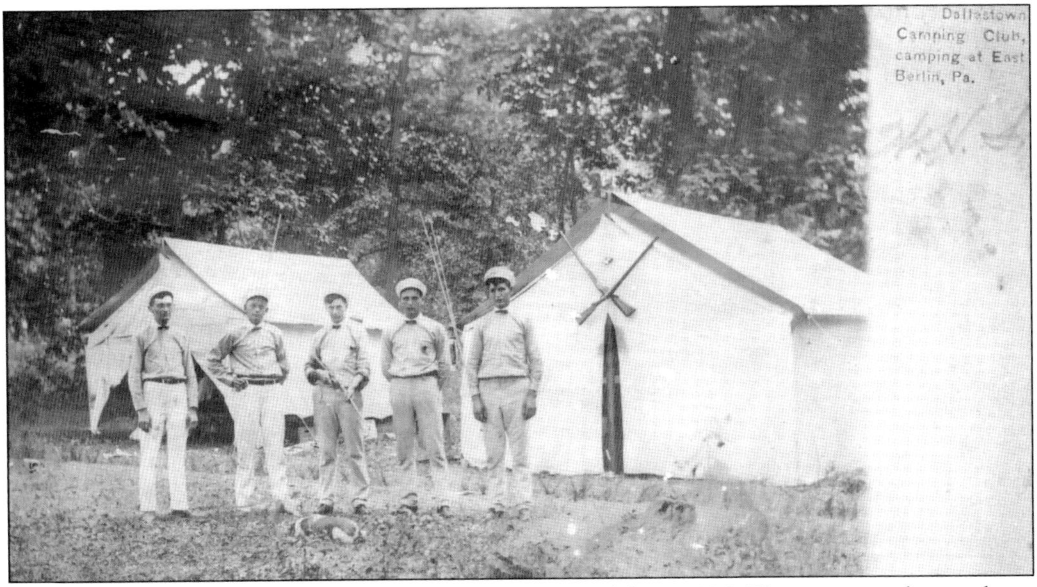

The Dallastown Camping Club is shown on this postcard from 1906. The campsite depicted was in East Berlin, Pennsylvania. The club members wear matching uniforms and hats. One of the five young men holds a rifle, while two other rifles are crossed and hanging over the entry flap to one of the two tents. (Courtesy of Tom Taylor.)

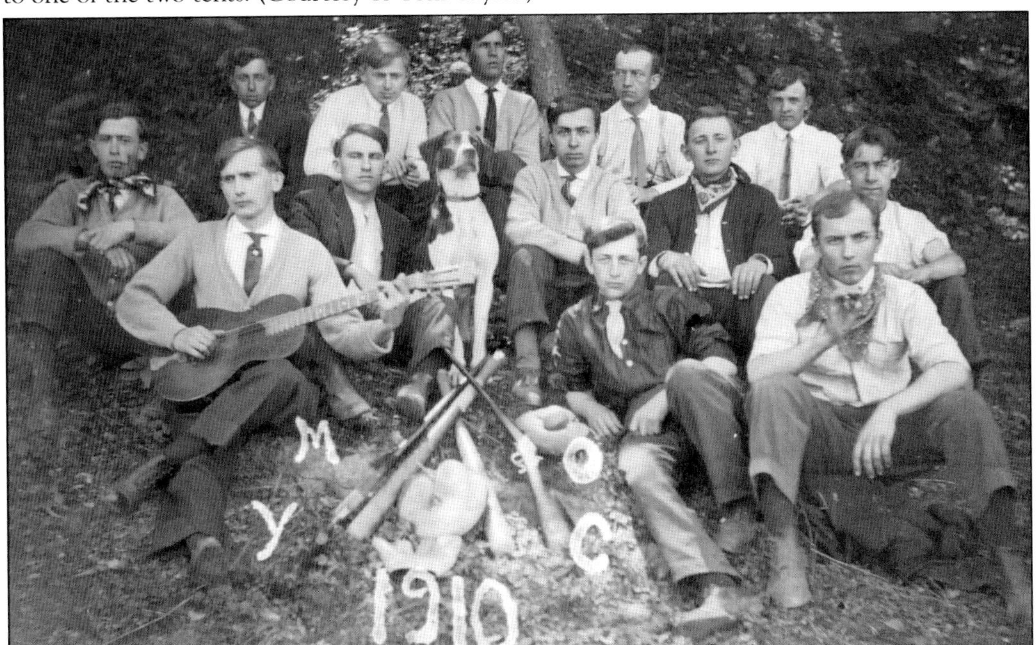

Depicted on this postcard is the Young Men's Outdoor Club of Dallastown in 1910. Crossed baseball bats, rifles, and mitts have been placed in front of the club members. From left to right are (first row) Walter Deller, John Knepper, and Allen Flinchbaugh; (second row) Wilber Barshinger, Austin Reidel, an unidentified dog, Marvin Koontz, Paul Zeigler, and Luther Reidel; (third row) Martin Knaper, Butch Geesey, Jerome Wagman, Jerome Keller, and Pete Williams. (Courtesy of Tom Taylor.)

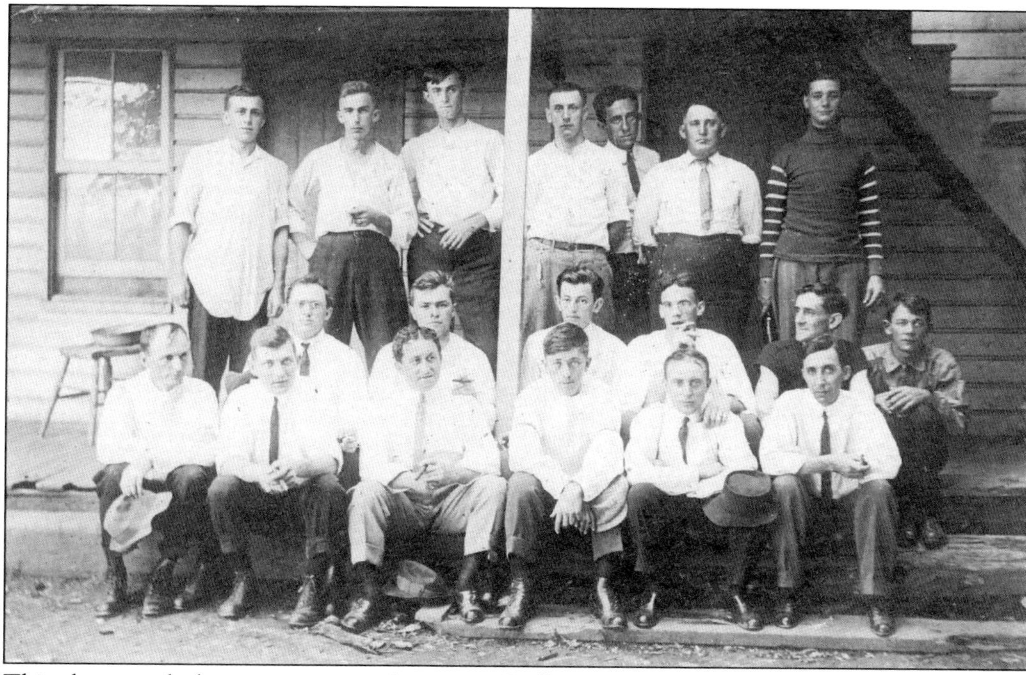

This photograph shows a young men's group in Dallastown around 1905, possibly a sports team or athletic association. From left to right are (first row) Kelly Ness, Bill Sechrist, Jacob Workinger, Gehra Shaffer, William Fuller, and Arthur Smith; (second row) Fred Minnich, Albert Benedict, Merle Rojahn, George Jacobs, Jess Ehrhart, and Wallace Warner; (third row) Lloyd Slenker, unidentified, Charles Ehrhart, Chauncey Seidenstricker, John Heisler, Sam Ness, and unidentified.

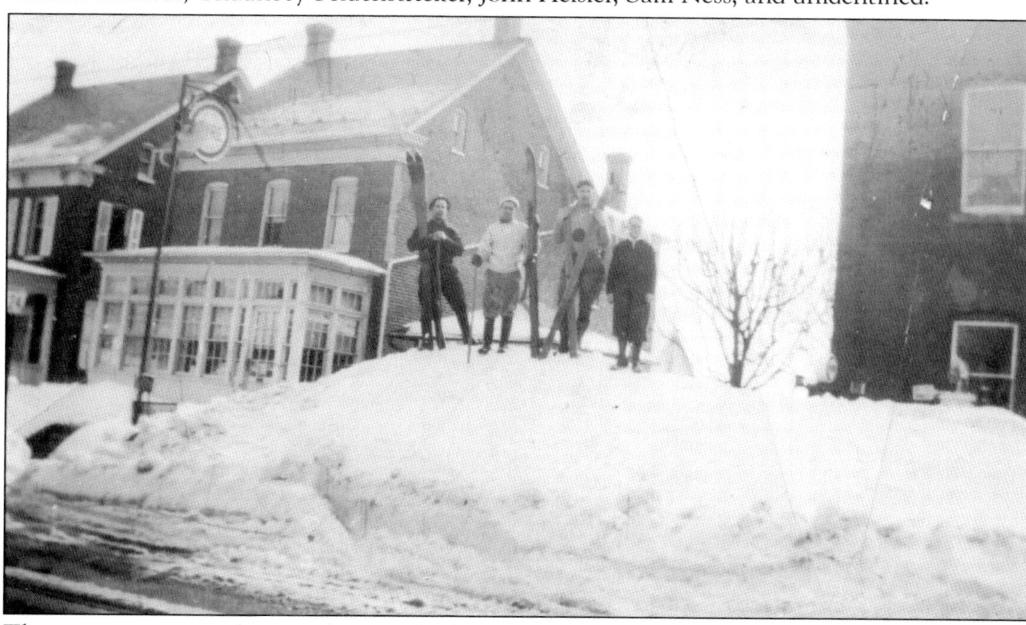

Three cross-country skiers and one onlooker pose on a giant pile of snow in front of the service station owned by Carson Landis at 400 East Main Street. The gas pumps are barely visible above the snowbank. The photograph was taken from the north side of East Main Street with a view looking south. The image was captured around 1935. (Courtesy of Cathy Bankoske.)

BIBLIOGRAPHY

Dallastown Official Centennial Program. York: York Pennsylvania Press, 1966.
Dallastown Story: 100 Years of Growth. York: York Pennsylvania Press, 1966.
Ellison, Ismar S., ed. *United States Tobacco Journal*. New York: Ellison Publishing, 1921
Gibson, John. *History of York County Pennsylvania*. Chicago: F.A. Battey Publishing, 1886.
Hilton, George W. *The MA & PA*. Baltimore: Johns Hopkins University Press, 1980.
Miller, Randall M., and William Pencak, eds. *Pennsylvania: A History of the Commonwealth*. State College: Penn State University Press, 2002.
Prowell, George R. *History of York County Pennsylvania, Vols. I and II*. Chicago: J.H. Beers & Co., 1907
Rhine, C. Stewart, "A Backward Glance," *Ma & PA Timetable*, Winter 1997.
Rohrbeck, Benson W. *York County Trolleys*. West Chester, PA: Ben Rohrbeck Traction Publications, 1978.
United States Census Records, 1850–1940
York City Directories, 1877–1935 (not inclusive)

About the Organization

Dallastown Area Historical Society was founded in 2000. Mayor Beverly Scott had the idea of creating a historical society for the borough and put a notice in the town's newsletter floating the idea and requesting that anyone interested in the proposal should contact her. Richard C. Saylor, a professional public historian, museum curator, archivist, and town native, responded to the newsletter suggestion. With Mayor Scott, Richard C. Saylor, who became the founding president of the society, held a series of town meetings where other like-minded residents interested in the history of the borough came together to establish a board of directors. The society was incorporated as a nonprofit organization in 2001. The first officers included Richard C. Saylor, president; Michael L. Sentz Jr., vice president; Kathryn M. Patterson, secretary; and Kimberly Edman, treasurer.

The society took up residence in the old fire company engine house at 118 East Main Street. Soon thereafter, archival records, photographs, and three-dimensional artifacts began to be donated and collected. Exhibit cases were purchased from a jewelry store and a movie theater at Delco Plaza in York, Pennsylvania. Themed exhibits were created in the cases, and the museum was opened to the public.

The society always welcomes donations of historical photographs or objects that are related to the history of the Dallastown area. Only through donations can the society continue to fulfill its mission of collecting, preserving, and interpreting the history of the Dallastown community.

The historical society has a web presence at the following:

http://www.dallastownboro.com/history/dallastown-area-historical-society
http://www.facebook.com/DALLASTOWN.HISTORICAL
http://dallastownareahistoricalsociety.tumblr.com/

Currently, the Dallastown Area Historical Society is open to the public the first Sunday of the month from 1:00 to 4:00 p.m. Other appointments must be made in advance with the society's president. The mailing address for the society is 175 East Broad Street, Dallastown, Pennsylvania, 17313. Public monthly meetings are held on the first Thursday of every month at 7:00 p.m. at the historical society museum at 118 East Main Street, Dallastown.

Consistent with our mission to preserve history on a local level, this book was printed in South Carolina on American-made paper and manufactured entirely in the United States. Products carrying the accredited Forest Stewardship Council (FSC) label are printed on 100 percent FSC-certified paper.

MADE IN THE USA